CYCLING IN THE GREAT WAR

PATRICK CORNILLIE

CYCLING IN THE GREAT WAR

LANNOO

CONTENTS

PROLOGUE

On 28 June 1914, two more or less simultaneous shots ring out. On precisely the same day that the 12th edition of the Tour de France starts in Paris, Crown Prince Franz Ferdinand of Austria is assassinated in Sarajevo by a Serbian nationalist. At first glance, these two events might seem to have nothing to do with each other. Not yet. However, the tension in the Balkans leads to a game of political bluff and counter-bluff with very high stakes. Before any one quite knows how or why, the game gets out of hand and suddenly all Europe is at war. The shot in Sarajevo is the starting shot for a conflict that will change the world forever.

The First World War is also destined to change the face of cycling forever. Its effect is almost immediate. Look at the list of winners for many of the world's great races — the Tour de France or Paris-Roubaix, for example — and you will see that there is often a gap from 1914 to 1919. Most sporting history books will tell you that this is because the war on the Western Front is fought over a region — Belgium and northern France — that is at the heart of the newly emerging but already highly popular sport of bike racing. As a result, no racing is possible until the war is over. What's more, nearly all the members of the peloton of 1914 are serving at the front, where many of them are among the nine million victims claimed by the war, symbols of a promising but lost generation. How could there be any thought of racing in these circumstances? Surely, cycling, so important in peacetime, becomes an irrelevance in time of war?

But is this true? Was there no bike racing anywhere in Europe during the years of the Great War? Did the occupying Germans allow no races in Belgium for four long years? Did soldiers on leave organize no competitions behind the front, if only to alleviate their own boredom? And what happened to the many velodromes that existed in 1914? After this difficult period in cycling history, very little research was carried out to answer these and other similar questions. It just seemed easier to assume that for four years professional riders had no option but to let their bikes gather dust.

Whoever takes the trouble to look will find a very different story. And the more you dig, the more it becomes apparent that there are interesting and informative connections to be made between the world at war and the world of cycling. In particular, approaching the war from the perspective of cycling makes it possible to understand the impact of the first global conflict at a more personal level. At the same time, the trials and tribulations of individual racers, both great and small, allow us to see the 'big picture', to understand what a world war truly means in social, political and economic terms. This is the aim of the 'Cycling in the Great War' exhibition, organized by the Tour of Flanders Centre (Centrum Ronde van Vlaanderen or CRVV) in Oudenaarde in 2018. The exhibition not only looks at each of the four war years, but also sheds light on the evolution of the sport before 1914 and its recovery after 1918. In addition to a virtual-reality experience based on the career of Paul Deman, winner of the very first Tour of Flanders in 1913 and later a spy in occupied Belgium, there is also a double time line that positions developments at the front and behind the lines against the cycling activities that were still possible during the war years. It makes for a fascinating comparison. In this way, supplemented by a series of artefacts that also make the link between the war and cycling, it is possible to survey the entire period between 1914 and 1918 in all its many different aspects: war, sport, social life, the economy, art and culture.

With this exhibition, 100 years after the signing of the Armistice, the CRVV is not only aiming to appeal to cycling fans, but also people who have a more general interest in the First World War. That applies equally to this book, which is published to coincide with 'Cycling in the Great War'. The book tries, like the exhibition, to answer a number of different questions. How seriously was the well-established pre-war cycling infrastructure damaged by the fighting? How was the bicycle used by the armies of both sides? Were cycling events organized in the unoccupied parts of Belgium and France? What happened to the racers? Which of them died on the battlefield and how did the others emerge from the worst conflict the world had ever seen?

What you can read in the following pages is not designed to be an 'erudite', scientific and highly detailed work of reference, but rather a chronicle of the years between 1914 and 1918 and how they affected cycling, in ways both great and small. Or as the French writer Jean-Paul Bourgier once said, it is the story of how the peloton went 'from flowers on handlebars to bayonets on cannons'.

PART I
THE PRE-WAR PIONEERS

Before 28 June 1914

The high bicycle — a two-wheeler for acrobats.

When the First World War breaks out, the bicycle — or bike — is still relatively new. As a result, bike racing — or cycling — is still a young sport. The modern two-wheel safety bicycle, with the diamond-shaped frame made from straight steel tubing that is still familiar today, only made its appearance in the years after 1885. This is surprisingly late, certainly in an era otherwise typified by remarkable scientific and technological advances, which sees the arrival of the steam locomotive, the telegraph and the telephone, the dynamo and the gas lamp, the automatic loom and balloon flight, photography and even the tin can!

But the evolution of the bike is much slower. True, at the start of the 19th century there is already the *draisine*, named after its German inventor Karl von Drais. However, this is no more than a heavy, cumbersome conveyance with two wooden wheels and a saddle. It is not powered by pedals, but by 'running' with your feet along the ground from a seated position, rather like toddlers do on their first bike today. For many years, the early 'experts' are convinced that it is impossible to maintain your balance on two wheels positioned one behind the other, as opposed to two (or more) placed alongside each other. This question of balance continues to plague bicycle development. How else can you explain that it is as late as 1861 before the first pedal bike appears?

The next major step forward is the invention of the two-wheel *vélocipède* — anglicized to

Charles Terront wins the 1891 Paris-Brest-Paris race on a safety bike with two wheels of equal size.

velocipede — by the Frenchman Ernest Michaux, who attaches pedals to the axle of the front wheel and handlebars that are directly connected to the front fork. A short while later, across the Channel in England, James Starley develops a further new variant. He reasons logically — or so he thinks — that if one rotation of the pedals is equivalent to one rotation of the front wheel, it makes sense to make this front wheel as large as possible. This should make it easier to cover greater distances and achieve higher speeds with just a few turns of the pedals.

This leads to the arrival after 1867 of the high bicycle, with a very large front wheel and a much smaller back one (known in England as a 'penny-farthing', because of the respective size of these two coins). The rider of this contraption is expected to sit high on top of the front wheel, which demands a degree of bodily suppleness that not everyone possesses. The imposing appearance and high degree of risk turns cycling from something ordinary into something spectacular. As a result, the popularity of the high bicycle is short-lived. As an alternative, the tricycle is developed for those with less athleticism (or more sense). However, their production is complex and expensive, so that just a few years later the tricycle also passes into history.

It is not until 1885, following the introduction of the bike chain, so that the bottom bracket and the pedals no longer need to have the same rotational speed as the wheels, that the safety bike becomes possible. The first model with a low frame and two wheels of equal size is designed by the British engineer Thomas Humber. Humber's design is transformed into a comfortable and easy-to-use means of transport by the further invention of the pneumatic tyre by John Dunlop in 1888. Their combined efforts result in one of the most important and most influential inventions in the history of mankind: the modern bicycle.

IF YOU CAN RIDE A BIKE, YOU CAN RACE A BIKE

There is cycling and there is cycle racing. The latter evolves from the former. New inventions automatically lead to competition, the desire to be fastest, furthest, longest, highest... It is no different with the bicycle. The high bike is largely a question of daredevilry. But the safety bike makes racing much more possible for many more people. Short races and demonstrations give way to competitions over longer distances. The newspapers quickly see the interest this might generate among their readers and encourage the riders to undertake ever greater challenges. Circulation figures are to the 19th century what viewing figures are to the 21st century: the be-all and end-all of everything. As a result, the press whips up excitement for the new sport. Certainly in France.

In 1891, the sports paper *Véloce-Sport* organizes a race of no fewer than 572 kilometres from Bordeaux to Paris, won by the British cyclist George Pilkington Mills, in a time of 26 hours and 34 minutes.

The race excites so much popular enthusiasm that other newspapers are quick to follow. In the same year, *Le Petit Journal* comes up with the idea for an even longer race, from Paris to Brest and back again: a total of 1,200 kilometres.

The winner of this cycling marathon is Charles Terront, who needs almost five days to complete the course. In 1896, the textile manufacturers Théodore Vienne and Maurice Perez launch their idea for a race between Paris and Roubaix. The first editions are simply viewed as training for Bordeaux-Paris, because the course distance is 'only' 250 kilometres long! However, the harsh conditions of the race mean that it is soon regarded as the 'queen of the cycling classics'. Until 1914, the finish is on the Vélodrome Roubaisien in the Parc Barbieux, which was built at the suggestion of Vienne and Perez especially for their event.

But it is not only the newspapers that do their best to promote the new sport: the bike manufacturers are soon jumping on the bandwagon as well. They want to tie the best racers to their brands and for a real champion are prepared to pay as much as 3,000 French francs per month, which in those days is higher than the salary earned by a minister of state! Everyone is curious to find the limits of human endurance on a bike. How far can they go? And how fast? What is the ultimate challenge? In 1903, *L'Auto* newspaper puts forward the most ambitious plan to date: why not send a group of adventurous souls on a journey around the entire country — a distance of 2,428 kilometres divided into six separate stages? And so the Tour de France is born. Most people think it is pure madness. Surely it will never catch on?

Report of the very first edition of Paris-Roubaix in the *Journal de Roubaix* on Tuesday, 21 April 1896.

Report of the fourth edition of Paris-Roubaix in the *Journal de Roubaix* on Tuesday, 4 April 1899.

THE ACATÈNES
OF FN HERSTAL

Thomas Humber's safety bike is such a success that in 1890 he is able to start his own company in Nottingham. He later moves to a larger factory at Beeston, which also produces motorbikes, motor cars and even aeroplanes during the First World War. Thomas leaves the company as early as 1892, but the Humber name carries on, even after the sale of the cycling branch to Raleigh in 1928.

England is destined to lead the way in cycle construction for quite some time, but France quickly becomes the leading country for bike sales and the mecca for professional bike racing. The Frenchman Armand Peugeot first develops an interest in bike design during his engineering studies in England. When he returns to his home village just outside

Besancon, he starts to manufacture his own two-wheelers. In 1890, Edmond Gentil does much the same in one of the outlying suburbs of Paris, where his factory produces the Alcyon bike — a legendary brand that begins sponsoring professional cyclists from 1906 onwards. Paris is also the home of the Sociéte La Française, which later becomes La Française-Diamant, another of the great pre-1914 names in bike construction. But the heart of the French bicycle industry is in Saint-Etienne, which is also the centre of the country's metal-working and weapons industries. The city in the Massif Central is responsible for launching several successful brands, such as Mercier, Automoto, Ravat and Panel.

During this period, there are also a number of bicycle makers in Belgium, but on nothing like the same scale as their French neighbours. The only manufacturer of any size is the Fabrique Nationale d'Armes de Guerre at Herstal near Liege — more popularly known as FN Herstal. Here from 1889 onwards they produce the so-called *acatènes*. These are shaft-driven, chainless bikes, where the power generated by the pedals is transmitted to the central axle of the back wheel by a system of interlocking rods. Also known as cardan bicycles after the name of their Italian designer, Girolamo Cardano, they are compact and require little maintenance, which makes them ideal for poor roads. However, the frame and axle construction makes them heavy, which means they need more pedal power to ride. More crucially, this also makes them much less suitable for the increasingly popular sport of cycling, especially as their more complex gearing makes changes in pace more difficult to achieve. As soon as modern production techniques are able to significantly reduce the cost and improve the quality of chain-driven transmission systems, the cardan bike quickly and quietly disappears from the scene.

FN, a trendsetting name during the pioneering years of cycling.

LUDWIG OPEL — A RACER WITH HIS OWN BRAND

Another producer of shaft-driven bikes is Dürkopp. The company is based in the German town of Bielefeld but soon has many distributors in Belgium and the Netherlands. One of their local rivals in Frankfurt am Main is Adler Fahrradwerke AG, which starts with the production of typewriters and bicycles in 1886. A third well-known German brand of two-wheelers is Opel. The company started by Adam Opel in Rüsselsheim initially specializes in sewing machines. Adam's five sons — Carl, Wilhelm, Heinrich, Friedrich and Ludwig — later make bikes and cars. The youngest sibling, Ludwig, is also a talented cycle racer. As an amateur, hc wins silver at the world sprint championships in Vienna in 1898. At the same time, he studies law at the universities of Giessen and Freiburg. He eventually becomes manager of the Opel factory in Berlin, but only after enjoying a seven-year career as a professional cyclist. When the First World War breaks out, he is called to serve *Kaiser und Vaterland*. Ludwig Opel becomes a lieutenant in the 24th Regiment of Dragoons and fights on the Eastern Front. On 16 April 1916, he dies at the Russian town of Hoduzischki. He is just 36 years old.

The five Opel brothers on a 'quintuplet'. Ludwig, the youngest brother, is at the front.

Carl, the oldest of the Opel brothers, poses with one of his first bikes, made at Rüsselsheim in 1899.

Thanks to the invention of the safety bike, the breakthrough of the bicycle is unstoppable. In a matter of years, the bicycle becomes both a popular pastime and an important mode of transport. It also becomes big business. Small-scale local workshops are replaced by modern bike factories. Mass production reduces the price of a two-wheeler dramatically. First introduced as a plaything for the sons of the rich and the famous, bikes are now an essential part of the everyday life of ordinary men and women. People are amazed by the wonderful sense of mobility it brings and, above all, by its tremendous practicality. It offers labourers the chance to find work further away from home. It offers children and young people the opportunity to seek education away from the church tower. The safety bike makes it possible to travel considerable distances quickly and even to carry loads. Errand boys or 'runners' are replaced by bike couriers. People who could never dream of owning a horse, cart or carriage are now able to make journeys of 20 or 30 kilometres with relative ease. The bike also revolutionizes a number of jobs. The Belgian government quickly decides to introduce the use of the bicycle in the postal service and in 1895 the first bikes are issued to village policemen working in rural areas. Firemen also rush to their stations on bikes and cycle units begin to make their appearance in the army. Between 1893 and 1900 the number of bicycles in Belgium increases from 20,000 to 115,000, with the *vélo* being seen with increasing frequency in the countryside as well as the towns.

The first cycling postmen and village policemen make their appearance in the years before 1900.

In spite of its name, the safety bike is not always that safe!

THE BICYCLE FINDS ITS WAY INTO THE ARMY

Italy is the first European country to experiment with bicycles in its armed forces. The safety bikes are a fast and easy means of transport and in many types of terrain are quicker than the infantry and even the cavalry. The first troops to use them are the *Bersaglieri*, the elite unit of the Piedmont (and later Italian) army. Even on the worst roads or in the deepest forests, the new bikes with two wheels of equal size are quick and manoeuvrable. At first, the army uses its cyclists as couriers and later for reconnaissance tasks. They are soundless and so do not betray their approach, as horses do with their hooves. They can also operate perfectly well at night, which is much more difficult for horsemen.

The Italian experiment is soon copied by other armies: Austria in 1884, France and Germany in 1885, and the Dutch and Swiss in 1886. In 1887, the English create the London Cyclist Corps, based on an idea by Lieutenant-Colonel A.R. Savile. The Belgium government also considers the introduction of military cycling units, although the high command is initially reluctant: the cavalry units, with their fine horses and glittering uniforms, are still seen as the pride of the army. Even so, the advocates of bikes continue to emphasize the potential advantages they can bring and in 1888 the Minister of War, Charles Pontus, asks a number of volunteers from the Fédération Vélocipédique Belge (Belgian Cycling Federation) to take part in that year's annual military manoeuvres.

This first test is a success and is repeated again in 1889, with equally satisfactory results. In 1890,

The Italian Bersaglieri are the first troops to experiment with bikes for military purposes.

Minister Pontus gives his permission for the setting up of a cyclists' section in the regimental school of the Carabineers at Waver, under the leadership of Captain-Commandant Hubert Soleil. The *vélocipédistes militaires* are selected on the basis of their physical and intellectual capacities. They must become the fast messengers of the army. Each year, 25 soldiers will be sent for special training. In a one-week course, they first learn how to ride a bike, following which they are sent on a series of rides to familiarize themselves with all the conditions and all the difficult terrains they are likely to face. As the training progresses, so the distances they are expected to cycle increases.

In the spring of the following year, the unit is ready to become operational. The first section sets off — by bike, of course — to Beverlo Camp, for further technical and tactical tests. The results are again more than satisfactory, so that soon afterwards the foundation of the *Korps der militaire Wielrijders* is confirmed by law. The regiment organizes its own final test ride of 350 kilometres, spread over three days. Again, all goes well and the cycling corps is finally given the green light.

In 1885, the German Army sets up its first *Radfahrer-Kompanie*.

"HUMBER No. II MILITARY"

JENKINSON

De Beste Safety voor Militaire Wielrijders is de

HUMBER SAFETY

The British engineer Thomas Humber designs the first safety bike
and immediately focuses on its possible military uses.

LEOPOLD II WANTS BELGIUM TO BECOME A CYCLING NATION

Like France, Belgium also quickly develops a great interest in cycling as a sport. As early as 1883, the cycling clubs in Ghent, Antwerp, Verviers, Leuven, Mons and Brussels come together to form the Fédération Vélocipédique Belge (Belgian Cycling Federation). Five years later, a rival Union Véloci-pédique Belge (Belgian Cycling Union) is set up. In 1889, they merge to create the Ligue Vélocipédique Belge, the forerunner of today's Belgian Cycling Association. The safety bike makes it possible to race on public roads and over much greater distances. Following the Italian and French examples, the Belgians also begin to organize events of 100 kilometres and more. On 29 May 1892, the Pesant Club Liégois hold the first edition of a race from Liege to Bastogne and back again — a bold undertaking for its time.

It is no coincidence that the first major cycling races take place in the province of Liege. The region has numerous cycling clubs and is home to some of the country's best racers, such as Léon Lhoest, Charles Van den Born and the track rider Robert Protin. In 1895, Protin even becomes the first ever world professional sprint champion. His duels with Hubert Houben from Brussels fill velodromes with thousands of enthusiastic fans. Above all, cycling is popular with the poorer sections of the population. By 1900, the country has almost 200 cycling clubs and the number of competitions and racers is steadily on the increase.

In 1893, the Paris newspaper *La Bicyclette* launches the idea of a race between the capitals of France and Belgium. The Belgian Cycling Association immediately sees the possible promotional benefit of the proposal and gives its full support. The Belgian press is also full of articles about the coming confrontation between the Belgian and French riders. The first winner of Paris-Brussels is André Henry, a bricklayer from Verviers, who immediately becomes a public hero. Five days later, he is even invited to an audience with the king! In his palace at Laken, Leopold II declares that he wants to make Belgium a sporting centre that will be attractive for international cyclists of all nationalities.

Charles Van den Born, here as winner of the Prix des étrangers (Foreigner's Race) in 1909.

Van den Born wins the Belgian sprint championship seven times and later becomes an aviation pioneer.

CYCLE-RIFLE VOLUNTEERS

WITH THE 'BELGICA' OVER HILL AND DALE!

For the English, it is clear: 'If we want to move our troops with a maximum of speed and a minimum of fatigue, then the bicycle has numerous advantages to offer.' The military authorities are aware of the importance of having cyclists in their ranks: 'They take full advantage of their mobility.' They are used mainly for reconnaissance purposes or as messengers and/or signalmen. Some larger mobile units even serve as advanced patrols. In 1890, the British Army has four different types of bikes at its disposal: the safety bicycle, the single tricycle, the tandem tricycle and the multicycle. Important lessons are learned during the South African War of 1899 to 1902, also known as the Second Boer War. In the fighting, the British seek to counteract the horse-based mobility of the Dutch-speaking Boers of the Transvaal and the Orange Free State by using for the first time a series of rapid-response cycling sections, which together form the Cape Colony Cyclist Corps.

During this same period, two military training schools for cyclists are also opened on the home front. A large-scale poster campaign is launched to recruit as many cycle-rifle volunteers as possible. Cyclists are also used with increasing frequency in the army's annual manoeuvres. They learn how to ride in columns, how to co-operate with the cavalry (the other mobile strategic arm), how to support the infantry, and how to rush to the defence of the coast when invasion threatens.

The bicycle is also becoming more commonplace in the Belgian Army. Following a ministerial decree passed on 10 August 1896, a first temporary cycling company is set up. The driving force behind this 120-man company is Lieutenant Gaston Beirlaen of the Brussels Carabineers Regiment, who is himself a fervent cyclist. In addition, he is also secretary-general of the Touring Club de Belgique and editor of the weekly publication *La Pédale Militaire*, which appears between September 1893 and December 1894. Many amateur cyclists will opt to join the cycling company during their compulsory national service, but the company also produces a number of promising racers.

Lieutenant Beirlaen thinks that his soldiers can be much more than just cycling messengers. He believes that they can be used to greater effect as a mobile fighting unit. When he hears that a French infantry captain, Henry Gérard, is experimenting with folding bikes, he wants to know more. Folding bikes make it easier to cross obstacles like walls and ditches and can also be carried across terrain that is too difficult for riding. In 1897, his company tests the Gérard bike and a number of other folding models. They must all weigh less than 15 kilograms, be quick to fold and easy to carry, and must not hinder the soldiers in the act of firing their rifles. For example, his sharpshooters must be able to

Recruiting poster to encourage the young men of Britain to join the Cyclist Corps.

The Belgian High Command also wants to make use of the Gérard system of foldable and portable bikes.

French infantry troops, with the folding bike of the French captain Gérard.

take aim while still sitting on the saddle with their feet on the ground, but without the pedals or the handlebars getting in the way. Beirlaen also wants it to be possible to link two folding bikes together to make a four-wheeler! Of the 26 models he tests, the 'Belgica' proves to be the best.

A French cyclist 'in the field'.

Het opvouwbare Rijwiel

Wat is het grootste bezwaar voor de militaire wielrijder? Dat hij niet overal kan rijden, evenmin als hij overal zijn rijwiel kan meenemen. Dat is wel mogelijk met het opvouwbare rijwiel. Het frame is geheel anders dan bij onze tegenwoordige modellen en doet denken aan het kruisframe van 4 à 5 jaar geleden. Het voor- en achterwiel zijn verbonden door een stalen buis, die in tweeën is verdeeld; de beide delen worden samen verbonden door een schroef, die als spil dienst doet. Teneinde te bewerkstelligen dat deze draaibare buis volkomen vast blijft zitten, is er om de spil een gespleten buis gemaakt, die men gemakkelijk over de gehele buis kan bewegen. Deze gespleten buis wordt echter, als men de machine berijdt, bij het draaiingspunt vastgezet, door drie handschroeven aan te draaien. Deze handschroeven bestaan uit ringetjes, die men zeer vast kan aandraaien. Zodra deze nu zijn aangezet kunnen de beweegbare delen van de buis niet meer heen en weer gaan, terwijl zo men de schroeven losmaakt men de gespleten stalen buis gemakkelijk kan verschuiven en het vouwen der machine plaats kan doen vinden.
Het rijwiel weegt slechts 12 kg; men heeft zonder hulp van een sleutel 25 seconden nodig om het rijwiel op te bouwen en 15 seconden om het op de rug te bevestigen.

In their advertisements, the makers of folding bikes emphasize their suitability for 'the discerning military cyclist'.

THE FIRST CHAIRMAN OF THE UCI IS A BELGIAN

The Fédération Vélocipédique Belge is not the first national cycling association. It is preceded by the British Bicycle Union (1878), the League of American Wheelmen (1880), the Union Vélocipédique de France and the Dansk (Danish) Bicycle Club (both 1881). Like the Belgians, the Dutch, the Italians and the Swiss all set up their national federations in 1883, followed a year later by the Germans with the Bund Deutscher Radfahrer. Cycling therefore already has a firm organizational structure at national level before the dawn of the 20th century. However, things go less smoothly at the international level, where early efforts to form an overarching world association all fail. The rivalries between the national associations are just too great, often reflecting similar tensions in the diplomatic and political relations between their different countries.

True, the International Cyclists Association (ICA) is set up as early as 1892. This is dominated by the Anglo-Saxon countries, led by Great Britain. Perhaps this is not surprising: with George Pilkington Mills (the first winner of Bordeaux-Paris), Arthur Linton, Jimmy Michael, Arthur Chase, Jack Stocks and Albert Walters, the British have most of the best riders. However, as time passes the British Bicycle Union becomes increasingly worried by the sport's growing professionalism. In England there is a strong belief that sport should be seen purely as a matter for exercise and relaxation, as something fundamentally different from work. Accepting money for sport is therefore 'not done'. Cycling must remain the sport of passionate amateurs, not greedy professionals!

The fractious debates in international cycling persist, so that the Belgians, French and Italians eventually decide to set up an alternative body of their own. On 14 April 1900, at a hotel in Paris, they create the Union Cycliste International (UCI). The first chairman is an Antwerp businessman, Emile De Beukelaer, whose family own the company that makes the famous Elixir d'Anvers liqueur. In his youth De Beukelaer was quite a decent cyclist and he is also a board member of the Antwerp Cycle Club and the sport committee of the Belgian Cycling Federation. Other national federations soon affiliate themselves to the UCI, so that in 1903 the ICA is disbanded. Even the British Bicycle Union finally admits defeat and becomes a member of the UCI.

Marshall Walter Taylor, who becomes world sprint champion in 1899, the only black man ever to hold a cycling world title.

THE 'SIX DAYS' IN AMERICA AND AUSTRALIA

With the absorption of the ICA into the UCI, England disappears from the world cycling scene for more than half a century. It is not until the emergence of riders like Brian Robinson and Tom Simpson in the 1950s and 1960s that Britain again produces racers of an international calibre, paving the way for a new generation of 'giants' like Wiggins, Cavendish and Froome. But this does not mean that professional cycling was devoid of Anglo-Saxon riders in the years before the First World War. The United States produces 'stayers' like Iver Lawson and Bobby Walthour, as well as world-class sprinters like Arthur Zimmerman, Eddie Bald, George Banker, Frank Kramer and Marshall Walter Taylor. Together, they were the 'kings of the track' and Taylor — known in those less politically correct times as 'the Flying Negro' — remains to this day the only black world cycling champion. On the other side of the world, the Australians Jacky Clark and the young Robert Spears are already making a name for themselves. The Americans seldom take part in road races, but indoor six-day events are hugely popular. Jim Morgan, Joe Fogler, Eddy Root, Charley Miller and Floyd McFarland are among the sporting superstars of their time. Their Australian counterparts are Reginald McNamara and Alfred Goullet.

Madison Square Garden,
here seen in December 1908.
This world-famous sporting temple
gives its name to the 'madison',
a two-man indoor track event
that is still ridden today.

Bobby Walthour in December 1909.

CYCLO-CROSS — A MILITARY INVENTION

To say that Flanders is the birthplace of cyclo-cross is to be highly economical with the historical truth! It is the French Army that first invents this new sporting discipline. It develops out of the friendly rivalry between a number of French cycle troops. They do what people all over the world love to do: test themselves against each other. After a large-scale exercise conducted by the French military in 1900, Private Daniel Gousseau issues a bold challenge to several of his cyclist colleagues. He suggests that the following Sunday they organize a race with their bikes across fields, over streams and through woods, for no other reason than to see which of them is best at it. And so a new branch of cycling sport is born: *cross-country*. But because 'competitors' in the new discipline soon discover that they spend as much of their time running and jumping over obstacles as they do on their bikes, the term *cyclo-pédestre* is added to the title.

What starts as a bit of fun amongst bored soldiers soon becomes a serious sporting activity. Gousseau, supported by his superiors in the army and encouraged by the journalist Géo Lefèvre (who is later one of the initiators of the Tour de France), approaches the French Cycling Union to discuss giving *cross-country cyclo-pédestre* formal recognition as a proper branch of the cycling sport. And with success! On 16 March 1902, the first official French cyclo-cross championship is held near the Kremlin-Bicêtre military base in Paris. In the following years, the discipline receives a further boost from the participation of non-military cyclists and even a number of leading professional racers. The young Octave Lapize, the first rider to carry his bike on his shoulder across difficult parts of the course, wins the national title in 1907. Between 1909 and 1914, Eugène Christophe is French champion for six successive years. It is also in France after the First World War, in 1924 at Suresnes near Paris, that the Critérium International — the first unofficial world championship — is held.

Cyclo-cross is invented in the French Army as a way to pass the time on a Sunday afternoon!

The riders slide down into the notorious Trou du Sable (Sandpit) on the spectacular course at Suresnes during the first official cyclo-cross world championship in 1924.

Because the racers run a lot during their cross-country, the term *cyclo-pedèstre* is added to the discipline's original French name.

THE IMPRESSIONS OF A SOLDIER-CYCLIST

While six-day events are the big thing in the United States at the start of the 20th century, in Western Europe it is speed competitions that attract the largest crowds. This is the era when the bike is still lovingly referred to as *'la petite reine'* (the little queen) and tests of pure speed are regarded as the absolute highlight of track cycling. Racers such as Thorvald Ellegaard, Willy Arend, Louis Grogna and Henri Mayer tear around the circuit like biking acrobats to the thrilled gasps of their thousands of fans, while from the sidelines they are watched by increasingly ambitious managers, keen to negotiate ever-bigger deals. The public love their sprinters — 'the aristocrats of the track' — and this popularity gradually spreads to the sport of cycling in general.

This is also the era that sees the first cars and the introduction of film and photography, all of which are new inventions demonstrated with pride at the 1900 World Exhibition in Paris, as are the moving staircase (escalator) and Rudolf Diesel's revolutionary engine. In fact, it seems as if Paris is the centre of the world, all the more so since the Olympic Games and the world track cycling championships are also held there that same year. One of the sprinters hotly tipped by a chauvinistic French public to lift the title is Edmond Jacquelin. His rise to the top of the sport is meteoric. He wins his first national sprint title at the age of just 20 and takes bronze in the world championships later that summer. In subsequent years, he triumphs at prestigious meetings in Vienna, Antwerp, Berlin and Paris. This not only earns him a small fortune, both in prize money and starting fees, but also elevates him to the ranks of the Parisian *beau monde*. The sprinter is the darling of the French cycling scene. The fans cheer him, the journalists write about him, and both are lyrical in their praise. The former baker's assistant from Burgundy is now held in the highest esteem. People have great respect for a man who is able to leave behind his humble origins and climb to the top of the social ladder through his own remarkable efforts. In short, he is a national phenomenon.

What's more, Jacquelin does not disappoint. He duly wins the world championship in Paris, beating Harie Meijers and Willy Arend along the way. Overnight, this gives him an almost god-like status. In the eyes of the public, he can do no wrong. During the day, he is the king of the track. At night, he flits from bar to bar and cabaret to cabaret. He has his own box at the theatre and drives through the streets in a striking carriage, drawn by two white stallions and driven by a coloured manservant. But his greatest victory is still to come. On Ascension Day, 16 May 1901, at the Parc des Princes in Paris, he beats the African-American Marshall — 'Major' — Walter Taylor, the 1899 world champion and perhaps the most legendary of all sprinters in this heroic age of sprinting, who many had thought was unbeatable.

Jacquelin carries on competing until 1914, but his fame slowly starts to wane. The popularity of road racing is on the increase, but Jacquelin sticks resolutely to the track, both as a stayer and as a six-day rider. What's more, his physical ability gradually declines as he gets older, so that he wins fewer races. The new stars of cycling are now Maurice Garin, Louis Trousselier and Octave Lapize. When war breaks out, Jacquelin is 39 years old. Even so, he joins the French Army, but is not sent to the front; instead, he serves as a driver. But the soldiers he drives often still recognize the man behind the wheel of the lorry. Some of them even cheered him to victory as teenagers. It is perhaps typical of Jacquelin that he is not content to be 'just' another driver. He keeps a diary entitled *Life in the regiment. Impressions of a soldier-cyclist* and his writings are later published in episodes in *La Vie Claire*.

Edmond Jacquelin, world sprint champion, who will later write for a newspaper during the Great War.

Edmond Jacquelin survives the First World War and returns home to Paris. But his glory days are over. Many men of his generation died at the front and the new generations of cycling fans no longer know who he is. He finds this difficult to accept and loses himself in an increasingly extravagant lifestyle that quickly eats up his remaining wealth. The great French sprint king dies on 29 June 1928 as a beggar.

Jacquelin before the start of the French 100-kilometre road race championship on 1 June 1913.

'FOLD BICYCLES! BICYCLE ON SHOULDERS!'

In 1898, the Belgian Minister of War Jules Vanden-peereboom decides to add a company of cyclists to each of the four battalions of Carabineers. They are equipped with 'Belgica' folding bicycles and are usually assigned guard duties or reconnaissance tasks by their cavalry colleagues. For training purposes, the companies are divided into platoons of roughly 50 men, which are further subdivided into sections. Each platoon has its own doctor, mechanics and lorries. From 1906 onwards, there is also an instruction manual: *Instruction pour les Compagnies Cyclistes*.

Each training exercise takes place over roughly 60 kilometres at an average speed of 12 kilometres per hour. However, the route always contains sections that need to be traversed on foot, which means that the bike needs to be carried on the shoulder (in addition to the soldier's full pack). There are also drill routines, where on the officer's command the soldiers must dismount, fold their bike, put it on

Carabineer Cyclists. The low height of the bike means that it is quick to get on and off.

their shoulder, take it off again, unfold it, and be ready to ride off as quickly as possible. It is even stipulated that the folded bicycle should be carried with the wheels to the left, the gear sprocket to the right and the saddle behind the left shoulder!

This detachment is ready to fire from a kneeling position, with their 'Belgica' bicycles folded on their backs.

An original 'Belgica' folding bike.

CYCLING CRISIS IN BELGIUM

During the UCI chairmanship of Emile Beukelaer Belgian cycling experiences a dramatic decline. The fall in interest in bike racing is just as spectacular as its sudden rise in the previous decade. The dream of King Leopold II to turn Belgium into a cycling nation looks destined not to be fulfilled — or at least not yet. After Protin and Houben, the supply of Belgian champions dries up. Of the 21 velodromes constructed in Belgium between 1891 and 1896, only six are still open in 1901. The malaise is so great that for the following three years no national track championship is organized. Until 1905, the Zurenborg cycling track in Antwerp is the only one that remains effectively operational. Ironically enough, this is where that year's world championships are held! The French professional Gabriel Poulain is the fastest sprinter and the American Bobby Walthour is best over the 100 kilometres (ridden behind pace-setters on motorbikes). The only Belgian entrant in the 100 kilometres is Arthur Vanderstuyft, who finishes sixth, some 24 laps behind the winner.

Belgian road racing is not doing much better. Liege-Bastogne-Liege is finding it hard to get off the ground. After three successive editions in 1892, 1893 and 1894, the fourth is only held in 1908. It is more or less the same story with Paris-Brussels. Ridden for the first time in 1893, it has to wait until 1906 for a re-run. In 1901 and 1902, the Belgian national titles are contested through lack of interest in the Netherlands, and in 1906 there is no championship at all. During this same period, the list of Belgian riders in the Tour de France can almost be counted on the fingers of one hand. There are just four Belgian cyclists in the very first Tour of 1903. Marcel Kerff finishes sixth and Aloïs Catteau is seventh. It is no surprise, perhaps, that both of them have strong French connections. As the son of a cattle salesman and butcher, Kerff regularly bikes from his home in Sint-Martens-Voeren with baskets full of meat to the market in… Paris! Catteau was even born in France, in Tourcoing, but is a Belgian national and lives in the border town of Menen.

The lack of top-class riders and the closure of the velodromes are certainly two of the reasons for the crisis in Belgian cycling. But the biggest reason is undoubtedly the advent of the motor car and the motorbike. The bicycle might have been a fine example of technological ingenuity back in the 1880s and the 1890s, but it cannot compare with the speed, style and comfort of motorized transport in the 1900s. The reign of *'la petite reine'* is brought to an abrupt end. The velodrome at Spa is transformed into a motordrome. The track meetings in Ostend have to make way for an annual automobile fair. The rich and the famous turn their backs on cycling: cars (and later planes) are now their new toys. Equally fascinated by the new inventions, a number of (the wealthier) professional cyclists also make the switch to the new machines. Léon Houa, a three-time winner of Liege-Bastogne-Liege, becomes a test pilot for Renault. Another Liege racer, Lucien Hautvast, takes up rally driving.

This evolution is perhaps best epitomized in the person of Jan Olieslagers. He first joins the Antwerp Bicycle Club as an amateur cyclist, before becoming a member of the Antwerp Motor Club and, finally, the Antwerp Aviation Club! In similar fashion, the Liege-born track racer Charles Van den Born, a professional cyclist from 1895 to 1910 and seven-time Belgian sprint champion, accepts a position as an instructor for the French aeroplane manufacturer Henry Farman. He later becomes the first man to fly a biplane over the uncharted regions of South-East Asia, but in 1914 returns to France at the request of the Belgian government to set up and run the Belgian School of Military Aviation for the training of fighter pilots. After the Armistice in 1918, he goes back to the Far East to take up an appointment as the director of the airport at Saigon (now Ho Chi Minh City) in Vietnam.

But if the wealthier classes have lost interest in bicycles and in cycling as a sport, the ordinary man in the street or field has not. As a result (in part, at least), the focal point for bike racing in Belgium undergoes a geographical shift. It is no longer focused on Brussels and Wallonia, but moves northwards into Flanders, and in particular to the provinces of West and East Flanders, albeit at a much more modest level. This is the era of 'poor Flanders', where people can only make a living by taking on hard and low-paid seasonal work in the brick ovens and chicory kilns of Northern France, or else by commuting to the textile factories in Roubaix or the coal mines in Wallonia. One of the few moments of respite from this harsh existence is the annual village fair. Clever innkeepers put a barrel at each end of their street, draw a finishing line in front of their door and hey presto: you

suddenly have a race track! In sporting terms, these
village races are modest in the extreme, but they
help to keep cycling as a sport alive. Just as impor-
tantly, they keep alive the love of cycling in poor
labourers who are used to sweating for a living and
have no problem in sweating to try and win their
local village race, if only to secure their own
'15 minutes of fame'.

Charles Van den Born (right) takes on the Frenchman Léon Hourlier
and the German Willy Bader in a sprint race at the Vel' d'Hiv circuit in Paris.

Hélène Dutrieu follows a pathway very similar to the one followed by Jan Olieslagers and Charles Van den Born: from cycling to motor sport to aviation. This is remarkable enough for a man. For a woman in the social climate prevailing at the start of the 20th century, it is nothing short of extraordinary! Like her male counterparts, Hélène also goes on to play a significant role during the First World War.

She is the daughter of a Belgian army officer, born in Tournai on 10 July 1877. At an early age, she moves with her parents to the nearby French city of Lille. This means that she is brought up more as a French child than as a Belgian one, although until her marriage in 1922 she has only Belgian nationality. She has a brother, Eugène, five years older than herself, who is an excellent sprinter and a professional cyclist between 1894 and 1901.

Hélène is also mad about cycling and from the age of 14 onwards risks life and limb on the race track in Tournai, where she later takes part in the few competitions that are starting to be organized for women at this time. She turns out to have natural talent and is soon breaking speed records. Sometimes she races with Eugène and in 1895 the siblings win a tandem competition at the velodrome in Ostend. A month later, Hélène sets a new world hour record with the help of human pacesetters. Her distance of 39 kilometres 190 metres smashes the old record (held by Debatz with 35 kilometres 936 metres) by a large margin.

Hélène is just 18 years old but already a star in the limited world of women's cycling. She crosses the English Channel to take part in the Ladies Cycle Races in the Royal Aquarium, a large indoor event hall in Westminster. Competitions for women are something completely new and also start to attract large crowds in Belgium. Dutrieu is seen performing by thousands in the Parc de la Boverie in Liege and in the Zurenborg velodrome in Antwerp, and in August 1896 she wins the Grand Prix d'Europe, a speed prize for ladies over 2,000 metres in Brussels. Later that same month, she is in the line-up for a meeting in Ostend that is billed as the *Championnat du monde pour dames* (Ladies World Championships). She triumphs in the 2,000 metres sprint, is second in the 1,000 metres and third in the tandem race.

By now, track racing for women is very popular, but it also meets with strong opposition from certain quarters. Cycling, say some doctors, will make the female racers infertile. The church regards it as a disgraceful voyeuristic spectacle. But the free-thinking Dutrieu doesn't care: she is making a good living on the track and has no intention of stopping! In 1897, she is back in the London Aquarium, where she is victorious in the Twelve Days' Lady Cyclists' International Race. In Ostend, she extends her (unofficial) world title. Notwithstanding public doubt about the sport in some quarters, King

LES VIEILLES GLOIRES DU CYCLE
ont toutes monté le " PNEU DUNLOP " le premier

Mlle Hélène DUTRIEUX

Hélène Dutrieu —
the Marianne Vos of her day.

The readers of the well-known magazine *La Vie au grande air* love Hélène Dutrieu's stunts.

LA "MOTO AILÉE"

Mlle Dutrieu dans la " Moto ailée ".

Voici en quoi consiste cet audacieux numéro, importé à Paris par Mlle Hélène Dutrieu, la charmante artiste, célèbre autrefois sur les vélodromes, et qui abandonna la piste pour la scène et les acrobaties sportives. Montée sur une légère motocyclette, elle descend du cintre en suivant une étroite piste qui, arrivée près du sol, se recourbe et s'arrête brusquement. Elle est alors projetée presque verticalement dans le vide et vient retomber sur une plate-forme située à 15 mètres plus haut. Ce numéro, que l'on a pu voir pendant quelques jours dans un music-hall parisien, a été interrompu par ordre de la préfecture de police, comme trop dangereux. Un soir, en effet, l'audacieuse cycliste dévia de la ligne droite, manqua la plate-forme et ne dut son salut qu'à sa présence d'esprit, qui lui permit de saisir de la main gauche une corde, pendant que sa machine allait s'abîmer dans les fauteuils d'orchestre.

Leopold II awards her the Cross in the Order of St. Andrew — with diamonds! As the icing on the cake, she is invited to take part in prestigious meetings at the famous Buffalo Velodrome in Paris and the following year at the velodrome in Berlin.

Later in her career, she is destined to return to these and other European capitals — not as a bike racer, but as a variety artist. By the time she is 22 years old, her sporting career is not as dynamic as it once was. For her, cycling has lost its excitement and its attraction. She needs a new challenge and so she becomes a comedienne in the Paris theatres. These palaces of entertainment are famed for staging large and spectacular acrobatic stunts. Dutrieu devises a stunt of her own that involves her sprinting down a ramp and then looping the loop on her bike inside a vertical track. She performs it for the first time in September 1903 at the famous Olympia in Paris to riotous applause. Many other theatre owners are happy to pay good money for a stunt as death-defying as this one, and she repeats it at theatres in London, Berlin and elsewhere. Later, she performs similar tricks on motorbikes, before taking up rallying, which makes her one of the very first female motorists.

The speed and excitement of motor racing leads her perhaps inevitably to the next and most dangerous mode of transport: the aeroplane, which is still very much in its infancy. Inspired by stories of the Wright brothers, Alberto Santos-Dumont and Louis Blériot, she starts training to be a pilot at the age of 31. After successfully completing a number of test flights, she gains her pilot's license on 23 November 1910. It is only the 27th license to be issued by the Belgian Aeroclub, and the first to a woman. She takes part in meetings and demonstrations in Russia and the United States, and in the Italian city of Florence she wins the King's Shield — a speed and consistency competition — ahead of 13 male aviators. In 1912, she becomes the first woman to pilot a flying boat and for her sporting results achieved in French aeroplanes on 9 January 1913 she is awarded the Legion d'honneur, France's highest civil order of merit. Not to be outdone, the Belgian government appoints her as an Officer in the Leopold Order.

At the age of 22, Dutrieu exchanges her cycle for a motorbike. Not much later, she is flying an aeroplane!

A TRIANGULAR RELATIONSHIP:
THE MANUFACTURER, THE PRESS AND THE RACER

By the start of the 20th century, the creed of amateurism, as stubbornly preached by the English sporting associations, is a dead letter in the rest of the western world. French cycle manufacturers like Alcyon, La Française and Peugeot understand that bike racing is the ideal 'shop window' to promote their products. And in the land of Molière there are plenty of opportunities, both on the road and on the track. As a natural progression, the big manufacturers are also keen to become the sponsors of the best racers. Good sporting results are not only a good advertisement for the winning rider and his bike, but also for accessories like saddles, tyres, chains and gear sprockets. In fact, after the big races like Bordeaux-Paris or Paris-Roubaix, the manufacturers and their products feature more prominently on posters and in newspaper adverts than the winners themselves!

These adverts provide papers like *Le Petit Journal*, *L'Auto-Vélo* and *La Bicyclette* with the money they need to organize new races and to lionize new champions. Their readers love heroic stories of triumph and failure played out by modern-day gladiators on two wheels, stories which in turn sell even more newspapers. In this way, the foundations for modern professional cycling are laid on the basis of an unholy alliance between three key players: the bike manufacturers, the well-paid professional racers and the 'gentlemen' of the written press. Spurred on by this mutually beneficial triangular relationship, cycling in France flourishes at an astonishing speed. There are four velodromes in Paris alone: the Buffalo track in Neuilly, the track at the Parc des Princes, the track at Vincennes and the Velodrome d'Hiver (usually shortened to Vel' d'Hiv). It is difficult to keep count of the number of new one-day classics and multi-day stage races, and in 1903 the greatest race of them all, the Tour de France, is launched for the very first time: 'an extraordinary challenge of human endurance', involving six stages each of more than 400 kilometres. This bold initiative will grow to become an unparalleled sporting and commercial success, transforming Tour winners like Maurice Garin, Louis Trousselier, Lucien Petit-Breton and Octave Lapize into 'the summer presidents of the republic'!

Italy quickly follows the French example. The bike manufacturers Bianchi and Atala and the tyre-maker Pirelli become the willing sponsors of the country's top riders, while the sporting newspapers *Corriere dello Sport*, *La Gazetta dello Sport* and the pink *Milanese Gazetta* compete with each other to organize the biggest and the best races. The first edition of the Tour of Lombardy takes place in 1905, followed by Milan-Sanremo in 1907 and the Giro d'Italia (Tour of Italy) in 1909.

Newspapers organize cycling races and cycling races fill newspaper columns — and so the cycle continues.

When Camille Fily starts in the second edition of the Tour de France on 2 July 1904, he is exactly 17 years and 15 days old. This makes him the youngest ever participant in *La Grande Boucle*, a record he still holds today. Journalists refer to Fily as *Le Gosse Lochois* (The Loches Kid), a reference to the cycling club for which he rides. With a total of 2,428 kilometres over six stages, it is one of the toughest and most memorable of the early Tours, not least because the spectators have no qualms about helping their favourites and hindering their rivals in ways that are anything but sporting. Only 44 of the 88 competitors succeed in reaching the finish in Paris, with Maurice Garin as the winner for the second year in a row. Lucien Pothier is runner-up and the young Fily ends in a creditable ninth place. However, so many irregularities have happened en route that the French Cycling Association feels obliged to amend the result. On 30 November 1904 — four months after the Tour has ended and for reasons that are far from clear — 19 riders are disqualified, including the first four finishers and Camille Fily! The new winner is Henri Cornet, who only arrived as fifth in Paris and is just 19 years of age, making him another of the youngest participants.

Undismayed, *Le Gosse Lochois* fights back in 1905. Still only 18 years and 8 days old, he is tenth in the 575-kilometre long Bordeaux-Paris epic and later ends fourteenth in that summer's Tour. It is his last ride in the race. He marries his childhood sweetheart and sets off for his three years of national military service. He never really picks up his cycling career after leaving the army, and when war breaks out in 1914 he is soon back in uniform. He survives for four years on the Western Front but is killed on 11 May 1918, just two days before his 31st birthday, during the Battle of Mount Kemmel. Ironically enough, he is shot while taking a message to a command post at the hamlet of Millekruis... by bike. His brother Georges, likewise a cyclist, also fails to live through the war, having already fallen at Verdun in May 1916.

Towards the end of the First World War, many French soldiers lose their lives at the Battle of Mount Kemmel. One of them is Camille Fily, the youngest ever rider in the Tour de France.

A WOMAN WITH BALLS

Immediately after the end of the first Tour de France for men in 1903, it is suggested that a similar race for women is held the following year. The idea is dismissed as 'unreasonable' or even 'immoral', but five years later a 33-year-old French woman demands to take part alongside the male competitors. Her wish is not granted, but she is not so easily put off. She rides all the same stages as the men, albeit the day after the official Tour caravan has passed. And she succeeds in reaching Paris and completing the 4,488-kilometre course. The name of this remarkable woman is Marie Marvingt — and she will show the same courage and determination during the First World War.

Born in Nancy in 1875, Marie — like her father Felix — loves sporting adventures. By the time she is four years old, she can already swim four kilometres in her local river. Later, she accompanies her father on long mountain treks and learns how to ride a horse, fire a gun and fence. Encouraged by Felix, she also tries her hand at gymnastics and athletics. When she is 15 years old, she cycles from Nancy to Naples, just to watch the eruption of a volcano.

In 1899, she is one of the first women to be awarded a driving license for the 'new' motor car. That same year, she climbs the highest peaks in the French and Swiss Alps, and two years later makes her first balloon flight. Still searching for new challenges, she switches from cars to planes and in 1909 becomes the first woman to fly across the English Channel. Her heroic deeds fill the newspapers and the public adore her. To cap it all, in her 'spare time' she successfully completes her studies to become a surgical nurse.

Marie is not a cyclist as such, but she adds the wish to become the first woman to ride in the Tour de France to her bucket list. What Alfonsina Strada will do in the Giro d'Italia in 1924, Marie wants to do sixteen years earlier in 1908. Not that she can rely on much support from the organizers. 'You're a woman, you can't possibly do this!' she is told. She doesn't listen. Marie is what we would today call 'a woman with balls'. She is determined to complete all fourteen stages and all 4,488 kilometres, following 24 hours behind the men. It is not simply that she wants to prove that women are capable of amazing performances, sporting or otherwise. She loves also the idea of the challenge and just wants to see if she can do it.

The 1908 Tour is won by Lucien Petit-Breton. Only 36 of the 114 participants make it to Paris. But Marie makes it as well, meaning that she does better than 78 of the men. In 1910, her lifetime's achievements are recognized by the Academy of Sports with

the award of the Medaille d'Or 'for all sports', the only time a medal is awarded in this way for performance in different sporting disciplines.

If Marie Marvingt wants to do something, nothing will stop her from doing it. She has proven this on a bike; she will prove it again during the First World War. Driven on by patriotism and her unrelenting quest for new adventures, she wants to help defend her country. She disguises herself as a man under the name of 'Marcel Beaulieu' and volunteers for the 42nd Regiment of Foot. She is quickly exposed (by her own cousin!) but is allowed to stay at the front as a nurse. In this capacity, she is temporarily attached to a mountain battalion of the Chasseurs Alpins in the Dolomites. But 'sister' Marvingt wants more. She helps to set up an air ambulance service and becomes the first trained and certificated 'flying nurse' in the French Army. In 1915, she is awarded the Croix de Guerre for bravery and she fully justifies her nickname in the press: *La Fiancée du Danger*.

Even after the Armistice, Marie continues to dedicate herself to ensure the fastest possible transport of the sick and the injured. She attends conferences all around the world and remains active in the field of medical aviation, also during the Second World War. Age seems to have no effect on her: she carries on searching for new challenges and adventures her whole life long. At the age of 85, she gains her license as a helicopter pilot. Even more remarkable, two years before her death in 1963 she cycles from Nancy to Paris in a single ride, a distance of more than 300 kilometres! In her native city, at Place de la Carrière 8, a plaque on the wall honours the memory of *La Fiancée du Danger*. Schools and streets throughout France are also named after this extraordinary woman 'with balls' from the pioneering age of aviation.

Marie Marvingt, the first 'flying nurse' in the French Army.

1907: THE REAL START
OF THE BELGIAN LOVE-AFFAIR WITH BIKES

During the early years of the 20th century, France is the cradle of professional cycle racing. The brief surge of interest in Belgium in the 1890s is of relatively short duration, so that cycling has become little more than a popular pastime, with an occasional race for fun at local village fairs. When the winner of one of these village races, a simple farm-hand named Cyrille Van Hauwaert, travels the 25 kilometres from his home in Moorslede to watch the arrival of Paris-Roubaix, he immediately knows what he needs to do if he ever wants to make it in the world of cycling racing: he must stop cycling 'around the church tower' and start cycling in France. That is where the big races are held. That is where the big money can be earned. In spite of a certain degree of French 'protectionism', Cyrille manages to gain selection for the 1907 edition of Paris-Roubaix. He finishes second behind Georges Passerieu, but ahead of Louis Trousselier, winner of the Tour de France just two years previously.

Fourteen days later, Van Hauwaert goes one step better: he wins the marathon race between Bordeaux and Paris. It is a victory that resonates around the cycling world, especially in his home country. Not only is he the first Belgian to win a race of international standing, but the poor farm worker also becomes a rich man overnight! All the big bike manufacturers are interested in signing him up and offer him lucrative contracts. He decides to leave La Française and cash in on his new market value with Alcyon. It is a move that neither the Parisian bike-maker nor the man from West Flanders will regret. Next spring he wins both Milan-Sanremo and Paris-Roubaix, and the sale of Alcyon bikes increases dramatically in Northern Italy and West Flanders.

120. Cyclisme
VAN HOUWAERT, *routier Belge*

Cyrille Van Hauwaert, the first Belgian to win an international classic.

1907 — the year in which Cyrille Van Hauwaert wins his first classic — is a turning point in the history of cycling in Belgium. It is the start of what we now regard as the Belgian love-affair with bikes. Cyrille becomes an instant superstar, the Peter Sagan of his day. In a single season he earns 40,000 Belgian francs, a sum for which a factory worker would need to work 12 hours a day for a quarter of a century. But the ordinary factory worker can now afford to buy a bike. And perhaps with a little luck and a lot of hard work, maybe he can win a fortune like Van Hauwaert. This, at least, is the dream that inspires many young Belgians. And it is this dream that helps to turn cycling into the country's national sport. Hundreds of young men turn their back on the hard labour of the factories and fields and follow in Van Hauwaert's footsteps to take part in great French and Italian races. Many of them fall by the wayside, but a fortunate few are able to turn their dream into reality and return home with pots of gold.

One of these new cycling celebrities is Odiel Defraeye. In 1912, he becomes the first Belgian to win the Tour de France. When he arrives home from Paris after his triumph, he receives the kind of welcome normally reserved for royalty. Not only in his native village of Rumbeke, but also in Brussels. His victory brings him prize money of 32,000 Belgian francs, more than enough to buy a large plot of land and build an impressive hotel: the Hôtel des Sports. It even has its own velodrome in the backyard! Defraeye also permits himself the luxury of being the first person in his village to own a motor car. Not bad for someone who just some years earlier was struggling to make ends meet as a brush-maker.

Thanks to the successes of Van Hauwaert and Defraeye, cycling in Flanders receives an enormous boost. The number of races increases spectacularly. And not just in village streets around two barrels! On 28 July 1907, the first Schelde Prize in Antwerp is organized. This is a race of more than 100 kilometres, which is long for the norm in Flanders at that time. In the meantime, Paris-Brussels is also resurrected. A year later, a multi-stage Tour of Belgium makes its first appearance on the calendar. Perhaps not surprisingly, all these events are won by Frenchmen: Maurice Leturgie, Gustave Garrigou and Lucien Petit-Breton. It shows that France is still ahead of Belgium — but no longer by quite so much.

The Belgians are catching up fast. Cycling has changed from being a fun pastime or a fairground attraction. Instead, it is now a professional top sport at its hardest and best. Inspired by Van Hauwaert, who is known in France as *Le Lion des Flandres*, a first Flemish championship is organized in Koolskamp in 1908. It is won by another West Fleming, Robert Wancour, who regains his title the following year. In 1909, Cyrille Van Hauwaert wins Bordeaux-Paris for a second time. His fellow villager Jules Masselis is best in the 1910 edition of the Tour of Belgium. In fact, the Belgians now dominate this stage race on home soil. René Vandenberghe from Roeselare wins in 1911, Odiel Defraeye in 1912, Dieudonné Gauthy from Liege in 1913 and Louis Mottiat from the Hainaut village of Bouffioulx in 1914. Vandenberghe also adds Brussels-Roubaix to his list of victories in 1910, Defraeye triumphs in the 1913 Milan-Sanremo and Mottiat in the last Paris-Brussels before the war.

Odiel Defraeye,
the first Belgian winner of the Tour de France.

Camp de Beverloo 1914.

A BELGIAN BATTALION OF CARABINEER CYCLISTS

During a reorganization of the Belgian Army in June 1911, the existing four companies of cyclists — one for each battalion of the Carabineers — are amalgamated into a battalion of their own, the 5th Carabineers under the command of Major Collyns. Two additional horizontal bars are added to the new model of folding bikes to give them extra stability. Officers note that field exercises go better when the bike is not folded but is carried on the back in the 'open' position. As in the French Army, the link to competitive cyclo-cross is quickly made.

From 15 December 1913, the 5th Battalion is attached to the Cavalry Division. It now acts independently from the regiment whose name it bears and is given a new title to reflect this: the Carabineers Cyclist Battalion. It also moves its home base to the barracks at Vilvoorde. The new commandant is Major Siron. In addition to a limited staff, he also has three companies each of three platoons at his disposal, plus a machine gun section. This section is armed with two light automatic weapons, fired from a folding bipod stand.

Members of the Carabineers Cyclist Battalion in battledress. A rolled shoulder cape is strapped to the handlebars.

A section of cyclists from the 1st Company in 1913, getting ready for action with their portable machine guns.

BERLIN, CRADLE OF THE EUROPEAN SIX-DAY EVENTS

Professional cycling is also active in Germany before the First World War. Very active. Especially in the field of six-day events. The first race of this kind to be organized in Europe is held in 1909 in the exhibition hall of the Zoological Gardens in Berlin, where a special temporary track is installed. The winners are the American couple McFarland-Moran (six-days have already been popular in the US for some time), but this hardly seems to matter: the public is sold on this new and exciting form of racing. The Berlin Six Day Race — which in 2018 celebrates its 106th edition — is an instant hit. Other circuits in Berlin — like the Berliner Sportpalast in Schöneberg — are soon organizing six-day meetings of their own. The craze also spreads to other German cities, with Kiel and Bremen leading the way in 1910, followed by Frankfurt, Mainz, Hamburg and Dresden in 1911.

The German Cycling Federation also programmes a number of road races. Nuremburg-Munich-Nuremberg is ridden for the first time in 1907 and from 1909 onwards a whole list of new events is added to the calendar: the Berlin Championship, Hannover-Berlin, Dresden-Berlin-Dresden and the Tour of Holstein. The opening spring classic is Berlin-Cottbus-Berlin, often referred to as the German Milan-Sanremo, and in 1910 the first edition is held of Berlin-Leipzig-Berlin, followed a year later by the Tour of Leipzig and the Saxony Grand Prix, the latter of which was won in 1912 by the Belgian Marcel Buysse, ahead of Charles Crupelandt.

Germany also has its own good crop of professional riders. The *Berufsradsport* is flourishing. At international level, their successes in the early years of the century are mainly on the track, with the stayer Thaddëus Robl and sprinters like August Lehr, Willy Arend and Henry Mayer. Later, they develop a number of excellent six-day specialists, such as Willie Lorenz and Walter Rütt, supported by a new generation of stayers, among whom Peter Gunther and Arthur Stellbrink lead the way.

The race track in the Zoological Gardens in Berlin, the setting for the first-ever six-day event in Europe.

Thaddëus Robl and Crown Prince Wilhelm of Prussia during the Berlin six-day event in 1909.

'LAD, IF YOU HAD NEVER RIDDEN ON THE TRACK...'

Cyrille Van Hauwaert is not happy when he has to share his leading position in the Alcyon cycling team with the French star Louis Trousselier. In frustration, he decides to branch out into track racing, where lucrative contracts are also waiting for him. He can earn more for a single track meeting than a bricklayer earns in a year. Many other Belgian riders decide to follow his example, so that track racing experiences something of a revival. It also undergoes a change in character. Ten years previously, it was a sport for the elite. It was watched by the wealthy middle class and the aristocracy from luxurious grandstands, and even the king had his own box at the track in Ostend. Now the velodromes become meeting places for ordinary men and women, who thrill to the excitement of the sprint races and team events. Several towns and cities build their own summer tracks. In 1901, there were only six tracks remaining in Belgium. By 1912, there are forty-seven — and, with the exception of the Ardennes region, they are spread over the whole country.

This revival also allows the cycling public to discover a new discipline: stayer or motor-paced racing. This type of racing demands great concentration and great bike control from the rider, since the speeds reached by the pace bikes sometimes border on the incredible. This makes for spectacular races and the crowds love them. The Ieper stayer Léon Vanderstuyft is a particular crowd favourite. In 1908, he is third in the world championship for amateurs and two years later he is runner-up with the professionals.

Another Belgian specialist in this discipline is Karel Verbist, who is national champion in 1908 and 1909. On the Zurenborg track, in his home town of Antwerp, he beats the Frenchman Paul Guignard, the first stayer to clock a distance of more than 100 kilometres in an hour. During this race Verbist sets new world records for the 100 kilometres (1 hour, 8 minutes and 57 seconds), the 50 kilometres (34 minutes and 15 seconds) and the hour (87.130 kilometres).

After his victory in the King's Prize on the Karreveld track in Brussels in 1909, Verbist is congratulated in person by King Leopold II. This race meeting is such a success that the organizers decide to programme a further meeting three days later on the Belgian national holiday. It seems

Poster for the Bundesfest Frankfurt in 1911. Cycle racing was very popular in Germany before the First World War.

certain that Verbist will win this race as well, since he enters the final lap well in the lead. However, a burst tyre causes his pace-maker Ceurremans to lose control over his motorbike, which starts to swing violently from side to side. Verbist crashes to the ground, but quickly gets to his feet, seemingly unharmed. Seconds later he is hit by the pace-bike of the German rider, Albert Schipke. This time his injuries are serious and within minutes he is dead. He is just 26 years old. The 'drama at Karreveld' plunges the entire nation into mourning and Verbist is given a funeral that befits a national hero.

A more popular tribute is sung in his memory by ordinary people at markets and fairs across the country: *Sjarelke, sjarelke, sjarelke Verbist, had jij niet gereden op de pist, had jij niet gelegen in uw kist...* (Verbist, lad, if you had never ridden the track, you wouldn't now be lying dead on your back...).

Karel Verbist is one the top stayer racers, who ride at dangerously high speeds behind powerful motorbikes.

Léon Van den Haute, the founder in 1912 of *Sportwereld*. After the First World War he also publishes an illustrated magazine with the same title.

'I CAN STILL HEAR THE SELLERS IN KOOLSKAMP!'

The successes of Cyrille Van Hauwaert and the resulting popularity of cycling is also noticeable in the Belgian press. The daily newspapers start publishing race results and it is no coincidence that 1907 — the year Van Hauwaert wins Bordeaux-Paris — also marks the appearance in Brussels of the first edition of *Le Vélo-Sport*. Within months, other sports journals fill the newspaper stands. Karel Steyaert, once a (mediocre) racer, now writes cycling articles for a living under the pseudonym of Karel Van Wijnendaele. Léon Van den Haute is the son of a public notary from Hemiksem, who lives and works in Brussels. Steyaert and Van den Haute become good friends, and when the Brussels publisher Patria proposes the launch of a Dutch-language sports paper aimed at a broad public, as a counterbalance to the 'elite' reporting in the French-language liberal press, they are quick to join the project. Van den Haute is the organizational brain, while Steyaert is the man with the literary talent.

The new paper is called *Sportwereld* (Sport World) and its first edition is scheduled to roll from the presses on Friday, 13 September 1912. Concepts such as 'product launch' and 'marketing'

have not yet been invented, but Van den Haute realizes that there is no better moment to promote a new sporting journal than on the day of a hugely popular sporting event. Thursday, 12 September 1912 is the day of the great Koolskamp Race, the Championship of Flanders, which since its inauguration in 1908 has attracted huge crowds. The editorial team decides to publish the first edition a day earlier than planned. As an extra touch, they print it on yellow paper, the colour that is traditionally associated with the Flemish people. The papers are collected from the railway station at Ardooie and taken by horse and cart to Koolskamp. Before the race has even started, the distributers are back on the phone to Brussels demanding a new delivery: the first batch has already sold out! Or as Van Wijnendaele later put it in his book *Het rijke Vlaamsche Wielerleven* (The rich world of Flemish cycling): 'I can still hear the sellers in Koolskamp, calling out the name of our first edition. Because *Sportwereld* was born on one of the great days of Flemish sport.' It is also one of the great days in Flemish journalism, since it marks the start of popular sports reporting in a part of the country that has previously been starved of this kind of media attention. Within weeks, the circulation figures for *Sportwereld* are through the roof.

The first edition of *Sportwereld*, dated 13 September 1912.

'GENTLEMEN, START!'

Léon Van den Haute is a born entrepreneur and Karel Van Wijnendaele knows how cycling works in Italy and, above all, in France. In these two great cycling countries the most important races are organized by the newspapers, which gain huge publicity as a result. If the Italians and French can do it, why can't a Belgian newspaper — *Sportwereld* — do the same! In terms of distance, difficulty and prestige, it will need to be something similar to Paris-Roubaix, Milan-Sanremo or the Tour of Lombardy. This rules out the Championship of Flanders, with its twenty 5-kilometre laps around the church in Koolskamp. But perhaps a longer race through the countryside of East and West Flanders; in other words, a true Tour of Flanders... Why not? Van den Haute and Van Wijnendaele are sold on the idea and set about turning it into reality. The former finds the money; the latter promotes the new race in their paper with as much bombast as he can.

With the legendary words *'Heeren, vertrekt'* (Gentlemen, start!), Karel Van Wijnendaele gets the very first Tour of Flanders under way at 6.15 in the morning on 25 May 1913. The race begins in Ghent, at the inn and cycle shop run by Frans Demeuyninck, on the corner of the Rooigemlaan and the Brugsesteenweg. Demeuyninck is the treasurer of the Ghent Cycle Club and his inn seems the perfect place for the participants to sign the pre-race registration sheet. In view of the early start, some of the riders have even stayed there overnight. The course is 324 kilometres long and passes through towns like Sint-Niklaas, Aalst, Oudenaarde, Kortrijk, Ieper, Ostend, Roeselare and Bruges.

Unfortunately, this first edition of 'Flanders Finest' is not a huge success. Of the 53 riders registered in advance to start, including twice Tour de France winner Lucien Petit-Breton, only 37 actually bother to turn up. The race itself is also disappointing. By halfway, 12 riders have an almost unassailable lead and the winner will come from this group. Six of the 12 eventually sprint for victory on the wooden circuit belonging to Oscar Braeckman in Maria-kerke. As the six enter the circuit, Arthur Maertens and Jan Van Ingelghem collide and are out of the running. Of the remaining four, Paul Deman is quicker than Jef Vandaele, Victor Doms and August Dierickx. 'That really was sport at its very best!' writes Van Wijnendaele in the following day's edition of *Sportwereld*.

The winner of the first Tour of Flanders is... French-speaking! True, Paul Deman is a Fleming, born and bred in the West Flanders village of Rekkem, but the village is so close to the Franco-Belgian border that more French is spoken than Flemish. The 24-year-old Deman has already won the Tour of Belgium as an amateur, but his victory in the inaugural Tour of Flanders hardly merits a mention in the foreign press. This is in stark contrast to his triumph in Bordeaux-Paris the following year. He is on the threshold of a brilliant international career, but unfortunately for him (and for the rest of Europe) the First World War breaks out just three months later. By October 1914, West Flanders is under German occupation and the world of cycling grinds to a halt.

Paul Deman, the winner of the first Tour of Flanders on 25 May 1913.

Sportwereld on 26 May 1913.

Most people assume — with, perhaps, good reason — that the Tour of Flanders is a publicity stunt devised by Van den Haute to boost the sales of his *Sportwereld* newspaper. But there might also be another reason for picking the spring of 1913 as the moment to launch a new cycling classic in Flanders. That year sees the World Exhibition come to the East Flanders city of Ghent. The Sint-Pieters-Aalst district — the site of the present-day Citadel Park and the Miljoenen quarter — is transformed into a temporary showground with broad avenues, each lined with the exhibition's palaces and pavilions. The 130-hectare site also contains parks, statues and a number of large water features. A new railway station — Ghent Sint-Pieters — is built especially for the occasion and wealthy visitors stay in the brand-new Flandria Palace Hotel on the Queen Maria Hendrika Square.

King Albert I and Queen Elisabeth are present on Sunday, 6 April 1913 for the festive opening of the *Exposition universelle et internationale de Gand*, which will run until the end of October. In the early years of the 20th century, these world exhibitions are spectacular extravaganzas of amusement and amazement, designed to showcase the achievements of individual countries. The Ghent edition is advertised as 'the greatest exposition ever held in Belgium, with no fewer than 25 nations represented!' The many popular features include the 'Old Flanders' precinct, a Congo museum, garden palaces and model farms. There are also foreign villages, where Europeans thrill to the sight of 'real' Senegalese or Filipino people, displayed almost like animals in a zoo. The exhibition also has an extensive programme of cultural and sporting events. There are fencing and tennis tournaments, a fight for the European heavyweight boxing crown between Georges Carpentier and Billy Wells, the European rowing championships and a football clash between the English Wanderers and the Dutch F.C. Haarlem. These events are all organized by a special Expo 'sports committee', chaired by the industrialist Albert Feyerick, captain of the Belgian fencing team at the 1908 Olympic Games in London (where his brother Ferdinand won a bronze medal) and the founder of the Latem Golf Club in 1909.

Not unnaturally, the committee feels that the sport of cycling should also be put in the spotlight during the Exhibition. The Belgian Cycling Federation and some of the leading bike manufacturers are given a stand in the Citadel Park, but Feyerick

also wants to have a prestigious race to add lustre to his reputation. In November 1912, he approaches Emile De Beukelaer, the Belgian president of the UCI, to ask him if it is possible to organize the 1913 world track cycling championships in Ghent. However, a meeting of the UCI in Paris in February 1913 awards the championships to Berlin and Leipzig. Feyerick will have to think of something else. Is the Tour of Flanders the result of his search for a possible alternative?

Little is known about the relationship between Feyerick, Van den Haute and Van Wijnendaele. What we do know is that Van Wijnendaele is a convinced Flemish nationalist, who sees cycling and sports journalism as weapons to be used against Belgium's French-speaking elite. Would he really collaborate with the organizers of the World Exhibition, which is dominated by that same 'bourgeois' elite? The pages of *Sportwereld* report once — and once only — that the inaugural Tour of Flanders is being organized *'in het kader van'* (within the context of) rather than *'in opdracht van'* (at the request of) the Exhibition. A nuance, perhaps, but a not unimportant one. The same article, published on 30 April 1913, goes on to say that agreement has been reached with three velodromes — Gentbrugge, Mariakerke and Evergem — to organize other cycling events during the Expo, but 'sufficiently spread to avoid competition between them.'

It is against this background that the inaugural Tour of Flanders takes place and it seems no coincidence that Ghent is chosen as the point of departure. After all, the eyes of the world are on the city in 1913. However, it is also worth nothing that Van den Haute and Van Wijnendaele do not choose to start their race among the elegant avenues of the Exhibition site, but opt instead for a working-class district on the Rooigemlaan. Is this intended as some kind of statement, to show that cycling is the sport of the ordinary Flemish people? True, the early kilometres of the race are routed through the Citadel Park, passing the Moroccan and Turkish pavilions, but soon after it leaves the Expo city — where all the posters and most of the presentations are in French, a language that the majority of ordinary Flemings cannot understand — and heads for the real heartland of Belgian cycling: the towns and villages of East and West Flanders.

The 1913 World Exhibition in Ghent. It is perhaps no coincidence that the city is also chosen as the starting place for the first Tour of Flanders.

A CYCLING ACROBAT BECOMES A SOLDIER

The Belgian Cycling Federation understands that the World Exhibition is an ideal opportunity to focus attention on its still relatively young sport. Small-scale competitions are organized in the Citadel Park, where the federation also has a stand, but perhaps more eye-catching still are the performances of some of the country's leading cycling acrobats. Perhaps the best of them all is Jean Van Camp, who performs tricks with his two-wheeler that almost defy belief: a kind of trial biker ahead of his time. Born in Jette on 26 November 1888, Van Camp has already built up quite a reputation for himself at village fairs and fetes, but the Expo is by miles his biggest stage so far. He is also a 'normal' racer, not perhaps of the highest calibre, but good enough to win the occasional race, like in Leuven in 1909 or in Boom in 1910. Less than a year after the Exhibition, Van Camp is more concerned with calibres of a different kind, as Private Second Class in the 1st Artillery Regiment. He is a gunner in the 12th Battery, defending the fort at Walem. It is here that he is killed on 1 October 1914, during the siege of Antwerp. After the war, his body is reburied in the civil cemetery in Laken, close to where he was born.

A document showing that Jean Van Camp was killed at Fort Walem.

THE FIRST TOUR DE FRANCE VICTORY
FOR PHILIPPE THYS

The organizing *L'Auto* newspaper announces a new concept for the 1913 edition of the Tour de France. For the first time, the course will run anti-clockwise around the country and the result will no longer be determined by the accumulation of points. Instead, the winner will be the rider with the best overall time, which immediately gives a huge advantage to the best climbers. One of these is the Belgian Philippe Thys. At first, however, he — and everyone else — is overshadowed at the start by the appearance of the Tunisian Ali Neffati, who is the first African to compete in the Tour and always rides with his fez! But once the real cycling starts, it is the Belgians who dominate. They win no fewer than ten of the fifteen stages: six for Marcel Buysse and one each for Jules Masselis, Firmin Lambot, Henri Vanlerberghe and Philippe Thys.

For Thys in particular, the new time-based results system is a godsend. He is an excellent uphill rider in the mountain stages and a highly consistent performer on the flat. Just as important, he is a clever strategist, who counts every second and saves energy wherever he can. He only attacks when he knows it can work to his benefit. In 1913, he is also helped by the fact that his closest rivals — Marcel Buysse and Eugène Christophe — both lose time with mechanical problems. His only serious challenger is Gustave Garrigou, but the clever Belgian keeps him at a safe distance and so wins his first Tour de France.

With this famous triumph, Philippe Thys — born in Anderlecht on 8 October 1889 — once again proves that he is a cycling 'jack-of-all-trades'. Not only does he win the first national cyclo-cross championships organized by the Belgian Cycling Federation in 1910, but he is also an excellent track racer, with numerous victories to his name.

Philippe Thys wins his first Tour de France in 1913.

LÉON AND LÉON: TRACK RACERS, PILOTS AND BROTHERS-IN-LAW

Wrestler and boxer Léon Hourlier later becomes a muscular bike racer.

On 18 January 1914, the duo Hourlier-Comès wins the six-day track event in Paris. The teammates both have the same first name — Léon — and they are brothers-in-law (Hourlier is married to Comès' sister). Sadly, they are both destined to die in the same plane, as pilots during the First World War.

Hourlier is the older of the two, born in Rheims on 16 September 1885. Before he becomes a cyclist, he also plays football, but is even better as a boxer and wrestler. His local wrestling trainer is former French champion Henry Caesar, who also trains a promising young cyclist named Maurice Brocco. Hourlier and Brocco do condition training together — gym exercises, running, skipping — and the latter eventually persuades the former to have a go on a bike. Hourlier turns out to be a natural talent. He makes his competitive cycling debut at the age of 18 and eventually becomes a good all-rounder, blessed with speed, strength, stamina and an abundance of self-confidence.

When he turns 20, he applies for a professional license. He decides to make the sprint his speciality

The Vel' d'Hiv, 18 January 1914:
Comès and Hourlier win the Six Days of Paris.

and moves to Paris, where he races at the Parc des Princes, the Buffalo velodrome and the Vel' d'Hiv against all the great sprinters of the day: Gabriël Poulain, Georges Decamps, the German Henri Meyer and the Italian champion Cesare Moretti. It is also in Paris that he meets his future wife. Alice Comès, an operetta singer, is the sister of another track racer, Léon Comès. The Comès family comes from Perpignan in south-eastern France, where Léon is born on 11 February 1889. At an early age, he moves to Paris with his parents. Like his sister, he also has a good voice and as a teenager he earns a living singing comic songs in Parisian clubs and cabarets. In his spare time, he knocks around with his friends from the 18th arrondissement, two of whom are cyclists: Maurice Schilles, who with André Auffray wins Olympic gold in the tandem discipline at the 1908 Games in London, and Henri Pélissier, the future winner of several classics, crowned by victory in the 1923 Tour de France.

Inspired and encouraged by his friends, Léon Comès also takes up cycling. He rides his first track race just after his 16th birthday. Three years later, he wins bronze at the French national sprint championships, behind his brother-in-law Léon Hourlier

and Emile Friol. The year after that, he triumphs in a sprint competition in Angers and also takes part in his first six-day event. In 1912, he is runner-up with Tour winner Lucien Petit-Breton is the Six Days of Brussels.

In the meantime, Léon Hourlier is also building up an impressive reputation for himself, with a string of victories in important sprint tournaments in Paris, Copenhagen, Antwerp, Brussels and Berlin. He wins three French national sprint titles (1908, 1911 and 1914) and takes the silver medal at both the world championship (1911) and the European championship (1913).

In January 1914, Hourlier and Comès decide to team up for the Six Days of Paris in the Vel' d'Hiv. All the great names of the day are there: Octave Lapize, Lucien Petit-Breton, Charles Crupelandt, André Perchicot, Oscar Egg and Walter Rütt. Even so, the brothers-in-law win by a convincing margin. The names of the riders they beat forces people to sit up and take notice. They are now stars in their own right.

Throughout the remainder of 1914, they cash in on their new-found status at various meetings across Europe. On 26 July, Léon Comès wins a

Jacquelin, Comès and Kreamer during the 1908 national championship on rollers in Paris.

tandem competition with Charles Meurger at the Parc des Princes, as part of the pre-programme for the arrival of the final stage in that year's Tour de France (which is won by Philippe Thys, ahead of Comès' childhood friend Henri Pélissier). On the same day, Léon Hourlier is the best in a prestigious sprint tournament at the Olympia circuit in Berlin. Eight days later, Germany declares war on France, but by then the cyclist has left the country.

The heroes of the last pre-war Six Days of Paris are now mobilized in defence of the motherland. Hourlier is first sent as a driver to a military transport unit, but he wants to be a pilot and on 1 February 1915 he applies for a transfer. Five months later, as a member of V97 squadron, he is flying over enemy territory and takes part in bombing raids on the German cities of Saarbrücken and Trier, for which he is awarded the Croix de Guerre. Comès is initially posted to the 89th Infantry Regiment, but he too wants to join the air force. Following his training, he is posted to the 19th squadron, where he flies a Voisin biplane on daily missions over the German lines, under constant threat from enemy fighters and ground fire from the trenches.

In the autumn of 1915, both the former racers are given a week's leave to rest, recuperate and visit their families. To boost the morale of soldiers on leave still further, the French Army organizes a number of sporting events for their entertainment. One such event is a boxing match on 16 October, featuring the famous French world champion Georges Carpentier, who is now also an aviator. Comès isn't really all that interested in attending the fight; he is happy to stay at home with his wife and child. What's more, the bout is taking place over 80 kilometres away, across roads badly damaged by the war.

But Hourlier keeps pressing his brother-in-law; he was once a boxer himself and doesn't want to miss the opportunity to see Carpentier fight. Besides, they don't need to drive; they can fly! That way, they can get back home to their families even quicker. Comès finally agrees and effectively signs their death warrant. Shortly after take-off, their plane crashes at Saint-Étienne-au-Temple. The precise cause of the crash remains unclear, but it seems likely they were shot down by the Germans. Comès, aged 26, and his brother-in-law Hourlier, aged 30, are buried in the military cemetery at Rheims.

THE WINNER WHO SHOULDN'T HAVE STARTED

Even though the first edition was not a great success, the *Sportwereld* paper decides to organize a second Tour of Flanders in 1914. This year the race will be held on 22 March, two months earlier than the previous year. This means that the Tour is now the first major event on the calendar. Although perhaps 'major' is something of an exaggeration. Van den Haute and Van Wijnendaele's race is largely unknown abroad and attracts very little interest from foreign teams. To make matters worse, the French bike manufacturers actually forbid their Belgian riders from taking part. Marcel Buysse has already given his word to his friend Karel Van Wijnendaele that he will be there, and so he decides to defy the ban. Alfons Spiessens and August Benoit, who ride for the JB Louvet team, do likewise.

Once again, the start is in the Rooigemlaan in Ghent, but the course as a whole has been shortened by some 45 kilometres. The loop around Ieper and Veurne has been scrapped, so that the riders now go directly from Kortrijk to Bruges. The finish has also been moved from Mariakerke to the summer circuit of Deesken De Poorter at Evergem.

As is so often the case, it is Henri Vanlerberghe who breaks open the race. Following an early attack near Zottegem, the man from Lichtervelde rides almost 100 kilometres solo. However, the group finally catches him on the road to Roeselare, but by the time they reach the wooden track at Evergem there are only eight of them left to contest the sprint. 'The grandstand was full and the sprint was bravely fought, but in the end Marcel Buysse won a well-deserved victory.' The irrepressible Vanlerberghe finishes as runner-up, although the story goes that Buysse pulls him back by his shirt in the last few metres 'to remind him of the deal he had made.' Pier Van de Velde is third and Aloïs Persijn fourth, followed by Arthur Depauw, August Dierickx, Georges Monseur and Alfons Spiessens.

Marcel Buysse, winner of the second Tour of Flanders, is the son of a family from Wontergem, which over two generations produces no fewer than 11 top-class cyclists. He is the oldest of four brothers. Jules and Cyriel are also professional riders and Lucien, three years his junior, is destined to win the Tour de France in 1926. Many people think that Marcel should also have won the Tour. In the 1913 edition he wins no fewer than six stages. After his victory in Perpignan, he is also ahead in the overall standings. However, four days later on the stage to Nice he breaks his handlebars in the descent from the Col de l'Estérel. This forces him to walk ten kilometres to the nearest village, where, according to the Tour regulations, he has to repair his own bike. This costs him two hours — and the race. In spite of this setback, he battles on gamely and manages to reach the finish in Paris in a remarkable third place!

When the First World War breaks out, a number of newspaper reports appear claiming that Marcel Buysse has been shot dead in Lotenhulle. Fortunately, it is not true, but the situation in the East Flemish village is far from safe. The village is occupied by the Germans on 17 October 1914. The troops also 'occupy' the local taverns and start drinking all the beer. Later that night, shots are heard. According some versions, the occupiers start arguing among themselves. The village priest confirms that he saw drunken Germans running

through the streets. Someone else says that one of the soldiers shouted out 'There is the enemy!' as a joke, which caused a passing Uhlan to open fire.

Whatever the truth of the matter, the situation quickly gets out of hand. Thinking they have been attacked by local civilians, the furious Germans now storm through the village, shooting as they go. An inn-keeper, the local baker and the village secretary are killed. Some of the officers threaten to burn down all the houses. They are persuaded to relent, but to ensure the population's future good behaviour they take a number of hostages. 'Including a renowned cyclist, the winner of many races. They were accused of supplying false information to the occupier, and some of them were later shot,' writes Virginie Loveling in her wartime diary. 'The cyclist', she continues, 'managed to escape and was given shelter.'

The renowned cyclist in question is Marcel Buysse. Together with a number of his fellow villagers, he is held captive for several hours. The Germans use this group as a living shield as they advance towards Tielt. Buysse somehow succeeds in slipping away and goes into hiding. As soon as things quieten down, he returns to his home village. Like elsewhere in the occupied parts of the country, spies and smugglers soon develop networks to work against the Germans. These networks can always make use of fast riders and in Lotenhulle 'Big Marcel' becomes their courier. Because he is well known as a famous racer (he won both the Tour of Saxony and the Tour of Kassel in 1912), the German sentries and patrols are usually willing to let him pass unhindered. Once, things nearly go wrong when he is caught in an ambush and wounded in the arm. But he manages to escape without being recognized.

After the Armistice, Marcel and his brother Lucien move to Italy, where they ride for the Bianchi team. Marcel finishes third in the 1919 Giro behind Girardengo and Belloni. In subsequent years, he wins a number of important six-day events in Brussels (1920), Ghent (1922) and New York (1924), before finally hanging up his bike and opening a hotel — the Hotel Continental — opposite Sint-Pieters station in Ghent. Later, it becomes a popular place to stay with foreign racers taking part in the Tour of Flanders.

Marcel Buysse, winner of the Tour of Flanders in 1914, is taken hostage by the Germans.

Henri Vanlerberghe, third from left, with his parents, Victor Vanlerberghe and Natalie Tampere, and his brothers, Gaston, Honoré and Amand.

THE DEATH-RIDER FROM LICHTERVELDE

Marcel Buysse is first across the finishing line in the 1914 Tour of Flanders, but Henri Vanlerberghe might just as easily have won. However, the man from Lichtervelde is a 'stamper' rather than a strategist. He often wastes his energy in ill-considered attacks and futile attempts to escape from the pack. That is also what happens in this race. He rides solo for more than 100 kilometres, but pays for his effort in the final sprint.

Vanlerberghe, born on 29 January 1891, has been a professional rider since 1909. In his home village he is known simply as *'Henri'ten'* or *'Riet'en de Coureur'* (Henry the Racer). His colleagues in the cycling fraternity know him as 'the Death-rider from Lichtervelde', from his habit of shouting at the start of every race: 'I'm going to ride you all dead today, you just wait and see!' Sadly, this bravura attitude seldom brings the hoped-for results. His impulsive way of racing means that his performance is wildly inconsistent. True, he manages to win a stage in the 1913 Tour de France, but that is about the sum of his achievement so far in his career.

Perhaps he might be on the point of winning more, but the war breaks out just as his best years are approaching. Because his older brother has already served in the army, Henri is exempted from compulsory military service. Once the fighting reaches Flanders, he is forced to flee with his family to France. Fortunately, he has raced there many times, so he knows exactly where to go. Later, the needs of war lead to a change in military regulations. New legislation creates the Special Contingent of 1915: men who have previously been exempted from national service are now called up. Vanlerberghe reports to the recruiting office in Montluçon on 10 July 1915. After nine months of training, on 16 April 1916 he is posted to the IJzer Front, as a private in a heavy mortar battery in the 9th Artillery Regiment. He sees action in the Diksmuide, Ramskapelle, Pervijze and Merkem sectors, but survives the war in one piece.

EXTRAIT-CONTROLE destiné à servir à l'immatriculation
du nommé *Vanlerberghe Henri Soldat M 15*

Père: *Victor*	Visage *Ovale*
Mère: *Tampere Nathalie*	Teint *coloré*
Né à *Lichtervelde*	Front { inclinaison *fuyant* ; hauteur *haut* ; largeur *large*
Province de *Flandre occid.*	
Le *27 janvier 1891*	Yeux: *gris*
Dernière résidence *Lichtervelde*	Nez { base *horizontal* ; hauteur *petit* ; forme *incurvé* ; largeur *étroit*
Province de *Flandre occid.*	
Taille d'un mètre *810* millimètres	
Profession antérieure : *coureur*	
Etat-civil : *Célibataire*	Bouche *moyenne*
	Lèvres *moyennes*
	Menton *moyen*
	Cheveux *châtains*
	Sourcils *châtains*
(Pour les militaires mariés iudication des noms et prénoms de l'épouse).	Signes particuliers *néant*

Le _____ 191 , engagé comme volontaire pour la durée de la guerre.
Le *10 juillet* 1915, incorporé comme milicien de 1915, *par la Commission de*
recrutement N°18 e canton. commune de à *Montluçon* le *10 juillet 1915* au service actif

Promotion. rétrogradation. privation
du grade. retrait d'emploi } _____

Chevrons et
Décoration militaire } _____

Antécédents judiciaires,
condamnations.
incarcération. libération } _____

Arrivée au C.I.A. le 8 octobre 1915, 1ère Bie venant du C.I. de la 1e DA
Départ du C.I. *le 4 février 1916 passé au C.I. des mortiers V.D.*

A *Saint Quentin* , le *4 - 2 -* 1916

Le Commandant *de la Batterie*

Manmeulle

Collationné

J'ai reçu lecture des lois militaires

Vanlerberghe Henri

Vanlerberghe's record of service in the army from 10 July 1915 onwards.

THE TRENDSETTERS IN THE SPRING OF 1914

On 5 April 1914, the Italian Ugo Agostoni wins Milan-Sanremo ahead of his compatriot Carlo Galetti and the Frenchmen Charles Crupelandt and Jean Alavoine. The Australian Donald Kirkham finishes ninth and Jules Masselis is the first Belgian in thirteenth place. A week later, the victory in Paris-Roubaix goes to home rider Crupelandt, making him the only native of Roubaix ever to win this famous spring classic. The other top placings go to the Frenchman Louis Luguet, the Belgian Louis Mottiat, the Swiss Oscar Egg and three other Belgians: Jean Rossius, Cyrille Van Hauwaert and Pier Van de Velde. Another week later sees yet another classic on the programme: Paris-Tours. This time, Oscar Egg is the fastest, with the Frenchman Emile Engel and the Belgian Philippe Thys trailing in his wake. The competitors in this race underline just how international professional cycling has become: of the 60 riders who reach the finish, five are Australian and three are German.

That year, Bordeaux-Paris is programmed for 17 May. The first two across the line are Paul Deman and Marcel Buysse, both past winners of the Tour of Flanders, followed by the 'Lion of Flanders' himself, Cyrille Van Hauwaert. Behind this Belgian trio comes a whole group of equally famous racers: Louis Trousselier, Emile Georget, François Faber and the ubiquitous Crupelandt. On 25 May, the scene of action for Belgian riders switches to home soil for the national championship in Dinant, won in 1914 by Victor Dethier. The French champion is (almost inevitably) Charles Crupelandt, who if not the best is at least the most consistent rider that spring. The last of the classics is Paris-Brussels on 7 June. It is a largely Walloon affair, fought out between winner Louis Mottiat, Louis Heusghem, Joseph Vandaele, Jean Rossius and André Blaise.

Are all these riders who give colour to the spring season in 1914 aware of the growing tension in Europe and in the international relations between the great powers? Can they sense the catastrophe that is approaching? Probably not. In the preceding decades, the bicycle and the sport of cycling have undergone a remarkable evolution. Thanks to the organization of lucrative races and the sponsorship of the bike manufacturers, the foundations of professional bike racing are firm and well structured. Van Hauwaert, Deman, Mottiat, Crupelandt, Egg, Rütt and all the other top riders, both on the road and on the track, earn the kind of money that ordinary people can only dream of. That is why they become racers. That is why they ride and fight so hard. They are professionals, and they live for their sport 24 hours a day. Would they really have the time — or the interest — to note the disturbing developments following the assassination of an Austrian archduke in Sarajevo, especially in an era when news reporting was confined to the papers and many people in the poorer sections of society — from which the riders are largely drawn — are barely literate? No, very few, if any, of the riders in the peloton of 1914 have any idea of the storm clouds gathering above their heads. Even so, many of them — like many hundreds of thousands of others — will be mobilized when that storm breaks. They will be required to exchange their bike for a gun: the cream of world cycling reduced to mere cannon fodder.

The Swiss Oscar Egg, winner of Paris-Tours on 19 April 1914.

PART II
DEATH
OR GLORY

28 June 1914 to 11 November 1918

A STARTING SHOT IN PARIS, A FATAL SHOT IN SARAJEVO

28 June 1914. At roughly the same time as the starting pistol is fired in Paris for the 12th Tour de France, 2,000 kilometres away in Sarajevo shots also ring out. The Serbian nationalist Gavrilo Princip assassinates Crown Prince Franz Ferdinand of Austria and his wife, Sophie Chotek. At the time, nobody imagines that this will also turn out to be a 'starting shot' of a different kind. After all, the Balkans has always been a powder keg. Surely this latest incident will blow over as well?

The news of the murder in Sarajevo has not (yet) reached Paris. With six former winners in the field — Lucien Petit-Breton, Octave Lapize, François Faber, Gustave Garrigou, Odiel Defraeye and Philippe Thys — the Tour of 1914 promises to be the most exciting ever. The list of 147 starters also includes Costante Girardengo, the first great Italian *campionissimo*. This year, *La Grande Boucle* will cover a distance of 5,405 kilometres in fifteen stages. The opening stage ends in Le Havre with victory for Philippe Thys. Two days later, the 1913 Tour winner and his teammates stay in the same hotel as Jean Jaurès, the leader of the French socialists and a confirmed pacifist. He tries to persuade the people not to listen to the politicians who are increasingly talking of war. Jaurès believes that diplomacy is the only way to avoid the terrible

violence that is threatening Europe. Just a month later, this belief will cost him his life. He will be shot dead in a Paris café by a young French nationalist who does want war with the German Reich.

The early stages of the Tour are ridden in a sweltering heat that persists for days on end. Meanwhile, temperatures are also rising in Europe's capitals. After the crown prince and his wife have been buried, the investigation into their assassination opens in earnest. How far was Serbia responsible for the attack? The newspapers report that the Russian Empire is ready to support its Serbian ally, if necessary. The riders in the race are worried by more mundane matters. Do they have enough water to drink? What will be the effect of the heat on their bikes and tyres? None of this bothers Philippe Thys. He seems to thrive on the heat. After the first mountain stage in the Pyrenees, he has a lead of 35 minutes over his only serious rival, Henri Pélissier.

By the time the Tour reaches the halfway point, the political tension is increasing in intensity. There are reports of large-scale military activity in Austria-Hungary, with troops massing on the Serbian border. In Budapest, the capital of Hungary, a man is arrested on suspicion of being a Russian spy. However, the Dutch newspaper *De Tijd* assures people there is no cause for alarm, because 'the Austro-Hungarian Minister of War is on his summer holidays'.

For the riders in the Tour it all seems so far away, a matter of no great concern. Blissfully unaware of the impending storm that is about to break over Europe, they race from Perpignan to Marseille. Although 'race' is perhaps an exaggeration. The blistering heat has taken its toll. Even when the leader Thys falls, no-one seems keen to try and exploit the situation. Octave Lapize triumphs in what is destined to be his last ever stage win. The biggest loser of the day is Emile Engel. The Frenchman, who only days before won the stage in Brest, gets into an argument with one of the Tour officials. He is listed as finishing fourth, but is convinced he crossed the line as third. It comes to a punch-up and Engel is sent home in disgrace. Tour organizer Henri Desgrange attempts to negotiate Engel's return, but the French rider is not seen again in that year's race.

The murder of Crown Prince Franz Ferdinand of Austria and his wife heralds in four years of misery for Europe and the rest of the world.

HENRI DESGRANGE, A PATRIOT THROUGH AND THROUGH

The Tour moves on towards the Alps. A revitalized Henri Pélissier now does all he can to try and cut the lead held by Philippe Thys. But the Belgian rider has things under control. He is still more than half an hour ahead in the standings. In the meantime, the government in Paris is starting to express concern about the state of readiness of the French Army and, in particular, the country's defences along its eastern border. It is there that the Tour riders bump into French cavalry. Literally. During the thirteenth stage, which starts in Belfort and follows the Franco-German frontier, the cavalrymen refuse to make way for the peloton. Some of the racers are forced into a ditch and lose precious time.

For François Faber, winner of the Tour five years earlier, this is a special stage. The finish is in Longwy, close to the point where the borders of France, Belgium and Luxembourg all meet. Faber's father was born in the Grand Duchy and his mother is a native of Lorraine, which is now part of Germany. He is determined to win this stage and attacks while there is still more than 200 kilometres to go. During this long solo, he is escorted the entire way by an armed French motorcyclist! The Luxembourger wins by seven minutes and is greeted as a hero by his fellow countrymen, many

of whom have crossed the nearby border to witness his moment of triumph.

This is the fourth time in the Tour's relatively short history that a stage ends in Longwy. Jules Masselis won there in 1911, Odiel Defraeye in 1912, and now François Faber for the second year in a row. Henri Desgrange does not route the Tour in this direction simply to please the Belgians and the Luxembourgers. He chooses Longwy as a symbolic finishing point for reasons that are more military than sporting. He would actually prefer to end in Metz, something he is only able to achieve in 1907. Following the Treaty of Frankfurt at the end of the Franco-Prussian War in 1871, the city is incorporated into the province of Lorraine, which is itself incorporated into the new German Reich. In 1907, Metz is therefore the first 'foreign' city ever visited by the Tour. However, the arrival is accompanied by such an overt display of French national sentiment that Count von Zeppelin, the German governor of Lorraine, is determined that no such thing will ever happen again. And so Desgrange has to settle for Longwy as the next best thing.

Lorraine is a sensitive border region between France and Germany and therefore a constant source of conflict between the two nations, not least because a hugely profitable iron and steel industry grows up around the region's coal mines in the 19th century. It was once part of Germany, but in 1766 became part of France, only to revert to Germany after its victory in the Franco-Prussian War. The treaty of 1871 creates a burning desire for revenge amongst the French. And also, it seems, in Henri Desgrange. Because he is no longer welcome in Metz after his 1907 'propaganda Tour', he focuses his attention in subsequent years on Longwy. The town's symbolism is obvious. It is the last customs post before entering 'German occupied' Lorraine, Desgrange's way of knocking on the Germans' door, to let them know that the French have neither forgotten nor forgiven. As a result, the 1914 passage of the Tour through Longwy is once again accompanied by a huge display of French national pride: flags, garlands, fireworks, marching bands... *'Allons les enfants de la patrie-ie-ie, le jour de gloire est arrivé.'* The First World War brings the 'day of glory' to an abrupt end. But the director of the Tour will have the last laugh. After the

Tour boss Henri Desgrange, who once calls the Germans 'cabbage-eaters'.

Armistice in 1918, Lorraine is returned to France and the first finish that Desgrange pencils in his route for the 1919 Tour is the 'liberated' city of Metz.

Henri Desgrange, the founder and the first great 'boss' of the Tour de France, is a remarkable figure in many respects. A man of nationalist sentiment at heart, he sees the Tour as the celebration of French superiority on France's roads. In his *L'Auto* newspaper, French riders are praised to the heavens, while foreign riders hardly get a look-in. When the German Empire declares war on the French Republic on 3 August 1914, Desgrange's editorial in *L'Auto* goes far beyond the normal scope of a sporting journal. 'The war is like a great race, in which we will need to fight very hard. But watch out for those Germans! If you point a rifle at their chest, they will beg for mercy. But don't let yourself be fooled. Finish them off without pity. (...) We need to deal once and for all with those imbecilic and villainous cabbage-eaters...'

The Tour director is a patriot through and through, and during the war publishes countless articles about military operations, prisoner of war camps, soldiers and their sports, etc. In 1917 — when he is already 52 years old — he volunteers for the French Army and even wins the Croix de Guerre for bravery while serving with the infantry. Yet throughout his time at the front, the energetic Desgrange also continues writing for *L'Auto* (under the pseudonym 'Desgrenier') and his thoughts are already fixed on the first post-war Tour. Less than two years after enlisting, those thoughts come to fruition. On 29 June 1919, just seven months after the Armistice, the Tour caravan sets off once again from Paris — but with no German riders allowed. Perhaps inevitably, he views the revival of the Tour in a patriotic light: 'It is the future of France, which now starts its most magnificent campaign and with powerful movement and graceful gestures will promote this beautiful sport wherever it passes. And I hope that the public, pouring in from all sides, will greet these heroes with respect, the heroes who must now take the place of our loved ones the Germans have stolen from us.'

23 July 1914. Austria-Hungary issues a series of demands to Serbia in the so-called July Ultimatum. The following day, during the finish of the stage in Dunkirk, Philippe Thys runs into trouble. A careless spectator causes him to fall from his bike and he breaks his front wheel. Thys panics and against the rules changes his damaged wheel for the wheel of his teammate, Louis Heusghem. He is given a time penalty of 30 minutes, so that his lead in the overall standings is cut to just 1 minute and 49 seconds.

Another day later, the world holds its breath. The July Ultimatum has got everyone worried. What will happen? The Serbian government meets to discuss the situation, which it describes as 'very serious'. If Serbia does not respond positively to its demands, Austria-Hungary threatens to attack 'with all its might'. Alliances that have been made during the previous decades now come into play. The German Empire supports Austria-Hungary. Serbia can count on the help of the Russian Empire. The Russians are also allied to France. The rivalry and tension between Europe's great powers escalates. War seems inevitable.

Back in the Tour, people are also expecting a war during the final stage to Paris on 26 July: a war between Philippe Thys and Henri Pélissier. But it doesn't happen. There is a strong headwind on the roads leading to the French capital and the experienced Pélissier knows that an attack in these conditions has little chance of success. He decides to save his strength for a last desperate effort to escape in the final 20 kilometres. He manages to open up a gap with the pack, but on a bridge over the Seine in Saint-Cloud he is surprised by a double row of spectators. He has to struggle his way through the crowd, but in doing so loses precious time. Soon after, he is caught by a group of eight riders — and one of the eight is Philippe Thys. Pélissier wins the sprint, but overall victory in the Tour goes for the second year in a row to Thys, who has led the race every day, from start to finish.

Given people's high expectations of a battle royal between Pélissier and Thys, this final stage is something of a disappointment. However, it is 'memorable' for other reasons. Although few people realize it at the time, it is destined to be the last sight of the Tour de France on French roads for four long and terrible years. Not until 1919 will the riders, team leaders, mechanics, helpers, organizers and journalists once again be reunited in the great Tour caravan. At least, those of them who survive the war.

That Sunday evening, 26 July 1914, all the world's great racers are in Paris. After a month of hard cycling, they can now go home and enjoy a bit of rest. Or so they think. Two days later, Austria-Hungary declares war on Serbia. On Friday 31 July, Britain and France announce the general mobilization of their armies. A day later, the German Empire, the ally of Austria-Hungary, declares war on the Russian Empire, Serbia's ally. Because the Germans know this will provoke a response from Russia's French ally, on Sunday 2 August they implement the first phase of the Schlieffen Plan. This foresees the rapid defeat of France by a flank attack through Luxembourg and Belgium. The Germans occupy the Grand Duchy and Kaiser Wilhelm demands right of free passage for his troops through neutral Belgium.

While all this happens, Philippe Thys is still in Paris. He is only expected to arrive back at the Brussels North Station at 11 o'clock on that same Sunday, 2 August. However, the welcome for the double Tour winner is understandably muted. After a short lunch, a meeting at the Karreveld track in Sint-Jans-Molenbeek is next on the programme, where Thys is scheduled to ride against Henri Pélissier, amongst others. In normal circumstances, a rematch between the numbers one and two in the Tour would guarantee a full stadium. But the circumstances are not normal. The news that the Germans have occupied Luxembourg and are demanding to press on through Belgium has suddenly reduced cycling to an irrelevant sideshow. The war is now very close. The meeting is cancelled and Pélissier takes the first train back to Paris.

Tour winner Thys is not called up to join the army. When he was 19, he cleverly managed to avoid his national service by taking a temporary job as a special policeman, an exemption he still holds. Even so, a number of the dignitaries at the reception at the Karreveld advise him to volunteer. As one of the few Belgians to own a motor car, he can easily get a posting as a chauffeur for the army staff. If the Germans succeed in invading Belgium and push along the coast, the army's senior officers will probably withdraw to England. As one of their drivers, Thys will be able to go with them. And this is what happens. By the time all Belgian citizens are ordered to hand in their cars just days later, the two-time Tour winner is already safely across the Channel.

Sunday, 2 August 1914. Just a week after the Tour, general mobilization is announced in France.

Philippe Thys has little time to enjoy his second Tour triumph.

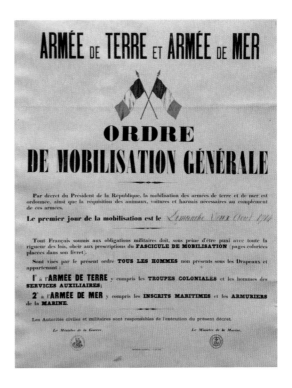

Charles Pélissier, Henri Pélissier, Francis Pélissier.

Henri Pélissier posing in his army uniform.

Like Thys, Henri Pélissier is not called up to join the army when war breaks out. However, his younger brothers Francis (who will later become a three-time French national champion) and Jean are both mobilized. On 11 March 1915, Jean is hit by a shell fragment while serving on the Marne front and dies of his wounds. The family is not aware of this tragedy and two months later even organizes a large celebration to mark Henri's marriage. In May 1916, his brother-in-law Eugène is killed in the terrible fighting at Verdun, a loss that finally persuades Henri to volunteer for military service. The two-time winner of the Tour of Lombardy (1911, 1913) and Milan-Sanremo (1912) is posted to a cyclist regiment in Paris. Later, he is assigned as a telegrapher to the air force. The former rider now sends and receives messages in Morse code from bases in Dijon, Bourget and Tréport.

His superiors regularly give Pélissier permission to train and take part in cycling competitions. On 19 August 1917, he wins Trouville-Paris ahead of Marcel Godivier and Charles Deruyter. In that year's Tour of Lombardy he finishes second behind

Philippe Thys, after a tumultuous sprint. In the following winter, he is active on the indoor circuit in Paris, and on the day that his daughter is born he wins a meeting at the Vel' d'Hiv track. During the final weeks of the war, Pélissier, still a telegrapher, moves up to Roeselare in Belgium, which has recently been liberated. There he meets other racers serving in the army, including Paul Duboc. On 11 November 1918, the day the war finally comes to an end, he is wounded in an accident with a lorry.

Fortunately, his injuries are not serious and while awaiting demobilization he is transferred to Paris as a driver for the military authorities. He is finally discharged from the army in the spring of 1919 and can once again focus all his attention on serious cycling. Henri Pélissier later wins a third Tour of Lombardy (1920), as well as the national road championship (1919), Bordeaux-Paris (1919), two Paris-Roubaix's (1919, 1921), Paris-Brussels (1920), Paris-Tours (1922) and — his crowning achievement — the Tour de France (1923).

Henri Pélissier on 5 October 1919 after the French 100-kilometre road championship, which for symbolic reasons started that year at Versailles.

GERMANS IN BELGIUM AND BELGIANS IN GERMANY

The prestigious meeting scheduled to take place at the Karreveld track just a week after the finish of the Tour has a truly impressive line-up. Not only is there the much-anticipated clash between Thys and Pélissier, but top names like the Frenchmen Louis Trousselier and Emile Georget, the German Walter Rütt, and home-grown favourites Cyrille Van Hauwaert, Firmin Lambot, René Vandenberghe, Julien Tuytten, Joseph Cassiers, Emile Aerts and Henri Vanlerberghe are all on the bill. But 2 August 1914 is the day on which the world changes forever, the day when the certainty and optimism of the new century are replaced by panic and fear. The meeting is cancelled and all the riders head for their respective homes as quickly as possible.

Other track competitions are also programmed for that fateful day, and some of them do go ahead. In Boom, the German Bruno Wehlitz is scheduled to race against the Belgians Albert De Belder, Jo Apostel and Louis Verbraecken (among others). Another German, Albert Schipke, rides in Halle, where his main rival is Henri Timmerman. On the velodrome at Anderlues, Gustave Garrigou, the 1911 Tour winner and the fifth-placed rider in the most recent edition, takes part in a 100-kilometre event that also includes Louis Heusghem, Camille Botte, Jean Mélotte, and Goupy father and son. The track meeting at Charleroi fails to attract the top international names, but still has a strong field of riders from the second tier, such as Hector Heusghem, Jean Rossius, Jean Alavoine, Ali Neffati, Aloïs Persijn, Georges Monseur, Florent Desanthoine, Paulin Louvion and Gaston Van Waesberghe. It is not clear how many of these meetings actually take place, since the following day's newspapers have more pressing things to report than sports results.

The Sunday edition of *Vooruit* also lists a number of foreign meetings that are planned for 2 August: in Zurich (with the German Jean Esser, the Frenchman Henri Fossier and the Swiss Paul Suter and Kurt Humann); in Cologne (with the Frenchman Paul Guignard, Willy Appelhans and Peter Günther); and in Nuremburg (with Paul Nettelbeck, Willy Arend and Oscar Peter). The paper also suggests that the planned three-hour race in Berlin has contracted as many big names to appear as the Karreveld meeting in Brussels. In addition to the Swiss Oscar Egg and home riders like Alfred Schrage, Eugen Stabe, Willy Tadewald, Bruno Wegener, Willy Techmer, Carl Rudel, Franz Krupkat, Hermann Packebush, Otto Pawke and Christian Stol, there are also a surprising number of Frenchmen, including the double Tour winner Lucien Petit-Breton, the 1910 winner Octave Lapize and leading racers Marcel Berthet, Charles Crupelandt and Emile Engel.

On that Sunday, 2 August 1914, the Antwerp-Walloon track cyclist Victor Linart is deep inside Germany; more particularly, in the city of Magdeburg, where he is on the programme to race against Jules Miquel, and Thomas and Clement Leviennois. Linart needs to leave Germany as quickly and as quietly as possible, if he wishes to avoid internment. The stayer, a professional since 1909 and twice Belgian champion, eventually arrives back exhausted in his home town, having followed a long and circuitous route to safety. However, just weeks later he is on the run again, when the invading Germans occupy Antwerp. This time he flees to the Netherlands, before travelling on to England.

In November 1914, Linart sets sail on the White Star liner RMS *Baltic*, bound for New York. He wants to carry on cycling and decides, like the Swiss racer Oscar Egg, to try his hand at the six-day events in the United States. Throughout the war he takes part in meetings at venues as distant as New York, Boston, Newark, Chicago, San Francisco and Kansas City. With the money he earns, he puts together aid packages that he sends to prisoners of war from his home village of Floreffe.

After the war, Victor Linart returns to his favourite specialization: stayer races behind powerful motorbikes. And with success, because the Walloon goes on to win four world titles (1921, 1924, 1926 and 1927) and is undefeated as Belgian national champion from 1919 to 1931. This results in a series of lucrative contracts, the proceeds of which he invests wisely in profitable ventures, including a large sawmill and a company trading in fine lace. He later moves to Paris and is naturalized as a French citizen in 1937.

Stayer Victor Linart is competing in the German city of Magdeburg when the war breaks out.

CRUPELANDT AND HIS FLIGHT
FROM BERLIN TO ROUBAIX

When the German Empire declares war on France on 3 August 1914, Charles Crupelandt is still in Berlin, where he was scheduled to race the day before. Like his fellow countrymen Lapize, Berthet, Engel and Petit-Breton, he is trapped in the lion's den and needs to escape as quickly as possible. On a train to Cologne, he hides all the way in the toilets and when he reaches the border crossing at Aachen he pretends to be a Dutchman — as a native of Roubaix, close to the border with Dutch-speaking Flanders, he has learnt a few words of the language. Via neutral Holland and Belgium, he finally makes it home, hungry and penniless but all in one piece. He has lost his costly bike, but that is not the worst of his worries. There is a letter waiting for him: his mobilization papers for the French Army.

By 1914, the 28-year-old Crupelandt is a popular and well-known racer. Brought up in a run-down area of Roubaix, where his mother ran a 'house of pleasure', he found escape in his love of cycling. Once he starts riding in competition, he soon establishes a reputation as a fast, energetic and sometimes impetuous racer. In part thanks to his imposing size, he is quickly known as *Le Taureau du Nord*: the Bull of the North. He is only 17 years old when he takes part in Paris-Roubaix for the first time in 1904 and he immediately finishes an impressive thirteenth. His great ambition is to be the first native of Roubaix to win this famous classic race. He achieves this ambition — in a way, at least — on 3 July 1910, when he wins that day's race from Paris to Roubaix with a lead of 20 minutes over Cyrille Van Hauwaert. Unfortunately, it is not the Paris-Roubaix, but the first stage in the 1910 Tour de France that follows roughly the same course.

But Crupelandt is not to be denied. He fulfils his dream and becomes a local hero by winning the 1912 edition of the real Paris-Roubaix, a feat that no other hometown rider from Roubaix has ever been able to repeat. The Bull's success helps to briefly brighten up the harsh existence of his fellow northeners in their grim industrial town: to celebrate his triumph, people are dancing in the streets for days. After victory in Paris-Tours in 1913, these riotous scenes are repeated on 12 April 1914, when Crupelandt prevails in the Queen of the Classics for a second time. Spurred on by 12,000 delirious supporters, he crosses the line first in

the Vélodrome Roubaisien in the Parc Barbieux, ahead of his compatriot Louis Luguet, the Belgian Louis Mottiat and the Swiss Oscar Egg.

Two months later, Charles Crupelandt also becomes French national champion, but he soon has to exchange his tricolour champion's jersey for an army uniform. Like millions of others, he is needed to defend the motherland. He is sent to the front, where he is badly wounded twice, but unlike several other great cycling champions he comes out of the war alive. He is honoured for his bravery with the award of the Croix de Guerre, but this does not prevent him from being called before a court martial in 1917 for a minor matter. The fact that he was in Berlin when the war broke out is still held against him, so that there is some doubt about his loyalty to France. For the same reason, the French Cycling Federation refuses to give him a license after the war. Crupelandt contests the decision, but the necessary legal documents that will allow the case to be reviewed in his favour have mysteriously disappeared. It is widely

When war breaks out on 3 August 1914, Charles Crupelandt is in Berlin.

Crupelandt is still the only 'Roubaisien' ever to win the Paris-Roubaix race.

Albert of Saxe-Coburg and Gotha, King of the Belgians, is the nephew of the German emperor, Wilhelm II. His wife, Elisabeth, is also a German princess and the godchild and niece of the Empress Elisabeth ('Sisi') of Austria-Hungary. The Belgian king begs the Kaiser to respect the neutrality of his country, 'on the grounds of our close family ties and bonds of friendship'. He closes his letter with the words 'your loyal and dedicated nephew'.

While awaiting the Kaiser's answer, the Belgian Army is put on a war footing. On 1 August 1914, the Carabineers Cyclist Battalion is ready for action at its barracks in Vilvoorde. Its battle strength is 428 privates and corporals, 31 non-commissioned officers, 15 officers, three doctors and a chaplain, making a total of 478 men in all. These figures suggest that cycling in wartime is seen as a high-risk activity. An ordinary infantry battalion of a thousand men has a complement of just two doctors; a cyclist battalion with less than half that strength has a complement of three! Be that as it may, the cycle unit, with its carefully selected young soldiers, is described as 'an extremely powerful fighting force'.

When a general mobilization is announced, other men who have previously completed their national service in a cycle unit are recalled to the colours. They are equipped with requisitioned bicycles, creating an extra company of cyclists used mainly for carrying messages and reconnaissance tasks. The commanders of the two army divisions responsible for the defence of Namur and Liege are also quick to set up cycling companies, to help maintain communications between their different units.

rumoured that the Pélissier brothers have something to do with this. Their involvement is never proven, but it is certainly true that the sidelining of the Bull means they have one less serious rival to face.

Denied the opportunity to race, an unemployed and penniless Charles Crupelandt returns to Roubaix. The north where he lives has never been France's most prosperous region, but now it has been devastated by the war and is largely in ruins. Poverty is rife and like many others Crupelandt is forced to turn to smuggling and petty crime, simply as a way to survive. Now that he has a criminal record, there is no hope of him being rehabilitated by the French Cycling Federation. His ban remains in place for the rest of his life. The man who fought bravely for his country and came home a wounded hero now gives up the fight. He takes to drink and later in life becomes a tragic figure. The final indignity is the amputation of his legs as a result of diabetes, caused in part by his excessive drinking.

Blind and alone, the man who was once the pride of Northern France dies in the anonymity of a shelter for the homeless in February 1955. It is only years later that the city of Roubaix finally recognizes the achievements of the sporting son it has ignored for so long. A section of the Avenue Roger Salengro, which leads to the André Petrieux velodrome, where Paris-Roubaix still finishes each year, is relaid with the cobblestones for which the race is so famous. This symbolic section is now the Espace Charles Crupelandt: 300 metres of tangible cycling history that brings posthumous and well-deserved honour to the old soldier and former racer, an honour that he sadly never knew in life.

The 'Belgica' bicycle no longer has a strengthened frame and now has a fixed gear sprocket with just a single brake operating on the front wheel.

A Belgian Carabineer Cyclist ready for action!

King Albert's plea falls on deaf ears. The Germany Army continues to insist on right of free passage through Belgium as a prelude to its attack on France. When the Belgian government rejects this urgent 'request' on 3 August 1914, war becomes inevitable. The next morning, German troops cross the Belgian border near Gemmenich. Twenty-two Belgian soldiers are killed before nightfall. The next day, the Germans establish a camp for 25,000 soldiers and several thousand horses close to the village of Moelingen in the Voer district.

Marcel Kerff, who was the highest placed Belgian in the very first Tour de France in 1903 (he finished sixth), lives nearby and decides to go and have a look. He has no ulterior motive other than curiosity, but he was always known as an adventurous rider and has lost none of his spirit. But war is not a cycle race. He is taken prisoner by the Germans on suspicion of espionage. The former racer denies categorically that he has anything to do with the army, either Belgian or French, but his furious interrogators refuse to listen. They torture him 'as long as is necessary', but when Kerff still refuses to 'confess' his crime, they cut out his tongue. But worse is yet to come. Convinced that Moelingen is a hotbed of *francs-tireurs* or resistance fighters, they burn the village to the ground. Any local people they find there are rounded up and forced to march as a living shield ahead of the German spearhead advancing towards Liege.

Marcel Kerff is also part of this shield. He watches in terror as the German commander selects three of his fellow prisoners and has them

shot for no apparent reason. On 7 August, it is his turn. Together with five other villagers, he is hung from an iron bar suspended between two poplar trees, while the remaining villagers are ordered to dig their graves. It is only a year later that their bodies are rediscovered and the tragic story becomes public. After the war, a monument is erected at the execution site, where the road between Eijsden and Battice is crossed by the road to 's-Gravenvoeren, not far from the present-day route of the Amstel Gold Race.

Kerff is not the first former professional cyclist to die in the war. The day before Jacques Julémont is executed in his home village of Labouxhe, some 20 kilometres south of Voeren. Once again, the Germans behave with great brutality and without obvious provocation. They pick ten houses in the village at random, drag the inhabitants on to the street, shoot them on the spot, and then burn their homes, before moving on towards the next village along the road to Liege, where they wreak similar havoc. In total, more than 300 Belgian civilians are massacred on that bloody morning of 6 August. One of them is Jacques Julémont, aged just 22. He has been racing as an independent rider since 1911, mainly on the circuits at Verviers, Mons-Crotteux and Wandre.

Marcel Kerff, seen here during the very first Tour de France in 1903.

KAREL VAN WIJNENDAELE, WAR CORRESPONDENT

The front page of *Sportwereld* on Monday 3 August 1914, the day before the Germans invade Belgium, carries a remarkable announcement. The impending threat of war has forced the editorial team to think about its immediate future and how it will respond to the situation on behalf of its readers. As a result, Léon Van den Haute and Karel Van Wijnendaele let it be known that from now on they intend to publish their newspaper in two parts. The first part will be called *De Telegraaf* and will report on international news (in other words, the war). The second part will continue to be called *Sportwereld*, but will be much reduced in size. The editors understand that for the time being there simply won't be all that much sport to report. And it goes without saying that developments at the front are much more important anyway.

De Telegraaf-Sportwereld covers the German invasion extensively. Men who were sports journalists only yesterday are now war correspondents. This includes Karel Van Wijnendaele, who twice travels to Liege to see things for himself. In the Saturday, 8 August edition he describes how the day before he took the train from Brussels to Tienen, using the same florid and often emotional style for which his sporting articles were already well-known: 'After much huffing and puffing and stopping and starting, our train finally reached Borgworm at about 10 o'clock. "Everyone off!" cries the conductor. I thought to myself: "Karel, lad, things are obviously getting much worse." Like everyone else, I got down from the train, only to be informed that it was going no further.'

Van Wijnendaele continues his journey towards Liege on foot. In Bierset-Awans: '… we hear the sound of guns for the first time. By now, it must be about half past one in the morning. If I live to be a hundred, I will never forget the impression those first cannon shots made on me. A shiver went through my entire body, as a vision arose unbidden in my mind of that hellish engine, which in the blink of an eye spits fire and fury, causing death and destruction among the ranks of our boys, cutting the thin thread of human life with a single devastating blow!'

He goes on to describe in detail how he manages to get to Ans, where he sees an escaped cow running through the streets, '… frantically trying to get away from the sound of the guns.' His ultimate destination is the fort at Loncin. 'Fortunately, I had my journalist's pass and after much palavering they finally let me inside the fortifications. At last, I was in Liege! (…) Here, then, was the flower of Belgian youth, the cream of our race, standing foursquare in defence of our national flag. So many terrible things have happened here in the last few days, and I unconsciously slowed my pace, taking step after careful step, as though I might be walking in a house where someone dead was lying at rest.'

In the following days Van Wijnendaele continues to report from Liege, where the first serious battle of the war in Belgium is being fought. The 12 forts around the city offer such resistance to the German invaders that their advance is slowed, giving the Allies precious time to prepare for the greater confrontations that lie ahead. For the 10 August edition, Van Wijnendaele writes the entire front page, which has no fewer than four main headlines: 'The French Army scores a great victory over the Germans'; 'The Germans lose 30,000 men'; 'The city of Liege in German hands'; 'But the forts are still ours'. The last of these headlines is not completely true, because after heavy fighting the fort at Barchon has been in German hands for the past two days. A week later, the garrison of the fort at Lantin will also surrender. Loncin is the last fort to fall: on 15 August a German shell penetrates its magazine, causing a massive explosion that kills 350 Belgian soldiers in an instant.

As soon as Liege falls, the Germans continue their relentless advance westwards. Léon Van den Haute 'retreats' in the same direction with his newspaper, moving it from Brussels to Ghent. Here *De Telegraaf-Sportwereld* is published for a further few days, but on 14 October 1914 the presses are closed down. The next edition will not be published until 1 January 1919, back under the original title of *Sportwereld*.

Jacques Julémont, the first Belgian professional cyclist to die during the war.

The front page of *De Telegraaf-Sportwereld* on Monday, 10 August 1914.

'CORPORAL' LENAERS, PRISONER OF WAR

One of the soldiers defending the forts around Liege is a bike racer. Victor Lenaers, just 19 years of age, is a member of the Vélo Club Tongrois. Between 1910 and 1913, he is the best in nearly every race for novices in which he takes part. Because he has nothing more to learn in the junior categories, he switches ahead of time to the independent category. But he keeps on winning. His nickname in the cycling world is *Caporal* or Corporal, after one of his ancestors who served in Napoleon's army. However, in 1914, it is Victor's turn to 'play at being soldier'. He is called up and sent off to defend the fort at Lantin against the German invaders.

Many people assume that the forts around Liege are impregnable and that the Germans will never be able to move further than the River Meuse. Even so, the people of Tongeren will be forced to miss their favourite local rider for four long years. From 10 August onwards, Fort Lantin is heavily shelled by the enemy. The concrete defences hold out, but it soon becomes clear that one important fact was overlooked during the construction: there is no ventilation. When they fire their own cannons, the gases released threaten to asphyxiate the garrison of 220 gunners and 82 infantrymen. Under constant bombardment and unable to fire back, the garrison commander decides to surrender on 15 August. The 300 survivors are taken prisoner and deported to camps in Germany.

Victor Lenaers is among them. Conditions in the German POW camps are atrocious. By the time he returns to Tongeren at the end of 1918, he is sick and totally exhausted. No-one believes that this emaciated young man, starved half to death for four years, will ever be able to ride a bike the way he used to. But they are wrong. Lenaers' rate of recovery borders on the incredible. He picks up the threads of his career as an independent rider and in 1920 wins the Schelde Prize. He gains his professional license the following year and immediately finishes sixth in Paris-Brussels and seventh in Liege-Bastogne-Liege. He also wants to take part in the Tour de France, but that is by no means evident in his debut year. Because he is not a member of a team, he will have to start as an *isolé*, which means he will be unsupported both financially and in sporting terms. However, his sup-

porters in Tongeren raise the money that will allow him to take part.

Their enthusiasm is rewarded. Lenaers rides a good Tour, finishing sixth in the final standings. The riders ahead of him — Léon Scieur, Hector Heusghem, Honoré Barthélémy, Luigi Lucotti and Hector Tiberghein — all ride for bike manufacturers, which means that Lenaers actually wins the Tour for *isolés*. This promptly wins him a contract with Automoto and he comes home with 20,000 Belgian francs in prize money in his pocket, enough to buy a house in the Jekerstraat in Tongeren. After his cycling career, which includes a fifth place in the 1922 Tour, he opens a cycle shop there. He promotes his 'Cycles Caporal' with the following advert: 'If you want a good bike, go to Victor Lenaers and ask for the one he won the Tour de France on!'

Victor Lenaers, seen here on the Col d'Aubisque with Félix Sellier during the 1922 Tour, survives four years as a prisoner of war in Germany.

FROM THE TOUR TO THE BATTLEFIELD

Because it infringes Belgian neutrality, the German Reich incurs the wrath of the British Empire. Thirty-seven days after the assassination of Franz Ferdinand, all of Europe's great powers are now at war with one another. As a result of various treaties and alliances, 33 countries and their various colonies will eventually be involved in the conflict. In each of these countries, men are mobilized to fight. In total, there are more than 20 million of them, a number that will increase as the war progresses. Never before in human history has there been a conflict on such a scale. It truly is the first 'world' war.

Nowadays, it is impossible to imagine that less than a week after riding in the Tour, Chris Froome, Romain Bardet, Fabio Aru or Marcel Kittel would be expected to exchange their rider's jersey for an army uniform, but that is exactly what happens in August 1914. One Sunday riding toward Paris in the peloton; the next Sunday marching towards the battlefield with a rifle in your hand. No fewer than 17 of the participants in the 1914 Tour fail to survive the war. The first to lose his life is the 25-year-old Emile Engel, who is posted as missing in action on 10 September 1914. On 2 July, he won the stage that finished in Brest, but he was disqualified after the eighth stage. As a member of the 72nd Infantry Regiment, he attempts to halt the German advance against Paris on the River Marne. Both sides lose thousands of men in a matter of days. Engel's body is never recovered and he is only declared officially dead on 25 May 1917.

Emile Engel, stage winner in the Tour on 2 July 1914 and missing in action on 10 September 1914.

The troops of Kaiser Wilhelm assume that their march through Belgium will be relatively unopposed and that they will soon reach the French border. However, the forts around Liege offer greater resistance than expected. The Belgians are also ready to put up a fight along the line of the River Jeker, between Tongeren and Bassenge. From the first day of the war, the Carabineer Cyclists carry out reconnaissance missions that often result in skirmishes with the advancing Germans. Not much later, they surprise a larger group of Germans in the fields to the east of the River Gete. The Germans probably expect to be opposed by cavalry units, who can be heard approaching from a long way off because of the noise made by their horses' hooves. And because of their bright colours — blue, white and yellow for the Lancers, green and red for the Rangers — you can also see them coming from miles away. But it is very different with the Carabineer Cyclists. They can approach quickly, quietly and almost unseen, with their dark green uniforms. The Germans soon have nickname for them: *Schwarze Teufel* or Black Devils.

It is only after ten days of hard fighting that the Germans are able to resume their advance. They move both southwards, towards Namur and Charleroi, and northwards, towards Hasselt and Borgloon. The German war machine now exerts its full pressure and the tiny Belgian Army is forced to pull back. In the north, the Cavalry Division takes up

Jean DEMARTEAU, de Verviers
sur Cycle LÉGIA et Pneu SOLY

1ᵉʳ d'Anvers-Menin, 1912. — 1ᵉʳ de Bruxelles-Esneux 1912.

positions behind the Gete. Three cyclist companies are with them.

The Belgian High Command hopes to use this naturally strong defensive line to further the delay of the Kaiser's troops. The bridge over the Gete in Halen is a crucial position. Convinced of their own superiority, on the early morning of 12 August German cavalry attempt to capture the bridge in an 'old style' frontal charge with sabres drawn. The attack is beaten off with heavy losses and the Belgian defenders hold on to the bridge until well into the afternoon. Two companies of the Carabineer Cyclists play a crucial role in this action, ably supported by regiments of Chasseurs, Rangers and Lancers.

The engagement at Halen, fought without the support of any of its allies, is a small but significant success for the Belgian Army, albeit a temporary one.

The emblem of the Black Devils is incorporated into all different kinds of brooches.

Cyclist Jean Demarteau is killed during the Battle of Halen on 12 August 1914.

It is now known in the history books as the Battle of the Silver Helmets. This name first appears in November 1914 in a poem (18 verses long!) written by August Cuppens, a priest in the nearby village of Loksbergen. Cuppens recounts how the silver helmets of the fallen German riders were scattered across the ground, in what seems a clear and romanticized reference to the Battle of the Golden Spurs, the great Flemish victory against the French in 1302.

Yet no matter how valiant the Belgian defence at Halen, the cyclists are soon threatened with encirclement from the flanks and are forced to pull back. Thirty Carabineer Cyclists are killed and a further hundred are wounded. One of the fatalities in this Battle of the Silver Helmets is a former bike racer: Private Second Class Jean Demarteau of the 1st Company of the 2nd Cyclist Battalion. Born in Verviers on 5 September 1893, he wins the Liege-Brussels race for amateurs in 1910 and as an independent rider he is also the best in 1912 in both Antwerp-Menen and Brussels-Esneux. His supporters in his home town soon see him as a

successor to André Henry, the legendary 'Verviers Bricklayer', who won the very first edition of Paris-Brussels in 1893 and after his remarkable victory was received in the royal palace at Laken by King Leopold II, who awarded him a gold clock. Sadly, the career of Demarteau is destined to be cut short. Notwithstanding his military service, he gains his professional license in 1913 and concentrates on track racing. This is the golden age of the Verviers velodrome, where riders can earn good starting bonuses and prize money. But then comes the war and the Battle of Halen, where Jean Demarteau's short life ends on 12 August 1914.

In 1924, a monument to commemorate the Battle of the Silver Helmets is erected in Halen, with King Albert attending the inauguration. It is no coincidence that the memorial is an initiative of the Touring Club of Belgium, the organization that first lobbied at the end of the 19th century for the introduction of the bicycle into the Belgian Army and was therefore instrumental in helping to create the Carabineer Cyclist Regiment.

An impressive Carabineer Cyclist!

STREUVELS: 'AS STUPID AS AN ASS AND AS IGNORANT AS A PIG'

Stijn Streuvels, the author of *De Vlaschaard* (The Flax Field) and twice winner of the five-yearly State Prize for Literature, reaches his 43rd birthday in the summer of 1914. Shocked by the German invasion of neutral Belgium, he decides to start a diary, which he plans to keep 'with all the accuracy and detachment of a medieval chronicler'. Perhaps better than any other sources, his notes show how he and, more particularly, those around him experience the war on a day-to-day basis. Streuvels lives and works in the West Flanders town of Ingooigem. In August, the war is being played out in distant Limburg and Wallonia, but the author wants to know what is happening. 'I envy men like Tolstoy, who made such good use of the opportunity offered to them to make new discoveries and to set aside a store of wonderful subjects for further treatment.' He hopes to be able to observe the battlefield from close at hand. 'In all quietness I promise myself that I will throw myself into it and try to get close to where heroism and recklessness, pain and misery can be seen.'

It seems that Streuvels is unaware of the acts of terror and reprisals being carried out in the Voer region, because having tried unsuccessfully to obtain a pass as a war correspondent, he nonetheless decides to go and see what he can find out for himself. Together with his friend Emmanuel Viérin, on 12 August he takes a train to Brussels and beyond. They get as far as Tienen, which is just 30 kilometres from Halen, where the Battle of the Silver Helmets is fought the same day. Two days later they move on to Landen. This is reckless behaviour indeed, because on 19 August in Aarschot and on 25 and 26 August in Leuven the Germans execute hundreds of innocent civilians, simply because they believe *franc-tireurs* are operating in the region where Streuvels is now travelling.

Their luck holds and they arrive back safely in their own Leie district, just as the first enemy reconnaissance troops are reported to be approaching. Even so, the author cycles alone to Kortrijk. On 26 August, he notes: 'On the way I became aware, because of all the posters hanging

For Stijn Streuvels the bicycle was the ideal way to see something of the war.

everywhere, that it is forbidden on pain of death to travel along this road! Bah! Do they really mean it?' And a day later: 'We are cut off from the world. Trains, trams, telephones, telegraphs: they have all ceased to exist.'

His curiosity continues to be greater than his fear of being picked up by the Germans or shot, because on 3 September he cycles to the badly damaged town of Tournai and on 27 September – 'a beautiful Sunday morning' — to Oudenaarde. On 3 October, he makes the trip to Tournai again, this time accompanied by three companions. This is highly rash, almost to the point of being inexplicable. The cycle-lover has become a thrill-seeker, impervious to the risks involved. On this occasion, they almost fail to make it home. A man walking along the road warns them that the Germans are letting no-one cross the bridge over the Schelde at Warcoing. 'The man tells us that they have just taken his bike. (...) We ask for information. "What about the road to Ronse?" "That way is full of them." "And Celles?" "There are 700 soldiers at Hérinnes and there has been fighting on the main road to Kortrijk, with patrols all over the place." It seems that we are in the middle of it with no-where to go!'

The daughter of a riverboat captain comes to their rescue. She ferries them across the river in the dark, '... and she was well rewarded for her trouble. She told her mother that she had never received so much for just taking people across the river. And now onwards! The Germans are behind us and the road ahead is clear. Like Faust and Mephisto on Walpurgis Night, we race over the cobbles at high speed through Helchin, Bossuyt, Autrijve, Avelghem, Ooteghem and, at last, Ingoyghem.'

Later, in *Ingooigem II*, the fourth and final part of his memoirs, Streuvels admits that in those days he was '...as stupid as an ass and as ignorant as a pig, and all to see something of the war, in the hope that it would live up to our expectations as a remarkable event, a spectacle of some importance. There is only one reason we can offer as an excuse: we thought that the Germans were only passing through and the rest of the war would be fought out in France, where Belgium would have nothing to do with it. We had to hurry if we wanted to see something while there was still a chance!'

Their fearsome 42-centimetre howitzers have forced the forts at Liege and Namur into submission. The next obstacle to the German advance is Antwerp. And it is a serious obstacle. The city on the River Schelde is surrounded by 47 forts and other smaller fortifications. To bring these to their knees, the Kaisers troops once again bring up their heaviest artillery. These cannons are so massive that they can only be transported by first dismantling them and then using lorries to move them in parts. The Belgian High Command is well aware of this. At the same time, they also notice a large increase in the rail traffic behind enemy lines. The German 1st and 2nd Armies are in difficulties on the Marne and are pulling back in disarray. As a result whole regiments are now being sent north by train via the Vosges region.

The dense rail network built up in Belgium before the war now works to the Germans advantage. The Belgium Army needs to disrupt these logistical routes — and needs to disrupt them fast. On 19 September 1914, the decision is taken to destroy the enemy's rail connections as systematically as possible. But how? It is agreed that each division will ask for 100 volunteers to take part in sabotage missions. And because this means operating in territory already occupied by the Germans, the bicycle is chosen as their means of transport. It is the ideal way to make use of the back roads and paths that will give the saboteurs the best chance of avoiding enemy troops and checkpoints before they reach their chosen targets.

On 21 September, Major Maglinse of the General Staff of the Belgian Army explains the plan in the town hall at Hoboken. Some of the saboteur groups will operate from Leopoldsburg, aiming to destroy the rail links to the south-east of Antwerp at places like Hoei, Hannuit, Gembloers and Ottignies. Other groups will operate from Ghent, targeting the rail junctions at Nijvel, Le Roeulx and Mons. The cyclists will be preceded by two men on motorbikes, who will act as scouts. Each group will also be accompanied by 12 explosives experts from the military engineers. The first target of the Ghent groups is the Halle-Edingen line, followed by the Brussels-Mons line. But it will not be easy. The Germans suspect something of this kind and have guards posted every

100 metres along the tracks. The saboteurs manage to get close to the line at Quenast and can see the trains passing almost nonstop. However, when they launch their attack, things go badly wrong. Some are killed and many more taken prisoner. Only about 20 manage to get away.

Another of the Ghent groups cycles towards Oudenaarde. However, their requisitioned bikes are of poor quality and on the first day they get no further than Deinze. They are also finding it difficult to carry their explosives by bike in an efficient manner. On the second day they travel via Ronse to Beloeil, where they just manage to avoid a group of some 400 German cyclists who have spent the night in the castle there. The Belgians lay explosives along a two-kilometre section of track between Edingen and Ath. They also bring down a number of telegraph poles, in the hope that these will derail passing trains.

On 25 September, they press on towards Mons. At Masnuy-Saint-Pierre, they explode a charge that brings down the railway embankment, blocking the line. However, German troops are working in the area and come to investigate. A fire-fight ensues and the Germans soon receive reinforcements from a train full of infantrymen that is forced to halt at the blockage. Heavily outnumbered, the saboteurs withdraw. Some are killed, but most get away. The Germans set off in hot pursuit along the road to Montignies-lez-Lens, but when they arrive there is no sign of the Belgians. As is becoming increasingly common, the frustrated invaders vent their anger on the innocent villagers. Several farms, houses and even the local vicarage are burnt to the ground.

The railway line between Mons and Valenciennes is of crucial importance to the German Army. It is one of their main routes for transporting men and material to the front in northern France. Consequently, the line is under constant guard. After the recent wave of sabotage attacks, the guard posts at key bridges have been increased to 50 men. The Belgians want to move north again, but the security checks at every river and canal crossing make this almost impossible. They risk being trapped in what seems increasingly like a suicide mission. They decide to try and fight their way out. On the night of 27 September, they attack the guard post on the bridge over the Blaton canal at Harchies. The attack is carried out silently with bayonets, so that the Germans have no advanced warning of their coming. Eight of the saboteurs are lost in the ensuing fight, but the rest make it over the canal and pedal furiously in the direction of Leuze and then on to Ath. Here, there are two more important tracks leading south: one to Saint-Ghislain, the other to Péronnes. They blow up the bridge at Chièvres to block the former, before moving on dynamite the track at Ormeignies to block the latter. Because they still have some 12 kilograms of explosive left, they search for a final target before trying to get back to unoccupied territory. They select the railway bridge at Tourpes, which they bring crashing to the ground. Their mission completed, they now head for home. Will they make it? Their luck holds. They encounter no further Germans and riding via Kortrijk and Pecq they arrive back in Ghent on 3 October.

A platoon of cyclists ride through Ghent on their way to sabotage railway lines in the area around Mons.

A BIKE WHEEL AS AN EMBLEM

It is impossible for the Belgian Army to hold back the massive German superiority in numbers. After the Battle of Halen, the Carabineer Cyclists again prove their worth at Werchter and Aarschot. The fast and mobile 'Black Devils' are clearly making a strong impression, on friend and foe alike. On 19 September, the High Command decides that every Belgian division must have a company of cyclists. This requires a degree of improvisation. For example, the cycling company from the Brussels civil guard is incorporated directly into the 6th Division. These cycling companies will play an important role in the defence of Antwerp. To assist in the army's controlled withdrawal westwards towards the city, on 4 October 1914 the 3rd and 6th Companies of the Carabineer Cyclists are transferred to the recently created independent Cavalry Brigade. The disadvantaged infantry divisions are later allocated replacement cycle companies. On 6 October, a further cycle company is formed within Fortress Antwerp, charged with the task of protecting the local railway lines.

When Antwerp also falls to the Germans on 9 October, the cyclists and the cavalry continue to fall back, covering the retreat as best they can. The 3rd and 6th Companies are now attached to the newly formed 2nd Cavalry Division. In the following month they see action at Merkem and Diksmuide, and later at Nieuwpoort, where they assist General Grosetti's French 42nd Division during the Battle of

the IJzer. Here they are later joined by the fortress company, which manages to escape from Antwerp.

When the IJzer plain is deliberately flooded to halt the German advance, the war of movement comes to an end and trench warfare begins. On 25 January 1915, the three companies of cyclists are amalgamated to create a new unit: the 2nd Battalion of Carabineer Cyclists, with the nickname *Diables Noirs*. The composition of this new battalion is diverse, including cavalrymen who are now fighting on foot, infantrymen from the 3rd and 6th Divisions, wartime volunteers, and cyclists from the class of 1913 (in other words, from the 1st Battalion in Vilvoorde).

In the trenches along the River IJzer the cyclists carry out numerous tasks in the changing sectors occupied by their division. Sometimes they operate in support of other divisions. The men are instantly recognizable, even without their bikes. They wear a 25 millimetre cycle wheel as an emblem on the 'IJzer kepis' of their transitional uniforms, with the same emblem later being added to the collar and shoulder straps of their replacement khaki uniforms. They are also equipped with new bikes for operating away from the trenches. These bikes are no longer Belgian, but British. They are ordered directly from makers like BSA (Birmingham Small Arms Company) and James and Son. The BSA 1915 model, with a frame height of 22 inches, continues to be used by the Belgian Army for many years.

The instantly recognizable wheel makes clear that this is the beret of a Belgian cyclist.

THE SAPEURS-PONTONNIERS ON BIKES

After receiving promises of French support, on 14 October 1914 King Albert I and the Belgian High Command choose the River IJzer as their last line of defence. The Westhoek, the last tiny western corner of Belgian soil in Belgian hands, must be held at all costs. Otherwise, the Germans will be able to push on to the vital French Channel ports. The bridges over the IJzer are equally crucial. The opposing armies bombard each other from the opposite banks of the river. Initially, a Belgian division is able to cling on to Nieuwpoort and a Franco-Belgian bridgehead is established at Diksmuide. But it is all to no avail. There are just too many Germans and they are too strong. By the end of October, all the IJzer bridges have fallen to the enemy.

It seems as though the Belgians are in danger of losing the Battle of the IJzer. However, the High Command has a dramatic plan that may rescue the situation. They decide to open the Ganzepoot (Goose's Foot) lock gates to the sea at high tide in Nieuwpoort. This will flood the low-lying fields between the IJzer and the raised embankment of the Nieuwpoort-Diksmuide railway line. Karel Cogge, a supervisor for the Veurne Waterways Company, understands perfectly how the hydraulic network in the coastal region functions and Hendrik Geeraert, an out-of-work skipper, knows how the lock gates work. The plan works and the Germans are forced to retire behind a wall of water 15 kilometres long and four kilometres wide. The Battle of the IJzer comes to a close, since neither side can attack in these conditions. Three months after crossing the Belgian border, the German advance is finally brought to a halt. Not in Paris, as people were starting to fear, but in Ramskapelle, Schoorbakke and Tervate.

The inundation of the IJzer plain is a turning point in the course of the First World War and, by extension, in the history of Belgium and all Europe. For now, however, the strategic action carried out by Cogge and Geeraert is just the beginning. It is followed by four years of bitter trench warfare. It is often forgotten that after November 1914 the flood waters — and the mechanisms to maintain them — had to be defended every single day: raising or lowering the level of the water, damming the culverts under the railway embankment, filling sandbags, laying duckboard tracks across the watery

wasteland, repairing damage from shell fire, breaking ice in winter so that the enemy cannot cross. Once again, the bike played a crucial role in all these tasks. It is the ideal mode of transport for moving quickly and quietly at night to the dykes, ditches and wooden piles that need attention.

Maintenance of the locks and the hydraulic system on the Belgian front is entrusted to Captain-Commander Robert Thys, who has a platoon of well-trained cyclists at his disposal. The cyclists are part of a specially formed company of *sapeurs-pontonniers* (bridge engineers). The company's workshops and quarters are just behind the front in Veurne, where each day the level of the flood water is carefully monitored. Sergeant Ballon and Privates Cop and Van Belle, who helped Geeraert to open the locks in October 1914, take the necessary measurements at different points in the line, travelling from place to place by bike.

Hendrik Geeraert, the skipper who helps to open the locks at Nieuwpoort in 1914.

In addition to his cyclists, Captain Thys can also call on a technical team and three sections of divers. One section works constantly on the locks at Nieuwpoort, while a second carries out necessary night repairs at Wulpen. This is heavy, exhausting work, carried out in highly dangerous conditions. What's more, throughout the four years they work to keep the flood waters at the right level, the 'bridge engineers' are under regular shellfire from the Germans. In total, 27 *sapeurs-pontonniers* are killed, 50 are wounded and 143 are affected by gas. In the Langestraat in Nieuwpoort, not far from the Ganzepoot, a bronze plaque on the wall of the house at number 5 marks the place where the brave cyclists of the Compagnie Sapeurs-Pontonniers sheltered during the war, so that they could carry out their vital work on the locks that kept the last remaining piece of unoccupied Belgium safe.

Sapeurs-pontonniers in 1915 on the road from Veurne to De Panne.

A FEMALE EX-RACER DESIGNS AN AIR AMBULANCE

Hélène Dutrieu, the Belgian ex-racer, stunt woman and pilot, is in Paris when the First World War breaks out. She immediately volunteers to become a pilot for the French Army. However, the brutal and underhand German attack has caused such disgust that the French, viewing themselves as a 'noble and civilized nation', refuse to allow women to take part in the fighting. Never one to be easily deterred, the former world hour-record holder keeps on pestering the military authorities — both in Paris and Brussels — to be allowed to fly. She finally gets her way: the French agree that she can fly reconnaissance missions as a volunteer.

During September 1914, Dutrieu takes off one or more times each day from an airfield near Paris to report on the positions of the advancing Germans and their own aerial strength. Brave as ever, she flies further and further, until she even goes beyond the Marne valley. 'When I was in the air, I never thought of the danger', she later comments to a reporter for an American magazine. 'I wish that I could find the words to describe the terrible things I saw when I flew for three days over the battlefield of the Marne, the battle that saved Paris and France. For a distance of 160 kilometres I only saw dead or wounded German soldiers, left lying where they fell — the French casualties had already been picked up. When I landed, we decided to ride back all those kilometres with ambulances to see if we could also help those German victims.'

Hélène even designs an 'ambulance-plane' that can carry a wounded soldier under its fuselage, but it is never put into production. What's more, a short time later she is forced to stop her reconnaissance flights. She is twice shot at by a Taube, an aircraft from the German *Feldflieger Abteilung*. It is only thanks to her flying skill and a good deal of luck that she is able to escape. But things are becoming too dangerous, certainly in her unarmed plane.

Because she was a famous personality before the war, the French authorities decide to send her to the United States. This is at the suggestion of General Gallieni, the future Minister of War. She takes part in propaganda events to promote the Allied cause, in the hope that the Americans can be persuaded to join the fight against the Kaiser and his German Empire. At the same time, she offers her services to help train American pilots. A year

later, during another of her propaganda trips, she visits a car factory in Detroit and returns home as an official distributer for the Chandler brand, soon followed across the Atlantic by a ship full of cars.

In the meantime, she continues to be active as a war volunteer. She is no longer allowed to fly, but in April 1915 she accepts a request from General Février to take charge of the Red Cross ambulances operating behind the front. The ex-cycle racer also becomes responsible for the Val de Grâce field hospital in Paris' 5th arrondissement. She continues to run the ambulance service and transport wounded soldiers for the rest of the war.

The Armistice brings an end to both her flying career and her stunt career. Cycling is also a thing of the past for her. Hélène Dutrieu marries Pierre Mortier, journalist, writer and member of the French parliament, and becomes his secretary. She does, however, later become the vice-president of the women's section of the French Aeroclub and in 1956 founds the Hélène Dutrieu-Mortier Prize, awarded each year to the female pilot who flies the longest distance in a straight line without intermediary landings. She dies in Paris at the age of 84 and is buried in the Batignolles Cemetery. There are streets named after her in both Tournai and Ghent.

Hélène Dutrieu is highly active as a wartime volunteer.

THE TOUR WINNER WHO NEVER GETS OFF THE GROUND

A few weeks after his Tour success and his short stay in England, Philippe Thys is back in Paris. He moves in with a cousin of his, convinced that the French will beat the Germans and that the war will soon be over. But it doesn't happen. The war drags on and there is no question of a resumption of cycling. Most of his fellow racers are already fighting at the front. When he walks along the streets of Paris, he can see what people think of him from the looks on their faces. Why is that young man here instead of defending his country? The attitude towards 'non-combatants' becomes progressively more hostile and in May 1915 the double Tour winner decides to report to the Belgian recruiting centre in Calais. After a short period of training, he is posted to Étampes, 50 kilometres south of Paris, where the Belgian Military Aviation Force has a flying school. But he never takes to the air. Instead, he is employed as a ground mechanic, working on the maintenance of the primitive aircraft.

Really, it is only half a job, so the racer still has plenty of time to train. His commanding officer is happy to let him. Each unit likes to show off with its sporting heroes and Thys' commander is none other than Charles Van den Born, who before he became an aviation pioneer was also a successful racer. Yet although his training keeps him fit, at first there are no races in wartime France for Thys to ride in. This gradually begins to change in the summer of 1916. A track meeting is held every two weeks in the Parc des Princes. In September, he beats Ali Neffati in a race behind tandems. On 18 November, he is second in a team event with Charles Deruyter behind Oscar Egg and Henri Contenet. But he gets back to winning ways in one of the last competitions of the year — an omnium — crossing the line ahead of Octave Lapize and Henri Pélissier.

Double Tour winner Philippe Thys (in the centre) as a military air mechanic at Étampes.

A BELGIAN VELODROME IN THE NETHERLANDS

The fact that King Albert and his army so stubbornly defend their country irritates the Germans. They take out their frustration on the civilian population. Hundreds of innocent people are shot and thousands of homes — sometimes whole villages — are burnt to the ground. Reports of the atrocities carried out by the invaders at Dinant, Tamines, Dendermonde and Leuven (among others) start to spread. Many people are so frightened that they decide to flee. There is a huge exodus, especially to the neutral Netherlands. Queen Wilhelmina appeals to her subjects to provide shelter and care for the homeless Belgians. The Dutch are a hospitable people and many families take the queen's words to heart. But after the fall of Antwerp the flood of refugees becomes so great that it is impossible to manage without some form of official organization.

At the beginning of October 1914, a Dutch population of ten million souls needs to cope with an additional one million displaced persons from Belgium, 40,000 of whom are soldiers cut off from the rest of the Belgian Army. To complicate matters further, international conventions require the Dutch to treat these soldiers as prisoners of war. To try and bring order to this chaotic situation, the authorities in The Hague can see only one solution: internment camps. The measure has, to some extent, the desired effect. Many of the Belgians decide to return home. Even so, more than 100,000 others will remain in the Netherlands until 1918. The civilians are treated as refugees, but for the soldiers there is no other option but to keep them interned. However, some 7,000 of them sooner or later escape to join their comrades on the IJzer.

To cope with both the refuges and the soldiers, the Dutch build barrack camps at top speed. There are military camps at Harderwijk and Soesterberg and civilian camps at Nunspeet, Uden and in Friesian Gaasterland. The camps are often larger than the towns and villages near which they are located. For example, Harderwijk has a population of 7,500 in 1914, whereas the nearby camp now houses 14,500 military internees. At first, the regime in the camps is strict and the Belgians soon get bored. But when the war shows no sign of ending quickly, things become more relaxed and a number of extra amenities are provided.

Schools, workshops, theatres and libraries are all built. The inmates also attempt to pick up the threads of their pre-war social and sporting activities — and this includes cycling.

In Harderwijk, they even build a cycle track. At first, it is very much an improvised affair, but by August 1917 there is a proper 400-metre circuit (complete with bends), constructed by troops from the Belgian military engineers. At that time, it is the only cycle track of near professional standard in the Netherlands. The men responsible for organizing cycling events in the camp are Jan Somers and Urbain Anseeuw. Anseeuw finished as amateur second in the last Tour of Belgium before the war and is a brother-in-law of Marcel and Lucien Buysse. Called up to fight in 1914, the West Fleming took part in the Battle of Antwerp but his unit was cut off from the main body of the Belgian Army, leaving it little option but to cross into the Netherlands to avoid capture by the Germans.

Somers and Anseeuw first race in Harderwijk against other internees, but it is not long before a number of Dutch racers ask to take part. For the camp's inmates this is a pleasing diversion from their normal dull routine. It also attracts the attention of local people in Harderwijk, who soon catch the Belgian cycling bug. It is not uncommon for there to be two or three thousand spectators gathered around the track. Amateur races are also organized on the 300-metre 'Vluchtorde Vooruit' circuit in Uden. At the end of 1916, the Dutch authorities even give permission for a road race through the Veluwe region, where Pier Van de Velde, already a professional rider before the war, is the pick of the pack. In the following year, Belgian soldiers from Harderwijk are also allowed to take part in a 24-hour race in Bergen-op-Zoom and in 1918 are even invited to attend a gala event for cycling professionals in Amsterdam, where a new velodrome is being opened.

On 22 September 1918, Alfons Spiessens and Piet Moeskops win a 100-kilometre team event on the velodrome in the internment camp at Harderwijk.

MINOR RACERS IN A MAJOR WAR

Philippe Thys, the great victor of the 1914 Tour, is now in uniform. But many other lesser cycling gods who rode with him in that final pre-war Tour are also serving their country. Some of them performed well in the race; some of them less well. Some of them didn't even reach the finish. This was the fate of the 34-year-old Félix Preignac, who lined up at the start in Paris for the very first time. Félix is only an average racer, riding as an unsupported *isolé*, and his first and only Tour turns out to be a bit of disaster: he doesn't even complete the first stage. But this is nothing compared to the disaster that will befall him just three months later. On 27 September 1914, Félix Preignac is killed while serving with the 220th Infantry Regiment somewhere south of Verdun, close to the place where five days earlier the well-known French author Alain-Fournier was also killed. Preignac is buried in the national necropolis at Lacroix-sur-Meuse.

Maurice Dejoie is another professional rider whose war is tragically short. The 25-year-old finishes 35th in the 1914 Paris-Tours and 22nd in Paris-Menen. In that year's Tour de France he is part of the Clément-Dunlop team, but is forced to retire after the third stage. As a soldier, he eventually finds himself in Gallipoli, a peninsula at the entrance to the strategically important Dardanelles that the British and French wish to capture from the Turks. In the insanitary conditions at the front, Maurice falls sick. He is evacuated to the hospital at Mudros on the Greek island of Lemnos, but there he dies. Several other riders who have taken part in past Tours — Jean Perreard, Marius Villette, François Cordier, Frédéric Rigaux and René Etien — also perish during the Gallipoli campaign.

Auguste Pierron also dies a long way from home. The 30-year-old rider has to give up during the second stage of the 1914 Tour. Less than a month later, he is a soldier in the 175th Infantry Regiment. He survives two years of war but meets his end on 21 November 1916 near the Serbian town of Suhodol-Raja.

One of the better known of these minor racers — if only by association — is Henri Alavoine. Henri has much less talent than his famous older brother Jean, who will eventually win a total of 17 stages in the Tour and twice be crowned French national champion. Even so, Henri manages to complete

La Grande Boucle on no fewer than four occasions. In 1913, he finishes in 25th place; in 1914, he is 52nd. Like many cyclists, during the war he serves in the air force, as a corporal in the 1st Aviation Group. In the summer of 1916, his plane is hit by enemy fire and crashes. The 26-year-old Alavoine dies of his injuries on 19 July in the hospital at Pau.

One of Henri's comrades in the same unit is another ex-racer, Emile Guyon. A year older than Alavoine, he also takes part in the 1914 Tour, in his case for the first and only time. He finishes in Paris in 43rd position. Although he lives not far from Geneva in neutral Switzerland, he volunteers for the French Army. Like Alavoine, his plane crashes near Pau on 6 September 1918, just two months before the end of the war.

Even closer to the end of the war, Louis Bonino dies at his home in Marseille from the effects of a lung infection he contracted at the front. He also started in the 1914 Tour de France, but gave up after the second stage. He is 38 years old at the time of his death — the oldest of the 1914 Tour riders to die in the war. But not really old at all.

Jean Alavoine, the more famous brother of Henri, finishes third in the 1914 Tour de France.

Victor Fastré gives his life for his country on 12 September 1914.

Fastré achieves most of his successes in the velodromes at Liege and Verviers. As a corporal in the reserve (he was drafted for national service in 1910), he rejoins the 25th Line Regiment when war breaks out in August 1914. On 12 September, his unit is ordered to move forward from Rotselaar, with instructions to hold the mill and bridge over the River Dijle against the advancing German Army. But it is a hopeless mission. The Belgian troops are decimated by the German artillery and soon find themselves surrounded and without ammunition. Superior numbers of German infantry close in for the kill and more than 900 men of the 25th Line Regiment are lost. One of them is Victor Fastré. He is posthumously awarded the Knight's Cross in the Order of Leopold II and the War Cross with Palm. He is buried in the military cemetery at Rotselaar.

One of the many soldiers reported missing after the heavy fighting at Nieuwpoort on 4 November 1914 is Charles Smits. Born on 9 February 1892 and originating from Schaarbeek, he has only recently become a professional rider. His license with the Belgian Cycling Federation is registered under number 173, but there is no record of his victories, for the simple reason that he was never given the chance to win any. The war starts almost immediately and he is rushed to the front as a Private Second Class in the 10th Cyclist Company, serving with the 26th Line Regiment. His body is never recovered, although like Fastré he is posthumously awarded the War Cross and the IJzer Medal.

A third cyclist who fails to see the first Christmas of the war is Jules Patou. It is not clear how or when he dies, but before the end of the year the newspapers are reporting that the 35-year-old ex-racer from Brussels will 'rest' forever on the IJzer. Patou is an all-rounder, who competes on the road and on the track, both as a stayer and as a sprinter. As an amateur, he finishes second in the 1906 Paris-Brussels, behind Albert Dupont. Five years later, he becomes Belgian sprint champion in the same category. At the 1909 world championship in Copenhagen he wins bronze in the stayer race. He also takes part in the road race at the Olympic Games in Stockholm in 1912, but doesn't make the finish.

A number of Belgian cyclists also die in 1914. Following Marcel Kerff and Jacques Julémont at the beginning of August and Jean Demarteau at the Battle of Halen, the next to fall is Victor Fastré. Born in Liege on 19 May 1890, he is a talented racer who in 1909 wins his 'home' race, when he triumphs in Liege-Bastogne-Liege (which at that time is only open to amateurs). Having turned professional, he is fifth in the same race in 1912. He rides for two seasons for the top French Alcyon team, and then later for Saroléa. He twice competes in the Tour of Belgium but soon switches to the track, where starting bonuses and prize money are higher.

Anselme Mazan (right) with his brother, Lucien 'Petit-Breton' Mazan.

THE 'LESSER GODS' OF THE TOUR

The First World War brings slaughter to Europe and also to the ranks of professional cycling. At least 222 French cyclists lose their lives before the Armistice in 1918. There are no exact figures, but it seems likely that 93 German, 18 Belgian, 14 Austro-Hungarian and 12 Italian racers meet the same fate. The statistics for the Tour de France alone are equally depressing. Of the 145 riders who appear on the start line in Paris in 1914, 17 will die. The same number of competitors from the 1910 Tour will also die, with a further 15 fatalities among the Tour peloton of 1909.

Of all the riders who take part in the Tour between 1903 and 1914, 53 will be dead by 11 November 1918. Some of them are great names; others are so-called 'lesser gods'. Like Eugène Mathonat, for example. Mathonat is a sapper in the 1st Regiment of Engineers and is already posted as missing on 22 August 1914, after the heavy fighting at Ville-Houdlémont on the Franco-Belgian border. His body is never found and it is only on 27 July 1921 that his death is confirmed by the court in Aix. Born in Auxerre on 1 April 1883, he turns professional in 1907 and rides for the Labor-Dunlop team in the Tour of 1910, finishing in 37th place. His younger brother Georges, a talented amateur racer, also dies during the war, just three days before the Armistice.

The 35-year-old Emile Lachaise from Lyon becomes a professional in 1909 and ends that year's Tour in a creditable 20th position. It is the only time he completes *La Grande Boucle*. In the following editions, he fails to get over the mountains. As a sergeant in the 52nd Infantry Regiment, he takes part in the Second Battle of Champagne from 25 September 1914 onwards. The battle rages for three days over a 24-kilometre front. By the evening of 27 September, the French have advanced four kilometres and taken 25,000 German prisoners, but at the enormous cost of 138,000 killed, wounded and missing. One of the missing is Emile Lachaise.

François Lafourcade, hero of the Aubisque, dies on 10 August 1917.

His remains probably now rest among all the many thousands of other unknown bones in the ossuary at Sommepy-Tahure, 30 kilometres east of Rheims.

Sometimes it takes several years before the deaths of missing riders can be confirmed. Charles Privas, born on 21 December 1887 in Jarcieu and a participant in the 1913 Tour, disappears on 22 October 1914 during the fighting at Saint-Laurent-Blagny near Arras. His death is only formally certified in court on 11 February 1921. Much the same is true for François Marcastel, a 41-year-old sergeant in the 116th Infantry Regiment, who dies as a prisoner of war in Hannover on 6 November 1914. It takes until 12 August 1920 before a judgement handed down by a court in Paris finally confirms his death. Marcastel took part in the second Tour de France in 1904, but retired before the end.

Another professional who is reported missing in action during the war is Raymond Didier. Didier serves as a Private Second Class in the 57th Infantry Regiment, which in 1915 takes part in the fighting to recapture the plain between the Meuse and the Moselle from the German invaders. On 30 March, his unit and others launch a fierce attack from the Bois-le-Prêtre. The fighting lasts for many days and claims thousands of lives on both sides, among them Raymond Didier, who is last seen on 8 April 1915. Born on 23 September 1891 in Foulain, he becomes a professional racer in 1908 and is ninth in the national championship in his debut year. He rides his only Tour in 1910, before ending his career just a year later. His death is confirmed by a court in Troyes on 8 December 1920.

Pierre Privat following his tandem pace-makers during the 1907 Bol d'Or in Paris.

Anselme Mazan is given a professional contract by the Peugeot-Wolber team in 1907 and starts in that year's Tour, although he gets no further than the seventh stage. Sadly, he does not have the same talent as his older brother Lucien, who will win the 1907 edition under his racing pseudonym of Lucien Petit-Breton. Equally sadly (if not more so), Anselme will not live to see the Armistice. In June 1915, this Private Second Class in the 265th Infantry Regiment finds himself in the Compiègne-Soissons region, where the French are anxious to break out of the Quennevières salient. They do not succeed. True, they gain a small strip of land, a kilometre wide and 500 metres deep, but this costs them 7,905 casualties, including the 31-year-old Anselme. The third and older Mazan brother, Paul, also a professional cyclist, has more luck than his siblings and survives the war.

Pierre Privat, a professional rider between 1906 and 1910, is a valuable helper in the Peugeot team. He takes part in the Tour four times, his best result being an eleventh place in 1907. Privat is a man of many talents: after his cycling career, he becomes a celebrated illustrator and caricaturist. In particular, his posters of other racers are in great demand. As a sergeant in the 274th Infantry Regiment, he is wounded by enemy fire in the hills of Artois and dies from his injuries in the evacuation hospital at Aubigny-en-Artois. He was 35 years old.

René Cottrel, born on 18 July 1885 in Saint-Ouen, is the 47th finisher in the Tour of 1914. Just weeks later, he is a soldier in the 298th Infantry Regiment and receives his first wound in the Battle of the Marne. In fact, for a number of weeks he is blind. As soon as he recovers, he is posted to Verdun as a cyclist and liaison officer. While he is riding to Fort Vaux on 5 November 1916, a shell explodes almost on top of him. He is hit by several fragments and dies of his wounds soon after.

One of the better known Tour fatalities is François Lafourcade. This is largely the result of Henri Desgrange's decision in 1910 to send the race over the Pyrenees for the first time. Lafourcade reaches the top of the legendary Col d'Aubisque with a lead of 15 minutes. But although he excels at uphill riding, he lacks the courage or the technique to go downhill at full speed. As a result, Octave Lapize catches him in the descent and goes on to win both the stage and the Tour. Lafourcade starts in *La Grande Boucle* seven times and reaches the finish in Paris on three occasions. In the 1911 Tour he is involved in a curious inci-

dent. After the first stage in the Pyrenees, Paul Duboc is the surprise leader, but then goes down with poisoning. Someone has put 'something' in his water bottle. The finger of guilt is pointed at his main rival, Gustave Garrigou, but others suspect François Lafourcade. Nothing is ever proven and Garrigou is allowed to continue in the race, which he eventually wins in Paris. In contrast, Lafourcade is banned from cycling for life. He continues his career with one of the unofficial cycling unions, but in 1914 is called up for service in the army. Initially, he serves as a sergeant in the 22nd Artillery Regiment, but in 1915 he transfers to the 485th Squadron in the 1st Aviation Group. On 10 August 1917, his Voisin 8 biplane is hit and catches fire. In a desperate attempt to escape from the flames, he jumps from his cockpit while still some way above the ground. However, he dies from his injuries soon afterwards. The 35-year-old Lafourcade is buried at Eu, in Normandy.

The very last rider in the Tour of 1906, Georges Bronchard, is yet another racer who fails to survive the war. Although he is the 'red lantern' in 1906, he is one of only 14 riders to finish that year. In other words, he is better than 68 other riders who never even reach Paris. In the 1907 Tour he finishes as 21st and in 1908 he is 29th. When war breaks out in 1914, he becomes a stretcher-bearer in the French Army Medical Corps. His task is to carry dead and wounded soldiers from the battlefield to the field hospitals behind the lines. This allows him to see all the horror and misery of war. In 1918, he is stationed at Villers-sur-Coudon, just north of Compiègne. On 27 April, he is hit by shellfire while tending a wounded comrade. The 31-year-old Bronchard later dies of his injuries at field ambulance no. 247.

Last in this line of less well-known Tour victims of the Great War is Albert Niepceron. Originating from Semblançay near Tours, he finishes tenth in the 1903 Bordeaux-Paris and also takes part in that year's Tour de France, as well as in the 1904 edition. He is killed in his 35th year while serving as a sergeant in the 206th Infantry Regiment at Coulommiers during the Second Battle of the Marne on 23 October 1918. It is less than three weeks before the war ends.

'LONG LIVE THE BIKE!' BECOMES
'LONG LIVE THE REPUBLIC!'

While the Germans are still attempting to capture Antwerp between 28 September and 9 October 1914, the car manufacturer Minerva makes the first armoured car by adding steel plating and either a machine gun or a light cannon to one of its most powerful models. This leads to the creation of another new unit in the Belgian Army: the *Corps Autos-Canons-Mitrailleuses* (Mobile Cannon and Machine Gun Corps) or ACM. Like all the army's other units, the ACM pulls back towards the IJzer after Antwerp falls. There they soon discover that there is little use for armoured cars in trench warfare, so King Albert decides to lend the ACM to Russia, following an official request from the Tsar, who wants to employ them on the more fluid Eastern Front. On 22 September 1915, the 351 men of the ACM set off from the French port of Brest. Among their number are the author Marcel Thiry and Constant le Marin, a world champion in Greco-Roman wrestling. By then, the ACM has at its disposal 12 armoured cars, 46 cars, 23 motorbikes and 120 bicycles. The convoy arrives in Archangelsk on 13 October. Via Petrograd (St. Petersburg),

the unit drives south to the region of the Carpathian mountains, where the Russians are fighting against the Austro-Hungarians.

Another member of the Belgian contingent is Henry George, born in Charleroi on 18 February 1891. He has only recently volunteered for the army, specifically with the hope of learning how to drive. Henry is an amateur cyclist, but he has always been fascinated by cars, the new toy of the rich. Consequently, he is disappointed when the ACM decides to use him as a cyclist, rather than a driver. So what does he do? He pretends he can't ride a bike! He deliberately keeps on falling off or bumping into things. However, his NCO, a certain Julien Lahaut, soon puts it to an end. He watches George like a hawk and forces him to keep on riding, until it becomes clear to all that his claim that he doesn't know how to ride a bike is nonsense.

In the summer of 1916, the ACM takes part in a major Russian offensive, but the attack is beaten off. A second offensive in July 1917 is equally unsuccessful. Sixteen of the Belgians are killed. By this time, the tsar has abdicated and in October

Henry George (third left) as a cyclist in the ACM Corps.

the Bolsheviks seize power. At the start of the following year, Russia makes peace with the German Empire.

The ACM is now associated with the discredited tsarist regime and is no longer welcome. But how can they get home? Travelling westward through Germany and Austria-Hungary is not an option and so they begin an odyssey that takes them eastwards, first to Siberia and Vladivostok, and then by boat to San Francisco. From there, they cross overland to New York, stopping to parade in several major cities along the way, where local people enthusiastically greet the soldiers of 'Brave Little Belgium'.

After an uneventful crossing of the Atlantic, the ACM arrives back in Bordeaux on 24 June 1918. The unit is immediately disbanded, but this does not mean the end of the war for Henry George. He fights as an infantryman during the final offensive of the war in Flanders and is wounded. He finishes the war as a decorated veteran and decides to resume his cycling career. By now, he is 28 years old and knows that a professional license is no longer possible. Even so, he scores a number of notable successes. In 1919, he is third in the Belgian road championship for amateurs. A year later, he is second in the same race. But he is an even better rider on the track. He breaks the national hour record with a tandem

The Mobile Cannon and Machine Gun Corps is created thanks to the inventiveness of the Minerva motor company.

Henry George is carried shoulder-high through the Zurenborg stadium after winning gold in the 1920 Olympic Games in Antwerp.

90

lots of pushing, pulling and falling. To make matters worse, the Italian supporters try to help their own riders by throwing them drink bottles tied to pieces of string, right in the middle of the peloton.

The British rider Thomas Harvey dominates the race and he starts his sprint as the bell for the last lap is sounded. However, in the final straight he falls, probably because his back wheel comes into contact with Henry George's front wheel. Another Englishman, Cyril Alden, falls over Harvey's bike but still slides over the finishing line. Has he won? No, Henry George has beaten him by 15 centimetres and is Olympic champion! It is the absolute highlight of his career. It is said that his old sergeant from the ACM, Julien Lahaut, was among the first to congratulate him with the words: 'It's a good job I taught you how to ride a bike in Russia!' George carries on cycling for a few more years, without much success, and then quietly disappears into anonymity.

The same cannot be said for Julien Lahaut. He enters politics and in 1932 is elected as a member of the Belgian House of Representatives. He survives the concentration camp at Mauthausen and after the Second World War becomes chairman of the Communist Party of Belgium (KPB), which at that time enjoys considerable popularity. On 11 August 1950, when the new king-prince Boudewijn I swears his oath of allegiance in parliament, someone is heard to call out *'Vive la République!'* (Long live the republic!). Although it is never proven, most people think that it is Lahaut who disturbs the ceremony. A week later, he is shot dead in front of his house in Seraing. The killers are never found. It remains the most important unsolved political murder in Belgian history.

pace-maker and is selected to take part in the 1920 Olympic Games to be held in Antwerp.

The opening ceremony is attended by King Albert, wearing the uniform in which he commanded the Belgian Army throughout the war. Doves are released as a symbol of peace and reconciliation. Henry George takes part in the 50 kilometre track race. There are 31 competitors, far too many for the relatively tight track at the Zurenborg velodrome. As a result, it is a tumultuous race, with

The odyssey of the ACM Corps is one of the most remarkable stories from the First World War.

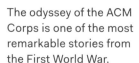

ODIEL DEFRAEYE, SOLDIER AND BRIDEGROOM

By mid-October 1914, the advancing Germans reach the borders of West Flanders. They quickly take a number of villages against only modest resistance. It is assumed that the rest of the province will quickly follow. Here and there, however, the retreating Allied armies put up a stiffer fight. In Rumbeke and Roeselare the Germans suddenly find themselves under fire from a rearguard of French snipers. The invaders think that their attackers are civilians and react with fury. Simply based on rumour and hearsay, they set about a series of savage reprisals. ln Rumbeke, 65 houses are plundered and burnt. Innocent civilians are herded together and shot. Before the German anger is cooled, 39 local people lose their lives: 30 men, six women and three children. 19 October 1914 will go down in the history of Flanders as *Schuwe maandag* (Black Monday). It is a shock for the whole region and the start of a complex relationship between the occupiers and the occupied.

Rumbeke is also the home village of Odiel Defraeye, the winner of the Tour de France in 1912. His success continues the following season, when he becomes only the second Belgian (after Cyrille Van Hauwaert) to win Milan-Sanremo. Luck, however, deserts him in the 1913 edition of the Tour. His preparation is hindered by injury and he is not properly fit. Even so, he leads the overall standings for three days but has to withdraw from the race after the first of the hard Pyrenean stages. He also fails to reach the finish in 1914.

Defraeye only learns about Black Monday and the happenings in his village after the war. In October 1914, he has already fallen back on Ieper with the rest of the Transport Corps of the 6th Division. Consequently, he doesn't know that his parental home has also been claimed by the Germans. A week after the reprisals, the invaders open an aerodrome near Rumbeke, from where Aviatiks and Fokkers fly missions to locate and bomb Allied positions. The castle in Rumbeke is also requisitioned for the headquarters of the 26th Reserve Corps, where *Freiherr* von Hügel and his staff take up residence.

On the other side of the front, Defraeye continues his work in the quartermaster's store, a low-risk task that basically involves looking after the supplies of food, drink and uniforms for his unit. Although a conscript, as a former winner of the Tour he enjoys a kind of 'protected status'. In military circles his sporting prowess is a source of pride and admiration. Even his officers look up to

Tour winner Odiel Defraeye works in a quartermaster's store throughout the war.

him. They treat him to beer in their mess and are happy to let him tell his tales about the Tour. As a result, Defraeye has a relatively comfortable war, as evidenced by the fact that after the Armistice he is not awarded a *vuurpas* (fire pass), which offers benefits to those who have been under fire or suffered the effects of a gas attack.

The racer is, however, given permission to marry, right in the middle of the war. His bride is Madi Stamper, a girl he has known for years. With her parents, she fled in 1914 from the war-torn village of Zonnebeke to the relative safety of Proven, just behind the front near Poperinge. It is there that Odiel and Madi are married on 13 October 1915, at seven o'clock in the morning. In spite of their apparent urgency to marry, the wedding is not a 'shotgun' affair: their first child is only born in December 1916. However, his new marital status wins yet even more benefits for Defraeye, since he is occasionally allowed to visit his wife at her temporary home behind the lines near De Lovie, a castle used by British and French units as a headquarters.

After the Armistice, Odiel Defraeye returns to competitive cycling. He renovates his Hôtel des Sport in the hope that a series of spectacular victories will attract new customers. But in contrast to riders like Thys and Lambot, who pick up their careers more or less where they left off in 1914, Defraeye finds it hard to get back into the groove. He gives up during Paris-Roubaix. He is back in the pack in the Tour of Belgium. Against his better judgement, he decides to ride in the Tour, but that too is a humiliating disappointment. He continues racing for another five years but will never reach his pre-war standard. Frustrated by his lack of success, he leaves behind his hotel with its own velodrome and moves to the south of France for three years. When he returns, he opens a tavern on the Belgian coast, first at Lombardsijde, later at De Panne. 'Fraeyke' remains a popular figure. He begins as a social drinker, but ends up as an addicted one. The first Belgian Tour winner dies on 21 August 1965 in the anonymity of a retirement home in the Walloon-Brabant town of Bièrges, where he is also buried.

'Black Monday' — 19 October 1914 — is the day on which the town of Roeselare learns about the cruelty of which the German invaders are capable. Everyone knows the town is likely to fall, but no-one expects the plundering, burning and massacre of innocent civilians. For fear that more acts of terror will follow, about a third of the town's population decides to flee. Among them is Jules Masselis, a protégé of Cyrille Van Hauwaert and one of his favourite helpers in the Alcyon team. He eventually finds shelter for himself and his family in Paris. By this time, Masselis is 28 years old, the age at which many riders reach their sporting peak. He has already put together an impressive string of results, with victories in the Tour of Belgium (1910), Paris-Menen (1912) and two stage wins in the Tour de France (1911 and 1913). He has also been on the podium for some of the classics, with third places in Paris-Roubaix (1909), Bordeaux-Paris (1911) and Milan-Sanremo (1912). However, like so many other riders, the war will hamper his further progress.

In Paris, he finds work in a city bakery. He is fortunate that his boss is a cycle-lover and gives him time off to train. But training is all he can do, since

Jules Masselis (right) alongside his fellow villager, Cyrille Van Hauwaert.

93

competitive cycling has more or less ground to a
halt in wartime France. It is only from 1916 onwards
that Masselis will once again be able to ride on the
track and, later still, in some of the limited number
of road races. On 19 September 1918, he is the best
in Bourges-Paris, a 'reverse' version of a race that
was organized in 1913 and 1917, and still exists today.
He covers the 263 kilometres in 9 hours, 2 minutes
and 10 seconds and at the finish in the Parc des
Princes has a lead of two minutes over Henri Pélissier, with Oscar Egg third and Charles Mantelet
forth. It is his last big victory. After the Armistice,
he rides twice more in the Tour (retiring on both
occasions) and has a number of top-10 finishes in
good races like the Tour of Flanders, Bordeaux-
Paris and Paris-Tours, but he never again matches
his pre-war level of performance.

Arthur Vanderstuyft is another racer who feels
the need to run from the Germans at the start of
the war. Originally from Ieper, he is brought up in
Essen, where his father Fritz is the stationmaster.
Vanderstuyft senior is one of the pioneers of Belgian cycling and his name appears in the earliest
results of both Bordeaux-Paris (1893-1896) and

Paris-Roubaix (1898-1899). His small but energetic
son races from a young age on the tracks at Zurenborg and Riverenhof. To pay for his bikes and his
other expenses, he works as a mechanic in the
Minerva car factory, where one of his fellow
workers is Jan Olieslagers, who is later one of his
pace-makers. Arthur becomes a professional racer
before his 18th birthday. Within two years he is

Stayer Arthur
Vanderstuyft flees
from Essen
to the safety
of the nearby
Netherlands.

British cyclists take the youngest refugees
on their bikes.

Belgian champion on the road, but he also excels in six-day events and is an outstanding stayer, in which discipline he also wins two national titles (1904, 1912). In 1905, he triumphs in the Bol d'Or on the famous Buffalo track in Paris, a race that involves completing as many laps as possible in 24 hours behind tandem pace-makers. His winning distance is an impressive 943.666 kilometres.

From 1912 onwards, Vanderstuyft rides a lot of his races in Germany. Some people hold this against him — German-Prussian militarism is already increasing political tension and the threat of war — but as one of the best stayers in Europe lucrative contracts await him on the circuits in Berlin, Leipzig, Dusseldorf, Dresden and Hannover. His compatriot Victor Linart, the American Robbert Walthour and the Frenchmen Jules Miquel, Paul Guignard and Georges Sérès all do much the same thing. With the German Deutschmarks he earns, he later buys large quantities of shoes, clothes and medicines, which, according to his grandson René Lux, he uses to help people in Antwerp during the war. Even so, at the end of 1914 he decides to flee to neighbouring (and neutral) Holland. He stays there for more than a year, but in 1916 returns to the city on the Schelde, where he rides in a number of track meetings, including a race against Cyrille Van Hauwaert.

Some racers don't even get the chance to run. César Debaets, a professional rider since 1913, is arrested by the Germans for reasons that are unclear and imprisoned in the fort at Sedan, just over the French border in the Ardennes. He is mistreated on several occasions by his guards, and when he is finally allowed to return home in 1915 he weighs just 45 kilograms. Even so, he starts cycling again in that same year and in September takes part in an 'ersatz' Tour of Belgium on the Karreveld track in Sint-Jans-Molenbeek.

His brother Michel, born in 1888 and second in the Belgian road championship at the age of just 22, fares little better at the hands of the Germans. He is ordered to report for work in one of their labour camps, but having seen how his brother returned from Sedan, he decides it is better to try and escape with his wife to the Netherlands, notwithstanding the risks involved. In December 1915, they manage with the aid of a barrel to find a way through the so-called 'wire of death' — the electrified fence the Germans have erected along the more than 300-kilometre long border between Belgium and Holland. After a short stay in a refugee camp, they sail to the United States and settle in Detroit. Michel Debaets rides for many years in American six-day events, often competing against Robert Walthour and Clarence Carman, among others. He is later granted US citizenship and opens a bike shop.

The youngest of the Debaets brothers is Gérard. He is just 15 years old when the war breaks out and cycles with the juniors. From 1916 onwards, he is forced by the Germans to repair railways, but he finds it difficult to tolerate being given instructions by his country's invaders. This leads to frequent beatings and occasional spells behind bars on a bread and water diet. One story tells how he once argued so fiercely with a German officer that the officer shot him in the leg. Be that as it may, after the war Gérard proves himself to be the most talented of the three brothers. He turns professional in 1924 and immediately wins his very first race: the Tour of Flanders. It is a feat he repeats three years later. In between, he triumphs in the 1925 Belgian championship and also in Paris-Brussels, before crossing the Atlantic for a first time the following winter to visit his brother in the United States. At the end of the 1920s he moves to America permanently and as 'Jerry' Debaets becomes a popular track racer and stayer. He wins no fewer than 17 six-day events, including seven in New York and four in Chicago.

César Debaets is imprisoned,
brother Michel moves to Detroit.

NO CYCLING — OR ELSE!

By the end of October 1914, the German advance has been halted on the River IJzer. The situation at the front will hardly change for the next four years. The line of trenches winds its way through Belgium over a distance of 75 kilometres, from the coast at Nieuwpoort, past Diksmuide and Ieper, to the ridges around Mesen and Wijtschate. West Flanders, East Flanders and part of Hainaut are officially designated as the *Etappengebiet* or rear zone of the German Fourth Army, where the troops come to rest, train and draw supplies. In short, it is a militarized zone and the invaders administer it with iron discipline. The civil population is under orders to limit their travel to an absolute minimum. Use of the main roads is forbidden to horses and carts, bicycles and cars. Even pedestrians are subject to strict control and to leave your village you need a *Reiseschein* or travel permit. The border with neutral Holland is also quickly sealed off.

As a result of these strict regulations, family and friends who only live 20 or 30 kilometres from each other are separated for the duration of the war. In these circumstances, it is hardly surprising that there is a general ban on all cycle racing on the road. 'Riding bicycles on the road without a permit is only permitted in towns and their surroundings within a limit to be set by the town commandant', according to a German order of the day that is reprinted in the *Volksstem* newspaper. 'Outside this town limit, the riding of bicycles is forbidden. Those who break this prohibition will be sent back, with a warning that any further infringement will lead to the confiscation of their bicycle.' *Het Vlaamsche Nieuws*, another local daily, even publishes a list of offenders and their punishments: 'Between the 22nd and 30th of July 1915, the following penalties were imposed: A.G., Poperinghe and D.D.K., Ghistel, wanted to cross the border without a pass; each two weeks imprisonment (...) L.K., Antwerp, riding a bike without a pass; 30 days imprisonment. A.V.B. and L.B., Antwerp, riding a bike without a pass; each 1 week imprisonment. M.S., Merxplas, carrying a false pass, 3 days imprisonment...'

Behind the *Etappengebiet*, movement of civilians is also restricted in the *Okkupationsgebiet*. For example, at the end of 1914 a general ban on cycling is introduced in Brussels. Some of the more creative local inhabitants decide that if they can't cycle on

the public streets and roads, they will cycle instead on private land. They transform a piece of waste ground on the Vierwindenstraat in the Scheut district into a cycle track simply by stamping down the earth. Within days, enthusiastic cyclists are queuing up to ride on it and it is not long before the first competitions are organized. This eventually comes to the attention of the German authorities, which is hardly surprising: the meetings are reported in the press! 'In Scheut, a fairly rideable cycle track in beaten earth, complete with banked bends, has been built on a plot of ground in the Four Winds Street. Frequent meetings are organized there. Last Sunday's meeting took place in front of a crowd of more than a thousand people. The main race was won by that excellent independent rider, Van Nevele.' On another occasion, the same paper — *L'Echo de la Presse* — publishes the results of another race on the same track. This time, the winner is a certain Wouters, followed by Léonard. The rider in third place is the young René Vermandel, who at the start of the 1920s will go on to win both the Tour of Flanders and Liege-Bastogne-Liege.

Of course, it goes without saying that the Germans are not amused. *Het Vlaamsche Nieuws* reports the inevitable outcome on 11 February 1915: 'Races had already been held on a number of the occasions and many young men came to ride there on an almost daily basis. This week, however, access to the new velodrome was cut off by German troops without warning and about a dozen riders were

—o—

VELODROME DE SCHEUT

Un bon millier de spectateurs ont assisté aux épreuves disputées dimanche après-midi au vélodrome de Scheut sous Anderlecht.

Course d'une heure : 1. WOUTERS; 2. Léonard, à une longueur; 3. Vermandel jeune, à deux tours. Jacobs, l'un des favoris a abandonné.

—o—

VELODROME DES QUATRE-VENTS

Tout comme à Scheut, une piste cyclable en terre battue, avec virages relevés a été édifiée dans un terrain de la rue des Quatre-Vents. De fréquentes réunions y ont lieu. Celle de dimanche s'est déroulée devant plus de mille personnes.

L'épreuve principale est revenue à l'excellent coureur indépendant Van Nevele.

From *L'Echo de la Presse*, 10 February 1915.

arrested. Why? Had they forgotten to apply for a cycle permit? We don't know. What we do know is that seven of these riders were taken to the office of the military commander and that the continued use of the cycle track will not be allowed... to the great disappointment of the many bike-lovers who have already tightened their chains and oiled their legs in the hope of riding there.'

There is furious protest against the general ban on cycling and following mediation by the Touring Club of Belgium it is lifted a few weeks later. Cycling is once again permitted in Brussels, albeit under strict conditions. 'In the municipalities of Sint-Pieters-Woluwe, Auderghem, Watermael-Boschvoorde and Ukkel riding a bicycle without a pass is only allowed within the following boundaries: the train line from Woluwe station to the station in the Woluwelaan, Boschvoordelaan, the built-up area of Auderghem, Souvereinlaan, the built-up area of Watermael-Boschvoorde, the road to Ter Hulpe, the road from Waterloo to the Kleine Hut and the area of the municipality of Ukkel west of the aforementioned road. Signed: the Governor of Brussels, Von Sauberzweig, Major General.'

STIJN STREUVELS IGNORES THE CYCLING BAN

The many prohibitions on cycling introduced by the Germans seriously reduce the 'field of operations' of Stijn Streuvels. But the Belgian writer is not easily intimidated; not even by the German Army. To begin with, he just ignores the cycling ban. As he later writes in his autobiographical sketch *Mijn Fiets in Oorlogstijd* (My Bike During the War): 'Even after the ban on cycling was announced on pain of a thousand mark fine, I rode to nearby villages on many occasions for urgent messages, and never met anyone.' He continues: 'As long as there were no fixed posts blocking the road and the German field police kept away, we lived as though we were a republic. Even if they came, we knew all the side and back roads so well that it was easy to avoid them.'

Even so, riding around in this cavalier manner is not without its dangers. It is better to apply for a *Reiseschein*, if you can get one. Most people are inventive when it comes to thinking up valid reasons. In 1915, Streuvels also applies for a cycle pass, 'to travel to Ghent "for business"'. As a result, he is issued a permit for the entire *Etappengebiet*. 'In those days, no mortal knew where that area started and where it ended. I took it to mean the whole of the occupied territories, up to the operational zone. This meant that I could now fulfil my main purpose and my greatest desire for having such a pass: to visit my brother and sister in Bruges, about whom I had had no news since the start of the war.'

Streuvels does indeed cycle from Ingooigem to Bruges. However, he does not realize that Bruges is in the *Marinegebiet* or coastal area, and therefore outside the *Etappengebiet* for which he has a permit. Nor does he know that the main Kortrijk-Bruges highway is restricted exclusively to military traffic. Blissfully unaware of these potential problems, he sets off in high spirits, happy that he can once again '...spread my wings. (...) I checked my bike the evening before, added all the things you might expect of a "tourist", tied a bag with something to eat around the handlebars, and set off bright and early the next morning. The road was flat and the wind was in my sails. It was the most glorious May weather: nature at its most beautiful, the peace and quiet of the outdoors, and that most wonderful feeling of freedom you always have when setting off on a long journey.'

When Streuvels turns on to the main Bruges road at Ingelmunster, he suddenly notices that people are looking at him strangely. He stops to ask why. 'I then learn that all traffic — even my humble bike — is strictly forbidden on this road.' In typical fashion, he is not unduly concerned. 'If it's so strictly forbidden, I imagine there will be control posts to stop me. If not, I ride.' Not surprisingly, the author has the road to himself and he starts to enjoy the countryside, '...those special things along the roadside, which I remember from having ridden here before'. He rides on untroubled until he is beyond Oostkamp. Then, suddenly, he sees two German soldiers. 'I could see they were reservists and not used to checking people's papers. (...) It seemed as though they didn't really know what they were doing. In the end, they simply asked me to explain why I was there and what my pass said, because by now it was clear to me they couldn't read!' Streuvels makes something up on the spot and is allowed to ride on unhindered. 'In Bruges no-one could believe that I had ridden all the way along the main road from Kortrijk. This whole experience strengthened my conviction that the most strictly forbidden roads are also the easiest to ride along, for the simple reason that they are the least guarded.'

René Vermandel, here seen in 1921 on the hippodrome at Longchamp, trained as a junior on the forbidden track in the Scheut district of Anderlecht.

DAGORDE

Het wielrijden is zonder bewijs toegelaten in de steden en omliggende tot eene door den commandant bepaalde grens. Buiten de gemeenten is wielrijden verboden.

Overtreders zijn terug te wijzen met de verklaring dat bij herniewing der overtreding, het rijwiel zal in beslag genomen worden.

A German order of the day reprinted in *Het Volksstem* on 8 November 1914.

THE LEGENDARY BIANCHI

In 1912, the British journal *Cycling* comments that no other army in the world is better equipped with bike soldiers than the Italian Army. 'The Italian Minister of War has just ordered 6,000 bikes, intended for use by the Bersaglieri in the Tripolitanian War.' The Bersaglieri are mobile infantry trained for special missions and advanced patrol work. They are skirmishers, although their name actually means 'sharpshooters'. 'The Bersaglieri are the ideal fighting unit on wheels', continues the same article. They prove the truth of this assertion time after time during the war in Tripolitania against the Ottoman Empire. What's more, they are instantly recognizable to friend and foe alike from the large bunch of feathers they wear in their hats or on their helmets. This headgear is always tilted to the right, so that the brim protects their right eye — so important for sharpshooters — against the sun.

The 1912 order referred to by *Cycling* is won by the company of Eduardo Bianchi. At the request of the military authorities, they are built with especially high frames. The front fork is fitted with suspension and the pedals are positioned 30 centimetres higher than usual, so that the soldiers will be less hindered by low-lying vegetation and stones when riding across country. To avoid punctures, the wheels are fitted with full rubber tyres. Its creator names this model with a simplicity that belies its sophistication: *Bianchi modello 1912*.

It is a folding bike, so that the Bersaglieri, if necessary, can carry its 14 kilograms easily on their back. Its typical Bianchi colour — the bluish-green that we still see today — is perhaps first developed as a kind of camouflage.

The 1912 model was also used during the First World War. The most famous Bersaglieri ever to ride and fight with such a bike is Carlo Oriani, the winner of the Tour of Lombardy in 1912 and the Giro d'Italia in 1913. Oriani, who is known by his fellow racers as *El Pucia* (The Glutton), because of his abnormally healthy appetite, is serving in the autumn of 1917 on the Isonzo Front, not far from Caporetto, near the present-day town of Kobarid in Slovenia. On 24 October, the Austro-Hungarians, supported by crack German Alpine troops, launch a surprise offensive that breaks through the Italian line. An entire division is captured by a single German mountain battalion led by Erwin Rommel, who will later win fame as the 'Desert Fox' in North Africa during the Second World War.

In the confused fighting, the Bersaglieri suffer heavy losses and are forced to pull back. Carlo Oriani is among them. However, all the bridges over the Isonzo have been destroyed by the Austrians. *El Pucia* has little option but to try and wade the ice-cold river. He manages to get across but later contracts pneumonia. In an effort to save his life, doctors transfer him to the warm south of the country, but it is all to no avail. He dies on 3 December 1917 in the hospital at Caserta, aged 29 years. His body is taken back north to his native region for burial in Sesto San Giovanni, not far from Milan.

A *Bianchi modello 1912*, mounted with a machine gun.

DAREDEVILS ON BIKES

When the First World War breaks out, a tide of nationalism sweeps through Germany. The recruiting offices are full to overflowing; everyone wants to fight for Kaiser Wilhelm II. Whole pelotons of riders volunteer to swell the ranks of the *Radfahrtruppen*. Just weeks later, the race reports and results in the pages of the *Radwelt* cycling magazine are replaced by exciting accounts of the exploits of the *Teufelskerle auf den Rade*: daredevils on bikes. The magazine reports accurately which riders are at the front and which ones win the Iron Cross.

What it doesn't do, is say anything — or at least, not much — about the riders who are *gefallen für Deutschland*. No fewer than 93 pre-war competitive cyclists die before the Armistice in 1918. Most of them are amateurs, but some of them are well-known professionals. The first to fall is probably Friedrich Treciakowsky, a two-time winner of the Tour of Dresden (1912, 1914). He is hit by a fatal bullet near the French village of Thin-le-Moutier on 28 August 1914, just three weeks after war is declared. Exactly three months later — on 28 November 1914 — Richard Dottschadis is called up to serve at the front. He has won a number of impressive podium places — second in Halle-Potsdam-Halle, second in the Tour of North-west Saxony — as well as finishing eighth in the 1914 edition of the classic Berlin-Cottbus-Berlin as recently as 24 May. But now he is off to war. He is posted to Mazuria on the Eastern Front, where the Germans and the Russians are soon fighting the Battle of Tannenburg. Dottschadis is wounded in the head and evacuated to a hospital at Magdeburg. It is there that he dies on 10 February 1915 from... a burst appendix.

In 1912, Georg Grosskopf is the best in Nuremburg-Plauen-Nuremburg. A year later he triumphs in the 'Across Bavaria' race. On 13 February 1915, he is racing across no-man's land as an infantryman near Quesnoy-sur-Deule on the Franco- Belgian border. The village is captured, but Georg is badly wounded and dies later that day at a field hospital in Komen. Other riders who fall in 1915 include track specialist Paul Bruns, a cyclist with the 2nd Guard Regiment, who dies on the Marne on 1 March, and road racer Josef Stübecke, a corporal with the 1st Company of the 236th Reserve Regiment, who is killed at St. Julien near Langemark on 1 July. It is said that Stübecke spent much of his

time out of the line billeted at the farm in Rumbeke belonging to the parents of the Belgian Tour winner, Odiel Defraeye.

When the war breaks out, sprinter Albert Ritzenthaler, a professional since 1908, exchanges the handlebars of his bike for the joystick of an aeroplane. It is a choice that costs him his life during his very first operational flight over the Polish village of Koszalin on 13 June 1916. A month later, road racer Jozef Rieder is fatally wounded by shellfire in the killing fields around Verdun. His most famous victory is in the 1912 edition of the marathon Basel-Kleve race (over 620 kilometres!), although in the spring of 1914 he also has podium success in both Berlin-Leipzig-Berlin and the Saxony Grand Prix.

Bruno Demke is another of the many cycling professionals who opt to join the air force. The Berlin stayer is popular with the public and wins numerous meetings in his home country. His venture into Belgium on 5 July 1914 is less successful, finishing only fifth in a race at the Zurenborg velodrome in Antwerp, but ten days later, back on home soil, he wins the German Grand Prix at the Treptow track in his native city. It is one of the last meetings before the war; a month later he is flying over enemy lines. On one occasion, his plane is hit

Bruno Demke competes on the track in Antwerp in July 1914, just weeks before the war.

and catches fire, but Demke still manages to fly it 40 kilometres back to his base and land safely — a feat for which he is awarded the Iron Cross, First Class. He recovers from his injuries and is ready to return to active service. Fate, however, intervenes. On 24 August 1916, he takes off from the Döberitz aerodrome, but something goes wrong. He collides with another aircraft and crashes to the ground. This time the 36-year-old pilot does not escape.

Alwin Vater is already 45 years old when the war starts. Even so, he volunteers to join the army. Vater is one of the pioneers of German cycling. He first learns how to ride a bike on a penny-farthing, but in 1887 he exchanges it for a safety model made by Opel. As an amateur, he wins two national (1890, 1891) and one European (1892) sprint title. He is a sporting all-rounder, also being an excellent fencer, footballer and ice-skater, even winning the German speed-skating championship in 1893. At the front, Vater is always in the thick of the fighting, but somehow manages to survive. Tragically, he is killed in an accident while on leave in Strasbourg, where he falls under a tram.

Albert Eickholl wins the 1911 edition of Hannover-Hamburg-Hannover and a year later is victorious in the Six Days of Frankfurt with Otto Rosenfeld. He serves throughout the war as a corporal in the Germany Army, but dies at the military hospital in Düsseldorf on 11 August 1918 from wounds he received at the front. The war has just three months to run.

Richard Dottschadis dies not from the wounds he receives at the front but from... a burst appendix.

RADFAHRTRUPPEN, CHASSEURS AND CYCLISTS

At the end of the 19th century, the bicycle is given a more or less permanent place in the armies of Europe. It is therefore only natural that they play an important role during the First World War. In 1914, every *Jäger Batallion* of light infantry — *jäger* literally means 'hunter' — contains an additional company of cyclists, consisting of three officers and 124 other ranks. These *Radfahrtruppen* are initially used as scouts for reconnaissance purposes and are often pushed forward ahead of the main units to capture bridges and other strategic points. 'At Spiere we find the civil guard from Tournai bivouacked nearby. They have been driven out of their city by 20 — yes, just 20! — German cyclists', records Stijn Streuvels in his war diary on 3 October.

It is a scene that is repeated as the Germans push on into France, where cyclists cross rivers, seize crossroads and locate enemy forces with a speed and surprise that confuses their opponents. They are equally effective on the Eastern Front. In 1915, the *Jäger* battalions are given a second mobile company. In 1916, the High Command decides to group all these companies together into five specialist *Radfahr-Batallionen*. In July 1917, a sixth of these cycling battalions is formed.

When the war starts, it is the Italians who have perhaps the most experience with military cyclists. Italy joins the conflict on the Allied side in mid-1915 and the Bersaglieri quickly find themselves in the thick of the fighting against the Austro-Hungarian Army on the Isonzo River, in what is now present-day Slovenia. No fewer than 12 battles are fought there between June 1915 and November 1917, and the losses suffered by the crack cycling troops are enormous. Toward the end of the war, ex-Giro winner Carlo Oriani and his comrades are joined by a number of American volunteers, including the writer Ernest Hemingway, who serves as an ambulance driver. He later records his experiences at the front in his semi-autobiographical novel *A Farewell to Arms*, which in the 1950s is made into a Hollywood film starring Rock Hudson (just one of three film versions).

The equivalent cycling unit in the French Army are the ten *Groupes de Chasseurs Cyclistes* or GCC (once again, the word *chasseur* means 'hunter'). They are officially formed on 1 October 1913 and

22 July 1916: French cyclists in full kit, ready for action.

French cyclists in the streets of Noyon on 24 March 1917.

one group is attached to each of the ten French cavalry divisions. Each group consists of three platoons, with two officers and 130 NCOs and light infantrymen. The unit is led by three senior officers and is accompanied by a doctor, nurses, drivers and mechanics. The cyclists are equipped with folding bikes, first designed in 1893-1894 by Henry Gérard and further developed by Peugeot. Captain Gérard was the pioneer of French military cycling, but he dies on 3 June 1908, so that he does not see the GCC in action during the First World War.

Gérard is later succeeded by Commandant Mordacq. When mobilization is announced in August 1914, Mordacq clearly foresees an important role for the GCC. The tasks he sets them in one of his first operational orders include: making sure the cavalry can pass through difficult areas; launching surprise attacks on the enemy; supporting attacks by friendly cavalry and artillery; preventing breakthroughs by enemy cavalry; acting on the flanks of neighbouring armies; and forming a focal point for support during offensive actions.

The GCC do not need to wait long before trying to carry out his instructions. Between 7 August and 13 September 1914, the *Chasseurs Cyclistes* are rushed forward to try and block the German line of advance in the Gaume region of the Ardennes and also take part in the disastrous Battle of the Frontiers, in which the French suffer a quarter of a million casualties. As part of their respective cavalry divisions, they also prove their worth in the crucial Battle of the Marne, but once trench warfare begins the High Command can no longer see the use of cycling units, so that their number is halved. It is only when the war of movement returns in 1918 that they are restored to their full complement, allowing them to make an important contribution to final victory during the last months of the fighting.

In 1914, the British do not send their cycling troops to France or Belgium, but keep them at home to defend the nation's coastline against possible German incursions. Even so, their commanding officers are every bit as ambitious for their units as Commandant Mordacq. The cyclists of the 25th Battalion, London Regiment are trained by their Colonel, Arthur Churchill, in infantry tactics, rearguard actions, specialist scouting and operations behind enemy lines. They are also initiated into the mysteries of the machine gun and learn how to ride quickly under wartime conditions. In short, '...they seemed destined for a very active and conspicuous role'.

In 1915, the 18 separate cyclist battalions are amalgamated into a single Army Cyclist Corps. From a complement of 13,000 at the start of the war, the British now have some 30,000 cyclists at their disposal. Six thousand of them will eventually be killed on the Western Front, but they also serve in many other theatres of war: at Gallipoli, in Kenya, during the 1916 Easter Revolt in Ireland, in German East Africa (where they fight alongside the Belgians), in Mesopotamia and along the Suez Canal in Egypt (an important route to India, the crown jewel of the British empire). A plaque in Canterbury Cathedral specifically commemorates the killed and missing of the Kent Cyclist Battalions.

A recruiting poster seeks to enthuse volunteers for the British Army Cyclist Corps by promising '... a quick trip overseas'.

HORSEMEN ON BIKES!

It is not just the cycling units in the Belgian Army that make use of bicycles. Other units also discover the value — or necessity — of two-wheeled transport. When the 1st Cavalry Division goes to war in 1914, one of its component units is a company of engineers known as the *pionniers-pontonniers cyclistes* (mobile pioneer and bridging company), or PPC for short. Although a cavalry unit, it only has three horses for riding and several draught horses for pulling wagons. But it also has 200 bicycles for its men. In February 1915, a PCC is added to the 2nd Cavalry Division. In addition, there will henceforth be a permanent squadron of cyclists in each of the division's ten 150-man regiments. In fact, as the war progresses, the cavalry — often to their great displeasure — make more use of bikes and less use of horses, which are more badly needed by the artillery. Behind the IJzer Front it is often possible to see former horsemen riding along on two-wheelers, sometimes with their spurs still attached to their boots. By the start of 1916, each cavalry regiment is also supplemented by a machine gun platoon. Once again, these platoons rely on the bike for their mobility. There is just one horse for the officer in charge, eight horses to pull the four caissons for the machine guns, and 31 bicycles for the crews to man them.

4. - Le Bataillon cycliste en ligne déployée

Librairie Militaire Guérin, Mourmelon

Belgian cavalrymen... on bikes.

A MARRAINE DE GUERRE

The *marraines de guerre* — the term literally means 'wartime godmothers' — are women who 'adopt' unmarried soldiers at the front. They send letters and occasional parcels, in the hope that this will ease the burden and the loneliness of those serving in the trenches. The idea originates in France, but a similar scheme is soon set up in Belgium by the Ghent composer Emiel Hullebroeck and his Dutch wife Anna De Vos. Their organization — *Werk der Vlaamsche Oorlogsmeters* — encourages women from Flanders, the Netherlands, France and even Switzerland to 'do something to help our brave Flemish troops on the IJzer'. By the end of the war, some 9,000 soldiers will be in contact with a *marraine*.

One of them is the cyclist Omer Verschoore. Like Cyrille Van Hauwaert and Jules Masselis, he comes from the West Flanders village of Moorslede. He is Belgian champion on the road in 1912, a year (as in 1923 and 1925) when the title is awarded on the basis of a points system. Thanks to victories in Liege-Bastogne-Liege and the Carolingian Star race, backed up by third place in Liege-Charleroi, sixth in the Tour of Belgium and eighth in Paris-Brussels, he proves himself to be the most consistent rider of the year. When war breaks out, Omer, together with his brothers, Alfons and Odiel, volunteers for the army. He serves at the front and is one of the soldiers who is allocated a 'godmother'. In his case, this is not a fellow Fleming, but a young Parisian woman called Germaine Dupont.

It is originally intended that the correspondence should only last for the duration of the war, but because the war drags on much longer than anyone expects and because the *marraines* always write to the same soldiers, the letters gradually become more personal and more affectionate. Very affectionate in the case of Omer and Germaine, because after the war they meet and in 1919 they marry. Verschoore follows his bride to Paris and gives up his cycling career. Moorslede almost forgets about its former champion, until the sad news of his death gradually filters through to the village in 1931. During a visit to the Colonial Exhibition at Vincennes, he is accidentally crushed between a tractor and a wall.

After the war, Omer Verschoore marries his *marraine de guerre*.

THE CANADIAN CYCLIST COMPANY

The bike is also used on a large scale in the Canadian Army during the First World War. The military cyclists are trained at Valcartier Camp in Quebec. As part of the 1st Canadian Division, the Canadian Cyclist Company leaves for England on the SS *Ruthenia*, arriving on 14 October 1914. The cyclists are posted to Pond Farm Camp near Salisbury and are attached to the British 1st Divisional Cyclist Company for further training under Captain R.S. Robinson. This training is more intense than anything they experienced in Canada: reconnaissance missions, bayonet fighting, topographical techniques, learning how to fire a Lewis gun, etc. It gives them a good idea of what they can expect at the front — or so they think.

British cyclists pass through the ruined village of Brie (close to Péronne and the River Somme) in March 1917.

By early 1915, the Canadian Cyclist Company is ready for active service in France, arriving by boat in Saint-Nazaire on 15 February. However, because trench warfare has now begun, they find themselves performing duties very different from the ones for which they have trained. They carry out traffic controls or man listening posts. They act as couriers between different units or help with demolition work or the digging of tunnels at the front. As a result of these many different tasks, the company soon becomes fragmented. One fifth of its soldiers are killed during that first year. Other cycling companies arrive in France from Canada, but are treated in much the same way. In May 1916, a major reorganization is carried out, leading to the formation of the Canadian Cyclist Battalion. Even then, the cyclists are not really used as cyclists, but are used to man the trenches for periods of four to six weeks at a time. Like all units at the front, they sometimes suffer heavy casualties. It is only during the last hundred days of the war that the survivors can uses their bikes in the manner that was originally intended. When movement returns to the Western Front, they follow close on the heels of the retreating Germans, reporting their positions and helping to maintain contact between allied cavalry and infantry units.

In 1914, Newfoundland is not yet a part of Canada, but is still an independent dominion within the British Empire. When war breaks out, the tiny island raises its own regiment of troops — including cyclists — to send to Europe. The Newfoundlanders serve first in Gallipoli but in March 1916 are sent to the Western Front to take part in the Battle of the Somme. On 1 July 1916, as part of the British 29th Division, they attack at Beaumont-Hamel. Ninety percent of their men are killed or wounded — a tragedy still marked by the Newfoundland Memorial Park, close to the village where they all died.

GUSTAAF MUS: SHOT BY FIRING SQUAD

By the end of 1914, numerous spy networks have been set up in the occupied territories in Belgium and northern France. These networks carry out tasks for the allied authorities and are often led by policemen, railwaymen, postmen or lockkeepers; in other words, married men with families who are exempt from military service by virtue of their profession. Some live close to the border with the neutral Netherlands, where they try to smuggle out the information they have gathered. Others live close to railways and other important lines of communication. By the end of the war, roughly 7,000 Belgian civilians will have worked for the Allied intelligence services. It is their way of getting back at the German occupiers — but it is not without risk. Almost a third of these 'spies' are arrested by the Germans and then imprisoned or deported. Two hundred and eight of them are executed by firing squad.

One of the men engaged in this dangerous work is Gustaaf Mus. Born in Dudzele in 1891, before the war he is a good (but not great) cyclist in the junior category. He mainly rides on the track and from 1910 onwards takes part in a number of professional meetings at Maldegem, Ghent and Roubaix. On 25 July 1911, with Maurice Leliaert as his partner, Gustaaf is in the starting line-up for a 24-hour race at the Arsenal circuit in Antwerp. The other teams include Henri Vanlerberghe and Marcel Buysse, Pier Van de Velde and Kurt Dierckx, and Constant Van Reeth and Frans Van

Eyck. Against riders of this calibre, the Mus-Leliaert combination has no chance of winning. It is one of the races that persuades Gustaaf he should give up the uncertain life of a professional racer and find a steadier job. On 23 September 1912, he joins the Mobile Brigade of the Gendarmerie and is sent to Brussels as a *wachtmeester te paard* (more or less the equivalent of a police sergeant).

When the war breaks out, Mus joins his cavalry unit and takes part in the retreat of the Belgian Army to the River IJzer. On 11 October, he is involved in a skirmish and gets shot in the thigh, but is able to escape from his German pursuers. His wound is treated and he is sent to a military hospital in England to recover. It is not until 2 May 1915 that he is fit enough to be discharged. Soon after, he is recruited by Major Mage of the Belgian intelligence service to set up a spy network on behalf of the General Staff in the *Etappengebiet*. Mus himself has let it be known that he is interested in this kind of work. As a native of Dudzele, he is familiar with the region close to the Dutch border and knows the port of Zeebrugge like the back of his hand. What's more, he is fluent in both French and Flemish.

The idea is that Mus will try to recruit other gendarmes — either retired or left behind by the German advance — to form the basis of his network. These operatives must then find other willing helpers in their own town or village to monitor and report on the movements of German troops and materials via roads, railways, harbours, aerodromes, etc. Mus is smuggled across the Dutch border into Flanders. He makes contact with an existing network, the *Service des Gendarmes*, which later becomes known by the less incriminating name of the *Service des Ambulants*. Mus is soon a leading figure in the network, which has a central 'letterbox' operated by a priest in Ghent, Father Octaaf Declercq. From here, information is collected by couriers, who risk their lives to take it across the electrified border between Zelzate and Sas van Gent. Via the Belgian consulate in Vlissingen, the documents are transferred to Folkestone for onward transmission to the headquarters of the Belgian Army or one of the other Allied armies.

At the height of his operations, Gustaaf Mus is running more than 100 agents. He is now the head of all the networks in West and East Flanders, which he coordinates from Father Declercq's vicarage in Ghent. His brother François is also in the Resistance and operates a similar group of networks in Brabant and Hainaut. A third brother,

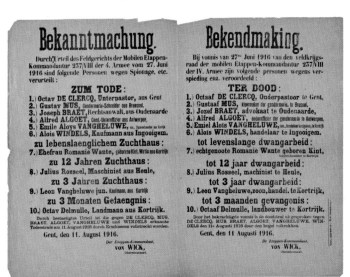

Public notification of the judgement handed down by the Germans on 27 June 1916.

Pierre, who was a tailor in the gendarmerie before the war, acts as a liaison between his siblings.

The Mus family soon discovers the heavy price that sometimes has to be paid by those carrying out this valuable but hazardous work. François is arrested by the Germans and executed for espionage on 5 September 1915. This makes Gustaaf more determined than ever to carry on. In fact, he intensifies his network's activities, moving on from the mere collection of information to acts of sabotage. Mus himself is directly involved in the disruption of tram and train signals, and even manages to derail a number of German troop trains. The network is also involved in the planning for a seaborne raid by the British Royal Navy on the port of Zeebrugge, although this raid is eventually postponed until St. George's Day — 23 April — 1918.

Sadly, Gustaaf Mus will not live to see it. In the spring of 1916, he is betrayed by one of his couriers, who is later identified as 'D.M. Fr. from the Dutch town of P'. The Germans use information from their informant to set traps for most of the network's leading figures and even many of the minor ones. The *Service des Ambulants* is in ruins and Mus is on the run. On 30 March, the German military police nearly catch him at the vicarage in Sint-Amandsberg, but he escapes through a back window. In spite of the risk, he insists on keeping an appointment the next day with another of his couriers at a newspaper kiosk on the Korenmarkt in Ghent. However, the courier's cover has been blown and Mus suddenly finds himself surrounded by eight Germans. This time there is no escape. Gustaaf is thrown into prison, where he is tortured to reveal all he knows about his own and other networks.

After a mock trial in front of a court martial held by the *Etappen-Kommadatur 237/VIII* of the German 4th Army, Gustaaf Mus is condemned to death. He is executed by firing squad with five others at the Ghent Rifle Range on 11 August 1916. 'One of the men shot was De Clercq, the curate of Sint-Pieters Aygem, a district in Ghent; in fact, my district. He lived with a sister and their 80-year-old mother', records Virginie Loveling in her war diary. She continues: 'Another of the victims was a gendarme, named Mus. He refused a blindfold and pushed the soldier who was trying to tie his hands roughly to one side with his elbow. There were dozens of people — sympathetic, outraged or just curious — in front of the clubhouse of the Shooting Club. They had heard what was going to happen and wanted for their various reasons to see the coffins come out.'

The third brother, Pierre, is twice sentenced to death but on each occasion is able to go into hiding. After the war, he accepts on behalf of his brothers the Order of the British Empire, the French Legion d'honneur, the Belgian Order of King Leopold and various other honours and decorations. Gustaaf and François lie buried side by side in the civil cemetery in Evere. The inscription on their gravestone reads: *'Aan de slachtoffers van hun plicht'* (victims who did their duty). After a long investigation, in 1921 the Court of Assizes in Ghent condemns their betrayer to life imprisonment. However, 'D.M. Fr. from P' never serves his sentence.

The obituary card for Gustaaf Mus, amateur cyclist, gendarme and wartime spy.

A TOUR OF FLANDERS WINNER
ALSO BECOMES A SPY

Paul Deman, the winner of the very first Tour of Flanders, also becomes a spy in 1915. He is approached by 'commissioner' Alphonse Lenfant, who is a member of both the *Oiseau de France* clandestine press and the intelligence network run by Louise de Bettignies. This 35-year-old woman is the descendant of an aristocratic French family and a former student at Oxford University. Fluent in English, German and Italian, in more recent years she has acted as a governess for some of Europe's leading families. By a strange coincidence, in the spring of 1914 she was asked to take up a position as governess for the children of... Archduke Franz Ferdinand of Austria, whose assassination just months later in Sarajevo will spark off the First World War. One of the conditions is that she must take Austrian nationality, but this she does not feel able to do.

By the time the war starts, Louise de Bettignies is in the employ of a German family. She quickly packs her bags and sets off to rejoin her mother in the French city of Lille, travelling via neutral Holland and England. In Folkestone, British Intelligence are monitoring the passengers to France, in the hope of finding people who may be of use to them in the occupied territories. Louise looks a likely candidate and they approach her to see if she is willing to train as a spy. She accepts and starts a crash course in secret writing, codes, observation techniques and everything else an agent behind enemy lines needs to survive. Her task is to set up an information-gathering network in Northern France and Belgium, with the resulting material sent to England via the Netherlands. This means that she and her operatives will need to recruit local people in key towns and villages and along key lines of communication, like the Kortrijk-Antwerp and Kortrijk-Brussels railway lines. Her network is given the codename 'Ramble' and she is known as 'Alice Dubois'.

The 'wire of death'. During the First World, the Germans erect an electrified fence along the Dutch-Belgian frontier to prevent people from crossing into the neutral Netherlands.

'Ramble' soon has more than 60 agents. Most of them live in the region Lille-Roubaix-Tourcoing-Menen. Perhaps it is not surprising that 'Alice' sends one of her people to approach Paul Deman. For 'Ramble', Deman has one huge advantage: he is a bike racer. In other words, someone who can ride great distances at high speeds — which are the ideal qualities for a network courtier in wartime. The man she chooses for the contact is Alphonse Lenfant, who lives in Tourcoing, not far from the Belgian frontier village of Rekkem, where Deman was born and where he still has family. The two men meet and Deman agrees to cooperate.

De Bettignies' operation is very similar to the one run by Gustaaf Mus. Her agents keep their eyes and ears open to collect all the information they can about Germans troop movements, ammunition depots, railways, military transports, aerodromes, etc. This information is then collated and assessed at secret locations in Tourcoing and Lille, before being taken by *passeurs* to the Netherlands, for onward transmission via ferry to Folkestone.

By now, Paul Deman lives in Outrijve. This means a ride of more than 100 kilometres to get to the Dutch border in Flemish Zeeland. Tough for an ordinary cyclist, but not for a former winner of the Tour of Flanders. Even so, as a *passeur* for Lenfant he needs to make his way as inconspicuously as possible through enemy-occupied territory. The very last thing he wants is to be stopped and searched by a German patrol or control post. True, the secret documents are well concealed. Some *passeurs* use a suitcase with a false bottom or a wig with a double lining. It is even possible that Deman hid his messages in the hollow frame of his bike. But none of these hiding places are foolproof.

Once at the Dutch border, it is necessary to get the information safely across the 'wire of death'. This is the electrified fence (2,000 volts!) built by the Germans along the Dutch-Belgian frontier to prevent people from crossing into the neutral Netherlands. Sometimes, the packages are just thrown over the triple wire at an agreed time and place. But more often than not, the *passeurs* need to crawl under the fence, risking electrocution. One of the most frequently used crossing points is at Boekhoute. From there, the *passeurs* arrive in Philippine, the first village on the Dutch side, before

travelling on to Breskens and Vlissingen or Middelburg, from where other couriers continue to Folkestone by boat. On their return journey, the *passeurs* smuggle butter, coffee and other foodstuffs back across the border, and sometimes even carry letters from refugees or interned soldiers intended for their families in the occupied zone.

This is, of course, a highly dangerous undertaking. If caught, spies face severe penalties. This is the fate of Louise de Bettignies. She is stopped and searched by a German patrol while in possession of incriminating documents. She is sentenced to hard labour for life and at the end of 1915 is sent to the prison at Siegburg, where she dies in September 1918 as a result of her constant mistreatment and poor medical care. But even without de Bettignies, 'Ramble' remains active and the ex-Tour of Flanders winner continues his espionage activities unhindered. But for how long?

Paul Deman, the winner of the first Tour of Flanders, works during the war as a courier for the spy network of Louise de Bettignies.

The first months of the war are chaotic. Some riders are mobilized; others are taken prisoner or flee as refugees. Life for ordinary people becomes a matter of day-to-day survival. In these circumstances, cycle racing is an irrelevance. But that's not the way it stays. By the start of 1915, the situation in occupied Belgium has stabilized, both for the occupiers and for the occupied. Thoughts turn again to social and sporting activities. From the spring of 1915 onwards, the Germans allow the resumption of some cycle races. There are, of course, plenty of restrictions. The total ban on road racing remains: in a country where you now need a *Reiseschein* if you want to cycle to the next village, the Germans are hardly likely to allow a 200-strong peloton to race across the countryside at high speed. In contrast, the velodromes are much easier to control, so that a limited number of track events are permitted. Some of the circuits in Ghent reopen their doors, as does the Zurenborg track in Antwerp and Garden City in Wilrijk. Meetings are even held amidst the ruins of Liege. Most are sprint competitions, although there are also a number of 'madisons', where teams of two riders race against each other over 100 kilometres or for a six-hour period.

Curious as it may seem, the Belgian Cycling Federation (BWB) is fiercely opposed to all these events and insists that all velodromes must be closed immediately (although for some reason it turns a blind eye to the frequent meetings at the Karreveld track). In fact, on 17 March 1915 the BWB even goes so far as to shut down its entire operations, as a protest against what it sees as unacceptable German interference in the sport. The relevant notification does, however, add that riders and meeting organizers will still need to pay their subscriptions to the federation for 1915 '...to cover administrative costs'. Not surprisingly, both these dubious decisions provoke a storm of criticism. The velodromes and the professional riders are worried about the income they will lose. The cycle-loving public are furious that one of the few pleasures still available in wartime is now to be denied to them. By their own national federation!

Faced with this situation, the Belgian people display their usual inventiveness. In Antwerp, events are organized on rollers and even on home-trainers. On 11 April 1915, '...a charity event on home-trainers [will take place] in the function room of the "Au Repos" tavern, Sint-Bernardsche-steenweg 232 (just past the Kiel Cemetery). The following riders are already registered to take part: Jef Geeraerts, Van den Bossche, Destombes, Van Wetter, Tyck, Lauwereyssens, Muys, Adolf Philibert, etc. Arthur Van der Stuyft will act as timekeeper. The prices at the door are: first terrace, 1.00 franc; second terrace, 0.50 franc; third terrace, 0.30 franc. N.B. To avoid any difficulties at the Kiel Gate, everyone is requested to bring with them a document confirming their personal identity, issued (free of charge) by the police office of the district where they live.'

The riders are ready for the start of a 100-kilometre race on the Karreveld track on 12 June 1915.

111 Notwithstanding these improvised events, criticism of the BWB continues. The professionals even go so far as to form their own rival federation, the Belgian Riders' Syndicate and are willing to help with both the organization of new meetings and the distribution of prize money. Above all, they just want to keep on racing. Eventually, the BWB is forced to yield to pressure from this and other quarters. It decides to lift its ban on competitions, but only under a number of conditions. These are set out in a circular letter to all clubs, delegates, track owners, organizers and riders, issued by the BWB Sports Committee on 20 May 1915. The circular first stresses that the tracks must pay their 1915 subscriptions in full. Secondly, the validity of professional licenses for 1914 will be extended temporarily and free of charge until the new licenses for 1915 can be issued. Thirdly, from now on juniors and independent riders will be able to take part in professional races. Fourthly, the members of the Sports Committee will no longer be permitted to fulfil official functions at race meetings, but are free to place their expertise at the disposal of track owners, organizers and riders for the settlement of any disputes. Last but not least, track owners are encouraged in these difficult times to donate part of their gate receipts to the National Food and Aid Committee.

None of these conditions are particularly contentious, so that the riders can look forward to 'real' races again, at least on the track. Because mobility from place to place is severely restricted by the Germans, most riders take part in events at their hometown velodromes. In Gentbrugge, this is Pier Van de Velde and Marcel Buysse; in Antwerp, it is Arthur Van der Stuyft. Some riders do, however, take the necessary trouble to obtain a *Reiseschein*. After all, cycling is their livelihood. In this way, the West Flanders brothers Michel and César Debaets and the future Tour de France winner Léon Scieur from Namur are seen on a number of occasions at meetings in Antwerp.

But perhaps the most active track is the Karreveld, on the Gentsesteenweg in Sint-Jans-Molenbeek, where a meeting is organized almost every Sunday throughout the summer of 1915. In addition to local riders like Jozef Van Bever and Jean Van Ingelghem, popular, crowd-pulling stars like Cyrille Van Hauwaert and Marcel Buysse also make regular appearances. Cycling is back, and the Karreveld is the focal point for its revival — at least for the time being...

The smuggling of secret information proves fatal for Pol Gabriëls.

THE HIGH-RISK LIFE OF A RACER-PASSEUR

Paul Deman and Gustaaf Mus are by no means the only pre-war racers who act as *passeurs* between 1914 and 1918. As men who can travel long distances quickly and quietly, their services are always in demand. For example, the Belgian Intelligence Bureau actively recruits Pol — officially Leopold — Gabriëls, a good amateur racer from Schilde. Gabriëls is 28 years old when the war breaks out and works as a diamond processor. Right from the earliest days of the occupation, he is a thorn in the side of the invader. On 27 November 1914, he is sentenced to three weeks imprisonment for stealing a load of planks from the fort at 's-Gravenswezel. But his spell behind bars does little to deter him. Quite the reverse. He becomes a *passeur*, operating in the frontier areas around Rijkevorsel and Merksplas.

His task is to smuggle secret information, letters and packages over the Dutch border and also to help Belgian civilians and even soldiers through or under the dreaded 'wire of death'. After his previous arrest, the Germans suspect that Gabriëls is still up to mischief and decide to search for him again. But he is nowhere to be found — until he is stopped by a patrol on 28 August 1915. Even though he is carrying false papers, the Germans soon recognize him. He tries to make a run for it but is shot down in a hail of 12 bullets. Two days later, a horse-drawn carriage brings him to his final resting place in Schilde. In 1922, his death certificate will be amended to show that he 'died for his country'.

Frans Vergauwen, born in Borgerhout in 1878, is another of the same breed: a racer turned *passeur*. As an amateur, he wins several races in and around Antwerp and on 6 September 1903 he is the best in Brussels-Ostend. He even has a world title to his name, but one won in a championship organized by an unofficial federation in 1910.

When the Germans overrun Belgium in 1914, Vergauwen is one of the first to help organize escape routes. He succeeds in getting 73 soldiers

and civilians to the Dutch village of Sluis, before he is betrayed and sentenced to death by the German military authorities. He is executed by firing squad on the National Rifle Range in Schaarbeek on 25 June 1917. His last wish is to be buried in Schoonselhof Cemetery in Antwerp, a wish that is granted. And there he lies still.

He is also commemorated in the Plot of Honour for the Executed in Schaarbeek, and likewise on a memorial plaque on the wall of the prison at Sint-Gilles, where he was held for trial, and on the wall of the Senate, where the German court sentenced him to death. He shares this 'distinction', among others, with Nurse Edith Cavell, who also helped Allied soldiers to escape to the Netherlands and was shot two years earlier at the same rifle range in Schaarbeek. Last but not least, there is also a small plate on the front gable of the house at Welvaart-straat No. 46 in Borgerhout, where he lived. The simple text reads: 'To Frans Vergauwen. Shot by the Germans for the motherland on 25 June 1917'.

Discovering spies was a priority for the Germans.

Cyclist Frans Vergauwen was betrayed as a spy and condemned to death.

JAN OLIESLAGERS, CYCLIST AND AVIATION PIONEER

The First World War sees the advent of a new weapon: the aeroplane. But who are the daring men who pilot these first planes, which in reality are little more than flying soap-boxes? A surprising number of them are former cyclists. Not only in Belgium, but also in France and Germany. Perhaps this has something to do with their love of speed and spirit of adventure? Be that as it may, one of their number is Jan Olieslagers. He is only a modest cyclist, but is destined to become one of his country's first great air 'aces'.

Olieslagers is a native of Antwerp, the second son in a family with two other brothers and three sisters. His father dies when he is just 11 years old. This means that Jan has little option but to become a breadwinner for his family. He works in a shipyard on the River Schelde and during the weekends helps with repairs at a local cycle shop, even though he has never ridden a bike — until then. He soon learns, using an old bike in the cellar of the shop or when he has to deliver a new one to a customer. When the shop owner again finds him practising in the cellar, he 'punishes' him by giving him an old second-hand model. Jan immediately converts it into his first 'racer'. He is fascinated by cycling and by the time he is a teenager is regularly seen working as a mechanic at the Zurenborg velodrome, which was opened in 1894 for the second World Exhibition in Antwerp. Each Sunday afternoon the circuit is packed with enthusiastic cycling fans and Jan wants nothing more than to one day cycle in front of them. He makes his debut under the pseudonym of 'John Max' and wins his first race when he is 16 years old. By then, he has a new job with Minerva, the Antwerp cycle and car manufacturer, which also becomes his first sponsor. He continues to perform well, so that he eventually comes to the attention of Emile De Beukelaer. De Beukelaer likes to think of himself as the biggest cycling promoter in Belgium and was the man behind the construction of the Zurenborg track. He is also the chairman of the Antwerp Bicycle Club. It would be unusual, to say the least, for him to allow a young lad fresh off the streets into this elite setting: at the time, cycling is still very much the preserve of the rich and famous. But clearly the chairman sees something in Olieslagers

and adds him to his stable of riders. From now on, he races under the ABC flag, both on the track and on the road — and with success. He also shows this same enthusiasm at Minerva, where he is promoted to 'bike salesman' at the age of just 17.

Everyone predicts a great career for Jan Olieslagers as a racer, but that is not the way things turn out — or at least not on a bicycle. When the first competitions for motorbikes are organized at Zurenborg from 1901 onwards, he immediately volunteers to give it a try. Like cycling, motorbike racing is only possible for someone poor like Jan with the help of a sponsor or manufacturer. In his case, this is again Minerva. At the start of the 20th century, mechanized sports — rather like Formula 1 today — are seen as a way to maximize technological advancement, while at the same time increasing brand awareness of the companies involved. In this sense, the first great 'motorized' heroes are both racers and test drivers. The fearless Olieslagers combines these functions perfectly and is the ideal front man for Minerva. He becomes the first person in the world to achieve a speed of 100 kilometres per hour on a motorbike, which brings him the nickname of the 'Antwerp Devil'. In 1904, he wins Paris-Bordeaux-Paris, a race for motorbikes over 1,200 kilometres.

His nerve and skill on a motorbike and the fact that he was once a cyclist himself also make him ideal as a pace-rider in stayer races. He appears on the track in partnership with quality riders like Julien 'Samson' Lootens, Karel Verbist and even the American Bobby Walthour. As the motorbikes become more powerful, the races become more dangerous. The pace-makers and their riders now round the bends at dizzying speeds and accidents are increasingly frequent. It is only a matter of time before Olieslagers is involved in one. He crashes on the velodrome at Scheveningen while pacing for

Jan Olieslagers standing next to his Blériot XI monoplane.

his fellow 'Antwerpenaar' Viktor Tubbax. The crash itself is not so bad, but while lying on the track he is hit in the back by a following motorbike. His injuries look serious and in a nearby hospital he is even given the last rites. But Jan is tough and makes a miraculous recovery.

After an experience like this, many people would think twice before continuing their relentless pursuit for speed, speed and more speed. But not Olieslagers. His passion remains undiminished — today, we would probably call him a 'speed junkie' — and he even wants to take things a stage further by moving into the world of aviation. This he does in September 1910. At his own initiative, he travels to Issy-les-Moulineaux to take flying lessons from the pioneer Louis Blériot, the first man to fly across the English Channel. A short while later, Olieslagers buys his own plane. He takes part in flying demonstrations in France, Spain and Italy and tours the Netherlands with a group of other pilots. Like in his motorbike days, he starts to break record after record, setting new figures for the longest flight at 7 hours and 18 minutes. In these pioneering days of aviation, the meetings and demonstrations are a lucrative source of income and Jan becomes a wealthy man. He also starts giving flying lessons of his own. His first pupil is his brother Max, followed later by his other brothers, Jules and Albert. Jan gifts each of them a plane and before long the flying Olieslagers brothers are celebrities throughout Europe.

Olieslagers as a young cyclist, sponsored by his employer, Minerva.

Most people see the outbreak of war as a disaster. A man of Jan Olieslagers' nature sees it as a great opportunity. On 1 August 1914, he writes a letter to Minister of War Charles de Broqueville in which he offers to place all his planes at the disposal of the government for the defence of the motherland. He also volunteers, like his brothers, for service in the aviation wing of the Belgian Army. He is posted to the *Escadrille Monoplane* and is initially used as an observer. But this fails to satisfy the thrill-seeker in him. He wants to take on the enemy in mortal combat, man to man. However, it is not until 1915 that the nascent Belgian air force is willing — or able — to engage in this kind of aerial fighting.

Jan Olieslagers scores his first victory as a fighter pilot on 12 September 1915. Flying a Nieuport 10, he shoots down a German Aviatik C over the village of Stuivekenskerke. This is followed by other 'kills': a Fokker D.II above Zuidschote on 17 June 1916; an Aviatik C above Schore on 14 June 1917; a Fokker D.II above Keiem the next day; a Fokker D.VII above Westende on 3 May 1918; and an Albatros D.V above Woumen on 19 May 1918. This total of six recorded victories makes him one of only five Belgian 'aces' during the First World War, a title given to pilots who bring down five or more enemy planes. In fact, he probably has other victories to his name, but it is not always possible for every kill to be confirmed. In total, he flies 491 missions and is engaged in combat 97 times. He survives it all and emerges from the war as one of Belgium's most decorated military heroes.

After the Armistice, Jan Olieslagers returns to Antwerp and runs a Minerva garage. But flying continues to be his great passion. He lobbies for the construction of an international airport in his home city. Thanks to his good relations with a number of ministers and even with King Albert I himself, he is able to help turn this dream into a reality: the aerodrome at Deurne is officially opened on 25 May 1923. Five years later, he is the driving force behind the foundation of the Antwerp Aviation Club and in 1929 is instrumental in the opening of the first international route for commercial flights between Deurne and Hamburg. Having defied death all his life — whether as a cyclist, a motorbike rider or a pilot — Jan Olieslagers dies peacefully in his bed on 23 March 1942, at the age of just 59. Even though it is the middle of the Second World War and such things are forbidden, the Belgian national anthem is played proudly at his funeral. A final tribute to a brave man and a good patriot.

ROLAND GARROS CRASHES IN HULSTE

On Sunday, 18 April 1915, two French planes swoop low over the station at Lendelede in an attempt to attack a German train. The Germans retaliate with ground fire and one of the planes is hit, forcing the pilot to make a spectacular emergency landing in a field near the village of Hulste. German troops close in to capture the unfortunate aviator and are amazed when they discover that their prisoner is none other than Roland Garros, who even at this early stage of the war is a great French hero. More important still, his plane is still intact. It is a Morane-Saulnier, the first aircraft on either side fitted with a deflector system that allows the pilot to fire his machine gun through the propeller while flying. Garros has used this system to establish quite a reputation for himself and the Germans are delighted to have captured one of France's leading 'aces' and the machine that gives him such an advantage in aerial combat. The plane is displayed as a 'trophy of war' on the market square in Izegem and inspires the German Anthony Fokker to design and perfect a similar 'interrupter' system for German fighters.

Roland Garros is not just any pilot. Even before the war, he is famous for his many aviation exploits. He is also an accomplished sportsman. At school he excels in rugby, but later switches to cycling — and with success: in 1906, he becomes the national university champion. He races under the name of 'Roland Danlor', probably because his parents are not all that keen on cycling. Even so, after completing his studies at commercial college he opens a cycle shop. The young Garros has learnt his les-sons well and business is soon booming, so much so that a year later he can already buy his own plane. He joins a group known as the Moisant International Aviators, one of the 'flying circuses' that are so popular in the pre-war years. With them, he takes part in air shows in the United States, Cuba and Mexico. In 1911, he sets a new world altitude record of 3,950 meters above Rio de Janeiro bay. Returning to Europe, he becomes a test pilot for Morane-Saulnier and two years later becomes the first man to fly nonstop from France to Tunisia across the Mediterranean Sea.

Like many former cyclists, in the summer of 1914 Garros volunteers for war service in the French Army as a pilot. His is promoted to lieutenant and in early April 1915 shoots down three enemy aircraft using his interrupter system. However, his crash in Hulste brings his war to a premature and unexpected halt. He spends three years as a prisoner of war, but at the start of 1918 is finally able to escape from his camp near Magdeburg. Via the Netherlands, he makes his way back to his squadron in France. Although his health has deteriorated during his captivity, he soon starts flying again. On 2 October 1918, he shoots down his fourth German plane, but three days later — on the eve of his 30th birthday — he himself is shot down in a dogfight over the French Ardennes. He crashes near Saint-Morel and is killed. His body is taken to the nearby village of Vouziers for burial. His name is recorded on an obelisk at the entrance to the military cemetery.

When in 1927 a new sporting complex is opened at the Porte d'Auteuil in Paris, the chairman of the prestigious Stade Français sports club suggests that it should be named after his fellow student and former club member, Roland Garros. It is in this stadium that the French open tennis championships are still played each year. The airport on the French overseas island of Réunion — his birthplace — also bears his name.

Air hero Roland Garros is killed on 5 October 1918.

Roland Garros, cyclist and French aviation pioneer.

THE FIRST ANZAC CYCLISTS
ON THE WESTERN FRONT

The starting line-up for the Tour de France in 1914 includes two Australians for the very first time: Don Kirkham and Ivor Munro. They both reach Paris. Kirkham is 17th, 11 hours, 36 minutes and 57 seconds behind the winner Philippe Thys. Munro is 20th, almost exactly an hour later. When the First World War breaks out a week later, both Australians are already on the boat taking them back home. When they arrive, Munro volunteers for the army, but is rejected, because he has... flat feet! Kirkham, who in 1913 won the Six Days of Melbourne with Bob Spears, returns to his farm and eventually resumes his cycling career in 1920. His older brother, Malcolm Kirkham, does become a soldier and dies at the French town of Peronne on 2 September 1918.

Like the world's other armies, the Australian Army also has cyclists in its ranks. As early as 1901, a cycling contingent is sent from Brisbane to South Africa, to fight alongside the British motherland in the Second Boer War, a war in which the British use no fewer than 13,000 cyclists. Having demonstrated their importance, cycling units are maintained in Australia in the run-up to the First World War. To ensure that their cyclists are in good physical condition, in 1909 the Australian Department of Defence organizes a 'practice ride' of 1,839 kilometres from Adelaide to Sydney, 'sponsored by the Dunlop Military Despatch Cycle Ride'.

It takes until 25 April 1915 before the first Australian troops, fighting alongside their Antipodean comrades from New Zealand, see action in the European theatre of war. With the British and the French, they take part in the landings on the Gallipoli peninsula, which aim to capture the strategically important Dardanelles straits and threaten the Turkish capital of Constantinople. The campaign is a fiasco and casualties are high. The Australian and New Zealand units are withdrawn to Egypt for reinforcement and reorganization. However, from then on the day of their first landing will always be known as ANZAC Day (ANZAC stands for Australian and New Zealand Army Corps, the unit in which they served).

By the end of 1915, the Australian Imperial Force (AIF) consists of five infantry divisions. Each division has its own company of 204 cyclists from the Australian Cycling Corps. The corps has many ex-cavalrymen among its volunteers, but also a number of former bike racers. The single New Zealand Division is also supported by a company from the New Zealand Cycling Corps. The cyclists are equipped with Birmingham Small Arms Company (BSA) bicycles and are armed with short-magazine Lee Enfield rifles and Lewis machine guns that can be mounted on their bike frames or fired from the shoulder.

From Egypt, the ANZACs are sent to the Western Front in the spring of 1916. The cyclists go with them and perform a variety of different tasks, first on the Somme and later in West Flanders. These tasks include patrolling, signalling, guarding prisoners of war, burying the dead, repairing roads, unloading trains, cutting down trees and laying cables. Most of this work is carried out in relative safety behind the lines, but sometimes they need to abandon their bikes and fight alongside the infantry in the trenches. The first Australian cyclist to die on the Western Front is probably Corporal Clifton Gordon Leslie, who seeks shelter in a dug-out during a German bombardment just before it receives a direct hit. He is buried in Bernafay Wood British Cemetery near the French village of Montauban.

Two members of the 1st ANZAC Cyclists Battalion in Henencourt, France, on 12 May 1917.

A TOUR WINNER DIES FOR HIS COUNTRY

François Faber — who won the 'provocative' stage to Longwy in the 1914 Tour de France and also triumphed in the next day's stage to Dunkirk — serves with the French Foreign Legion during the First World War. As the son of a Luxembourger father, he also has Luxembourg nationality and therefore does not need to become a soldier. But because he was born and raised in France, he regards himself as a Frenchman and therefore feels morally obliged to fight. This patriotism will cost him his life.

Faber grows up in the small town of Colombes (Île de France). He leaves school at an early age to work as a removal man and as a dock labourer. These are both heavy jobs, but Faber — 1.88 metres tall and weighing 88 kilograms — has strength to spare. Like his elder foster brother Ernest Paul, he becomes a rider. With his impressive physique, he soon starts winning races at the highest level. At the age of just 21, he wins four stages in the 1908 edition of the Tour de France and is second in the overall standings behind Lucien Petit-Breton. This the same season he also wins his first classic, triumphing in the Tour of Lombardy.

In the 1909 Tour François Faber dominates the race from start to finish. To some extent, he is helped by the weather. That summer is one of the worst on record in western Europe, with 14 days of torrential, nonstop rain. This deluge turns many of the French roads into muddy tracks that are barely passable. In these extreme conditions, the riders are pushed to the limit. They finish each stage in a state of near exhaustion, all except for one man: François Faber. The muscular 22-year-old Luxembourger powers his way through the slush with apparent ease. His energy and endurance seem limitless. Rain or wind, cobbles or gravel: it all makes no difference to him. In his black and yellow Alcyon jersey, he destroys the field, winning five successive stages (the only man in cycling history to do so). In the stage to Metz, he wins by 33 minutes over Lapize. Next day, in the stage to Belfort, ridden in near freezing conditions, he again wins by 33 minutes, this time from Garrigou, after a solo of 255 kilometres through the wind and snow. Although he carries much more weight than many of the other riders, he survives climbs in the Alps and Pyrenees with little difficulty and arrives in Paris with a massive lead of 20 points. To make the family celebration complete, his foster brother Ernest Paul finishes sixth. The best Belgian is Cyriel Van Hauwaert in fifth place.

Between 1908 and 1914, Faber wins a total of 19 Tour stages. But he also has regular success in the classic one-day races: in 1909, Paris-Tours and Paris-Brussels; in 1910, Paris-Tours again; in 1911, Bordeaux-Paris; and in 1913, Paris-Roubaix. Thanks to his humble background and his modest nature, he is hugely popular with cycling fans. His final

Tour winner François Faber is a Luxembourger, but still joins the French Foreign Legion.

victories as a cyclist were gained in the Tour of 1914, as mentioned above. On 26 July, the 'Giant of Colombes' rides into Paris to complete his seventh Tour. Few people could have realized it would be his last.

Just weeks later, he signs on for the Foreign Legion and is posted to C Company of the 2nd Battalion of the Legion's 1st Regiment. On Sunday, 9 May 1915, the battalion, with a newly promoted Corporal Faber in its ranks, is one of the units charged with capturing the German positions on Vimy Ridge and at Notre-Dame de Lorette on the opening day of the Second Battle of Artois. This is no easy task, because the Germans on the high ground have a clear view of the French line of attack. By the end of the day, his unit has been decimated and the ex-Tour winner is dead. There are two versions of how he meets his end. The first version claims that Faber receives a telegram in the trenches at Carency just before the attack, saying he has become a father. Overjoyed, he leaps into the air in celebration, but is seen by an enemy sniper and shot through the heart. The second — and perhaps more likely — account says that he is killed while attempting to bring in a wounded comrade from no-man's-land.

Author Pascal Leroy, who has extensively researched the circumstances surrounding Faber's death, is convinced that the romanticized 'jumping for joy' story is a fabrication. He says that Faber had a premonition he would not survive. On the day before the battle, he collects together all his belongings and hands them to his comrade, Georges Miron, who before the war rode motorbikes in stayer races. It is almost as if Faber knows he will not be coming back. During the attack, Miron stays in battalion headquarters and watches with horror as the massacre unfolds. By lunchtime, the ground in front of the ridges is covered with dead and wounded Frenchmen. When the fighting dies down, Miron goes in search of his friend, asking for information about him among the wounded in the first aid posts. He eventually finds someone from the battalion, Sergeant Marteau, who tells him: 'He fell, just a few metres from Colonel Noiré. He called out "I'm hit!", clutched his hands to his stomach, and then toppled forward. After that, I heard nothing more of him.'

Miron continues his search but can find no other survivors from C Company. Perhaps it is not surprising. That day, the regiment suffers 1,950 casualties from its total strength of 2,900 men.

The news that François Faber is missing spreads fast. Another racer, Louis Darragon, scours the battlefield in the hope of finding the Luxembourger's body, but without success. Later, Charles Cruchon, another cyclist serving on the staff of the 279th Infantry Regiment, searches through the graves of all those brought in from no-man's-land, but he is unable to find the name 'Faber' among the many crosses. Twenty days later, the military authorities confirm that 'Corporal Faber was killed by the enemy'. Like so many others, he is 'missing in action'. His body will never be recovered, although he is posthumously awarded the Military Medal.

So ended the life and career of one of the first great Tour de France racers. But he was not alone. The murderous fighting in Artois continues for another week and claims 100,000 French lives for very little gain: the crucial ridges remain in German hands. Forty thousand of the victims of this slaughter are later buried at Albain-Saint-Nazaire in the Notre-Dame de Lorette National Necropolis. Almost half of them have individual graves, but the bones of 23,000 unidentified soldiers rest together in a massive ossuary. Nearby there is a small chapel. One of its stained-glass windows is dedicated to the spy, Louise de Bettignies, and the walls are covered with memorial plaques. One of them reads: *François Faber. 1er Regiment Étranger. Cycliste, mort pour la France.*

François Faber on 1 August 1909 in the Parc des Prince in Paris, following his victory in the Tour de France.

THE TOUR OF FLANDERS... IN A VELODROME!

The outbreak of the First World War is also a disaster for the cycling plans of Léon Van den Haute and Karel Van Wijnendaele. The men behind *Sportwereld* have ambitious plans to turn the Tour of Flanders into one of the great spring classics. True, the first two editions in 1913 and 1914 were not a great success. The number of riders was disappointing, as was the lack of international interest. But now that Europe is at war, it seems as though they will be denied the chance to correct these failures and finally get their race off the ground.

Because the course runs through the *Etappengebiet* and even in places through the *Operationsgebiet*, it seems impossible to organize a Tour of Flanders for 1915 — at least not on the road. But the stubborn and inventive Van den Haute is determined not to throw in the towel. In spite of the difficulties, the man from Brussels (who spends most of the war in Ghent) continues to do everything he can to promote 'his' sport and 'his' race. As soon as the Germans relax the ban on track cycling, he contacts Désiré De Poorter, the owner of the track in Evergem, to discuss a number of possibilities. They eventually decide to organize a race meeting on 15 August 'for the benefit of the Prisoners of War Welfare Fund'.

The race is publicized in the *Gentenaar* newspaper: '50 kilometres with five prizes for the professionals — 30 kilometres with three prizes for the 10 best newcomers — The prizes will be awarded by well-known sportsmen.' Unfortunately, 15 August is a washout. It pours with rain the whole day, so that the wooden track is too slippery for racing. It is decided to try again the following Sunday, 22 August. During that intervening week, Van den Haute has a bright idea. Why not do things bigger and better than they originally planned? Instead of a 50-kilometre race, he makes it a 150-kilometre race — and he decides to call it the Tour of Flanders!

The newspaper *Het Volk* reports that the race '… has been so organized that the riders will be faced with all the trials and tribulations they usually encounter on the road: flying checkpoints, fixed checkpoints, the need to fix their own wheel if it breaks, etc.' What's more, even though the race is taking place on a track, it will be ridden over an imaginary course. 'The signs have been arranged thus: start, Ghent; flying checkpoints, Aalst and Zottegem; fixed checkpoint, Oudenaarde; flying checkpoints, Kortrijk and Torhout; fixed checkpoint, Bruges; flying checkpoint, Eeklo; and the finish on the velodrome in Evergem. All the fixed control points will be indicated on the track and the riders will need to dismount from their bikes for three minutes to receive their stamp. It is certain that thousands will flock to Evergem on Sunday!'

WIELRIJDEN. — Velodrom van Evergem. — Zondag laatst eindelijk hebben we schoon weder gehad, en kon de *Ronde van Vlaanderen*, 150 km. op piste, dan ook den bijval genieten, welke zulke belangrijke koers verdiende.

26 renners namen het vertrek. Het was een mooie groep. Aloys Persyn had de eerste bandbreuk weldra gevolgd door Cocquyt. Tot aan de vliegende kontrool van Aalst valt er echter niets belangrijks voor tenzij dat een paar rijders opgeven. Achter Aalst schiet Fernand Maertens een paar malen geweldig uit en neemt tot 200 m. voorsprong. 't Is de rekordman Desmedt die het meeste en schoonste werk doet om den vluchteling in te loopen.

Achter de kontrool van Audenaarde zijn het Dhondt, Maes, De Jaegher en K. Maertens die wat voorsprong nemen, doch Desmedt, Cocquyt en Van Rentergem brengen heel de bende weder zamen. Juist vóór de kontrool van Thourout, Leon Buysse en de kleine Goetgebuer verschalken al hunne tegenstrevers en nemen eene ronde voorsprong onder de daverende toejuichingen der menigte.

Pol Verstraete vol moed, beproeft verder ook 't zelfde spel, doch het lukt niet, en op het einde der koers schiet Marcel Buysse menigmaal uit om zich te ontdubbelen, doch de anderen waken en er komt geen verandering meer, tenzij dat Desmedt een halve ronde neemt op de groep en ze behoudt tot aan de aankomst, wijl de beginnelingen hem achterna zetten en de *groote bazen* als Marcel Buysse, Verstraete, P. Vandevelde en Persyns lamlendig aan 't steertje hangen en in de laatste ronden opgeven.

De uitslag is dus :
1° Leon BUYSSE, Thielt, in 4 u. 34 m. 30 s.; 2° Oscar Goetgebuer, Gent, op 10 m.; 3° Albert Desmedt, Assche, op 333 meters; 4° F. Martens, Gent, op 150 meters; 5° Ariel Cocquyt, Mariakerke, op 1 wiel; 6° Henri De Jaegher, Somergem, op 1 lengte; 7° Reyniers, Sleidinge, op 1 lengte; 8° Jules Dhondt, Gent, op 50 m.; 9° Jules Van Rentergem, Evergem, op 1 wiel; 10° Fonteyne, Eyne, op 1 lengte; 11° Bauwens, Doornzeele, op 50 meters.

De premies werden gewonnen door De Jaegher (6); Persyn (3); Leon Buysse (2); Marcel Buysse (2), Pol Verstraete (2); Cocquyt (2).

Leon Buysse, winner of the ersatz Tour of Flanders in 1915.

Het Volk reports on the race on 25 August 1915.

Thirty-five riders register to take part in this ersatz Tour of Flanders. True, it is not a huge number, but mobility in occupied Belgium is still difficult. In part for this reason, only 26 riders line up at the start. Most of them are from East Flanders and a few from neighbouring West Flanders. 'Even so, it was a fine group', comments *Het Volk* in its report of the race on 25 August. The report continues: 'Nothing of importance happened before the flying checkpoint in Aalst, except that a few riders gave up. (...) Just before the checkpoint in Torhout, Leon Buysse and little Oscar Goetgebuer surprised their rivals with an attack that put them a lap ahead, to the loud applause of the large crowd (...). Towards the end of the race Marcel Buysse tried on several occasions to gain another laps but now the other riders were on their guard. As a result, there was no change, except that Albert Desmedt gained half a lap on the pack and held it to the finish.'

Leon Buysse crosses the finishing line first, completing the 150 kilometres in 4 hours, 34 minutes and 30 seconds. He is by no means an unknown rider. In 1911, the man from Pittem won the Championship of Flanders in Koolskamp, as well as finishing second in both 1910 and 1912. Although exempt from military service, he flees to the neutral Netherlands when war breaks out in 1914. Riding on a Dutch license, he takes part in a number of local events and also races on the track in the internment camp for Belgian soldiers at Harderwijk. In the summer of 1915, he returns to his home in West Flanders and resumes, as far as possible, his cycling career. Following this victory in the track version of the Tour of Flanders, he will later finish second behind Henri Vanlerberghe in the first 'real' Tour of Flanders held after the war in 1919.

The war has clipped Stijn Streuvels' cycling wings for more than a year. The urge to take to the road, 'to master the endlessness of our country lanes', becomes irresistible. In August 1915, he decides to make a six-day bike journey with two friends, Emmanuel Viérin and Jozef De Coene, through the occupied territories. 'We will make a series of short day trips. Nothing too strenuous, of course. (...) We submitted applications to each of the relevant military commands to travel by bike to different cities: Brussels, Mechelen, Leuven, Antwerp, Ghent. But we always gave different reasons. In one case, it was for a business trip, in another to visit museums and libraries, and so on.' What they really want to do is visit the places where there was heavy fighting last year. 'For anyone who was able to read between the lines, it wasn't difficult to work out what had planned; in other words, to visit Aalst, Diest, Halen, Aarschot, Lier and Dendermonde. Although we made our applications to three different commands, in the passports from all three places the word 'Leuven' was crossed out with a thick, blue pencil as *"nicht genehmigt"* (not approved). This was a blow, because Leuven was the one place we most wanted to see, the main reason for our journey.'

The three friends cycle via Oudenaarde and Ninove to Brussels. 'By nightfall we had arrived in the capital, a little bit tired, a little bit sweaty, and with a ravenous hunger', Streuvels would later write in *Onze Fiets in Oorlogstijd* (Our Bike in Wartime), his account of their adventures. Brussels, he finds, has been completely Germanized; the sooner they can leave, the better. Next morning, they set off for Mechelen. 'In Eppegem, Zemst and Hanswijk we see the first ruins. (...) Their pitiful appearance made a powerful impression on us and it was with a feeling of awe and diffidence that we approached each place.'

In Mechelen, they pass a German military cemetery. 'And on the other side of the city, much simpler, much more sober, we find the cemetery for our Belgian soldiers. (...) It was an emotional moment. All three of us had a lump in the throat, tears in our eyes. Boys of twenty, twenty-five years, in the flower of their youth, full of hope, full of spirit , cut down in their prime and here laid to rest.' A portrait of the dead soldier hangs on one of the crosses. Streuvels thinks that he can read in his face 'a deep contempt for mankind, which sends its children to their death with words like "courage" and "heroism" on their lips'.

Leuven is still off limits. A year earlier, it had been subjected to a reign of terror for three nightmarish days. The Germans executed more than 200 innocent civilians and burnt down over 1,100 buildings, including the town hall, St. Peter's Church and the magnificent university library. They try to enter the city, but are turned back by a member of the civil guard. Once they are out of sight, they double back along a canal and still manage to reach the city centre. Streuvels compares Leuven to the ruins of Pompeii. 'Everything has been flattened, as though there has been an earthquake. (...) We stared open-mouthed in amazement, walking without words, stunned by the impact of that terrible scene, trying to imagine what had happened here, trying to imagine what the people must have felt when this hellish fury was unleashed upon them.'

After visiting a few professors of Streuvels' acquaintance, the three friends ride on in the direction of Aarschot. Streuvels has read newspaper accounts of last year's dramatic events in the town,

played out on 19 and 20 August 1914. 'We knew the tragic story of the burgomaster and the brave demeanour of his son and his other housemates, and we were aware of the cruel fate suffered by several of the local inhabitants.' Their next stop is Scherpenheuvel, where they spend the night in a tavern called 'De Zwaan' (The Swan). In Diest, they climb the old ramparts, which is not to the liking of '... a kind of *feldwebel*. It seems that the ramparts are now part of a military zone and that we were treading on forbidden ground. It was fortunate that our travel documents were in order; otherwise, we might all have been deported to Germany as spies'.

Their odyssey continues towards Halen, where the Battle of the Silver Helmets was fought on 12 August. The graves of the fallen Belgian soldiers are visible wherever they look. In Lier, Streuvels is saddened that '... the pleasing aspect of the town centre has been battered, bruised and torn apart. The venerable St. Gummarus Church has been damaged. (...) The larger part of the population has left, driven away, forced to live as refugees in strange places for more than a year'. On the fifth day of their journey, the threesome arrives in Antwerp, where, to their disgust, they find a German flag flying from the tower of the Cathedral of Our Lady. From Antwerp, it is on to Dendermonde; like Leuven and Aarschot, another of the martyr towns. Here innocent civilians were massacred over several days, their possessions looted, their houses burnt. By the time the German bloodlust was cooled, fewer than a hundred buildings were left standing. Via Aalst, Streuvels, Viérin and De Coene arrive in Ghent, where they plan to spend a restful Sunday, before '...on Monday morning each setting off to his own home, via Deinze and Kortrijk'. And so their six-day epic comes to a safe and satisfactory conclusion.

In 1915, Stijn Streuvels publishes *Mijn Rijwiel* (My Bicycle), in which he professes his love of cycling.

When Léon Van den Haute organizes his imaginary Tour of Flanders at the velodrome in Evergem, he does so with Désiré De Poorter and probably not with his partner Karel Van Wijnendaele. His name is not mentioned in any of the newspaper articles about the race. Perhaps this is because Van Wijnendaele — real name Karel Steyaert — lives in Torhout, just 20 kilometres from the IJzer Front on the German side of the line. The invaders turn the town into an important military centre, surrounded by field hospitals, rest camps and supply depots for their troops. For this reason, it is governed by a strict military regime throughout the war. In theory, Van Wijnendaele cannot cross into another town or village without prior German permission, which is seldom given.

In his later memoirs *Het rijke Vlaamsche Wielerleven* (The rich world of Flemish cycling), Van Wijnendaele hardly mentions the war. If he talks about the spring of 1914, it is only to praise the victories of the great Flemish riders: 'From January to July, you could read it every Monday morning in the weekend's results from the velodromes: victories for Van Lerberghe-Depauw, De Baets-Persijn or Leon Buysse-Pier Van de Velde. You could count on it!' But the German invasion of Belgium is covered in a single sentence: 'The month of August came and with it the war, which would set the whole world alight.' Following which he carries on with sporting matters, by skipping the next four years as though they never happened: 'After the war, we had the Six Days of Brussels in 1919'.

How did Karel Van Wijnendaele live through those four years of war? What happened to him? Because he purchased his exemption from military service when he was drafted as a young man, he certainly does not need to join the army. And we have seen how he reports from Liege in the early days of the fighting. But after *Sportwereld* closes down for the duration, the 32-year-old Van Wijnendaele once again becomes just plain Karel Steyaert. True, the unemployed journalist is still 'director of the velodrome in Torhout' but this means very little: during the occupation no meetings can be held at the track on the Bruggestraat, close to the Bruges-Ostend railway line. This 'iron road' is used for military purposes and the Germans won't let anyone near it.

Steyaert tries to keep his head down, but few people living so close to the front are able to avoid doing forced labour for the occupiers. The Germans decide to open an aerodrome in the nearby hamlet of Twaalf Gemete — where the St. Rembert's hospital stands today. 'Koarle' (as everyone knows him locally) is conscripted to help with the work. But not for long. The story goes that he was recognized by one of the German soldiers, the six-day racer and 1913 world sprint champion, Walter Rütt. The rider puts in a good word for the journalist with his commander.

Steyaert is able to return home and after that probably helps his wife, Helena Allemeersch, in the little grocer's shop she runs on the Burg, in the centre of Torhout. There is nothing else he can do. The entire neighbourhood is overrun with soldiers. It is the place where they rest and train before marching westwards to the front. For those who are fortunate enough to come back, Torhout — the first town behind the lines in the *Etappengebiet*

During the war, Karel Van Wijnendaele is forced by the Germans to help build an aerodrome at Torhout.

— is a breath of fresh air. It is here that they can forget the mud and misery of the trenches, knowing that a hot bath and a warm bed will be waiting for them. For the less fortunate, it might be a hospital bed. Between 1915 and 1918, the buildings of the 17th-century Ten Walle infirmary and the teachers' training college, all close to Steyaert's home, are used to house a major evacuation hospital. One of its most famous patients is Erich Paul Remark, wounded on 31 July 1917. IIe will later become famous under the pseudonym Erich Maria Remarque as the author of *All Quiet on the Western Front* (1929), a groundbreaking novel about the horror and futility of war.

Like all the citizens of Torhout, it cannot have been easy for Van Wijnendaele/Steyaert during the war. Requisitions are frequent and freedom of movement is almost non-existent. Farms and factories are damaged or closed. Because normal traffic on the railways is cut back to allow more military traffic, the inflow of essential supplies — food, coal, etc — into the town is severely reduced. The people are cold and hungry. The constant booming of the guns in the distance creates an atmosphere of gloom and despondency. Sometimes, Steyaert and his fellow citizens can even feel the ground shake under their feet.

And then there is the danger. The Germans transport munitions and troops through the station in Torhout almost 24 hours a day. The Allies are well aware of this and from 1916 onwards carry out air raids over the town. The first target is the station, but later the hospital in the school buildings will also be bombed. Karel and Helena live in between these two locations, so the chance of being hit by a stray bomb is very real. Perhaps this helps to explain why Karel Van Wijnendaele begins his first post-war article in *Sportwereld* on New Year's Day 1919 with the following words: 'Phew! At last we are rid of those terrible brutes from across the Rhine! We want to live again, be free again and move at will through the clean and healthy air of our liberated Belgium!'

A 'REAL' TOUR OF BELGIUM — ON THE TRACK!

In 1915, the Karreveld track becomes the epicentre for cycling in the *Okkupationsgebiet* or the occupied part of Belgium beyond the *Etappengebiet*. More and more meetings are organized — and with success. In these difficult times, the people of Brussels seek solace in their pre-war pleasures, especially if they are close to home. Cycling fits the bill. Just as local cinemas flourish between 1915 and 1918, so too do the local velodromes. But Karreveld leads the way and its meetings are often attended by thousands of people.

One of the big public attractions is the so-called 'road races', which are copied in ersatz form on the track. In July 1915, Jan Van Ingelghem wins 'Bordeaux-Paris' at Karreveld — not the real marathon race, of course, but a mock version ridden on the boards. A month or so later, much the same thing is done with the 'Tour of Belgium', again organized on the track but with 'stages' spread over five days, using the names of pre-war start and finishing towns to add a touch of 'realism' to the event. *L'Echo de la Presse* describes it as 'the finest competition of the season'.

On Sunday, 29 August, the opening stage in what we would now call a 'virtual' Tour of Belgium takes place — in people's imagination, at least — from Brussels to Liege over a distance of 150 kilometres. The Monday stage is from 'Liege to Arlon' over 100 kilometres. Tuesday sees the riders cover another 100 kilometres from 'Arlon to Namur'. Wednesday is a rest day, followed on Thursday, 2 September by a penultimate stage of 125 kilometres from 'Namur to Ostend'. The climax is on Sunday, 5 September, with a 150-kilometre ride from 'Ostend to Brussels'. 'The distances between the towns have been calculated "as the crow flies" and there will be a sprint prize at each of the control towns.' The winner of each sprint gets one point, the second two points, and so on. The rider with the fewest points at the end of the race wins the prize. Riders who are lapped are given an extra five points. Riders who get a flat tyre or have other mechanical problems are allowed a bonus lap.

As far as the participants are concerned, *L'Echo* describes them as '…an outstanding group of riders. (…) Twenty-five top racers have been called together to dispute the Tour of Belgium on the track'.

LE TOUR DE BELGIQUE SUR PISTE

'Van de Velde held on to his lead and his victory was loudly and enthusiastically applauded. Here are the final results of this remarkable Tour of Belgium: 1. Van de Velde, 151 points; 2. Rossius, 165 p.; 3. M. Buysse, 195 p.; 4. Desmedt, 206 p.; 5. Verbist, 201 p.; 6. Tuytten, 215 p.; 7. Van Isterdael and Beths, 217 p.; 9. Coolens; 10. L. Buysse.'

In 1916, a second wartime edition of the Tour of Belgium is organized, but this time as a one-day race. This 'mini-Tour' takes place on 20 August 1916 at the Arsenal velodrome in Ghent. There are 19 riders at the start and spectators are offered a choice between four different kinds of entrance ticket: 'Grass, 1.75 francs; grandstand, 1.25 francs; banking, 0.60 franc; back terraces, 0.30 franc. The riders will compete for prizes of 150, 120, 100, 80, 60, 50, 40, 30 and 20 francs'. The race starts at half past one in the afternoon and is scheduled to cover a distance of 175 kilometres in seven separate 'stages'. In the sixth stage, Lucien Buysse and Pier Van de Velde gain a lead of a lap over the pack. But once again, the rain spoils things. The 'Tour' is abandoned after 140 kilometres, with Van de Velde once again the winner. Buysse is second and a lap behind come César Debaets (third), Avile Cocquyt (fourth) and Basiel Matthys (fifth).

The organizers even make sure there is a good balance between the different parts of Belgium: '...six Walloons and six Flemings'. The list includes famous names like Louis Mottiat, Jean Rossius, Noël Hubert, Leon Scieur, Jacques Coomans, Marcel and Leon Buysse, Pier Van de Velde, Pol Verstraete, Julien Tuytten, Joseph Van Isterdael, Albert Desmedt and Pierre Everaerts, 'the popular crack rider from Sint-Gillis'.

The first stage is abandoned after 94 kilometres. It starts to rain and the track is too slippery to be safe. It is decided to ride the remaining 56 kilometres before the start of the next day's race. But on Monday it pours again, so the second stage is now moved to Tuesday. It is won by Pier Van de Velde, who also takes the lead in the overall standings. Sadly, the bad weather persists. The third stage is called off after just 30 kilometres. It is now proposed to ride on both Wednesday — the 'rest' day — and on Thursday. But the weather gods are unrelenting and it continues to bucket down until Saturday. The fourth stage is switched to the Sunday, with the grand finale now on Monday. Van de Velde wins the shortened third stage and is also the best in the fifth stage. 'It was a battle between the Walloon and Flemish riders, the latter being cheered on by thousands of their fans, who came from near and far to support their sporting heroes', reports *Het Vlaamsche Nieuws* on 9 September.

The race is announced on the front page of *L'Echo de la Presse* on 29 August 1915.

Paul Van de Velde, the winner of the Tour of Belgium at the Karreveld velodrome.

When Stijn Streuvels and his friends arrive home at the end of August 1915 after their six-day adventure, they are only just in time, because '...a short time later it was announced that no further passports will be issued to ride through the country'. The occupiers feel the need to control everything. Potatoes and meat are already rationed. Cattle are branded, ringed, counted and registered. The Germans decide which farmers can plant how much of which crop, when they should sow it and when they should harvest it. At the end of 1915 and the start of 1916, the number of these bureaucratic restrictions and interferences increases dramatically. Farmers now have to apply to plant crops and many see this as a step towards the confiscation of the harvest and its compulsory sale to the occupier at fixed (and relatively low) prices. At the same time, the list of resources and materials of economic and military value gets ever longer, almost to the point of absurdity. Wool, cotton, cars, motorbikes, their spare parts, petrol, oil, wood, electric machines, batteries and all copper, bronze, nickel and tin in private possession are all likely to be requisitioned at a moment's notice. And now even the humble bicycle is to be added to the list.

The Germans are particularly keen to have the steel from their frames and the rubber from their tyres. In September 1915, people living in the *Etappengebiet* are instructed to hand them in to the authorities. Stijn Streuvels notes in his war diary: 'And then came the order: all bicycles, fitted with an address label, must be deposited in the village square, with the threat of a fine of a few thousand marks for those who keep their bikes hidden after the stipulated date. The pile that steadily grew in front of the town hall on the appointed day looked like a heap of old scrap iron. It seems that everyone tried to find something that vaguely resembled a bike, so that they could hand that in instead. This was the end of biking history. In theory, bicycles no longer exist.'

As Streuvels records, most people tried to find a way around the new rules and regulations. Many things on the German lists were hidden in barns and cellars, or even buried under the ground. New bikes were concealed in the most unlikely of places and old ones were surrendered instead. 'Anyone who had a suitable hiding place filled it to the brim with their copper, wool, tobacco and other valuables, in the hope they would be safe from prying eyes. And now they had to find a place for their bikes! A big, stupid thing that takes up a lot of space and can't be made any smaller.'

Streuvels has four bikes to hide. '...one for every member of the family. (...) Off come the tyres, the wheels, the fork, the chain, the pedals, etc, all neatly greased and wrapped in cloth against the rust, before being entrusted to our hiding place. (...) I carefully studied the entire topography of our house and decided to use an attic no-one knew about, whose door could be plastered over so that it was smooth with the wall, making it almost invisible. This was all carried out in the most nerve-wracking of circumstances, not in the least because a dozen or so soldiers, including five officers, were billeted with us and could have disturbed and ruined our plans at any moment.'

The poster confiscating bikes, dated 15 September 1916.

Bekendmaking

in aansluiting met de verordening betreffende het

in beslag nemen van de

Rijwielbanden

en het opnemen van de stapels.

Met goedkeuring van den heer Gouverneur-Generaal van 14-9-1916 worden de volgende termijnen verlengd :
in § 5 : aankoop bij de verzamelkantoren tot op 20 September 6 uur 's namiddags ;
in § 6 : verplichting tot aangifte van de tot op 20 September niet afgeleverde banden tot op 25 September 1916.

Er wordt bijzonder de nadruk op gelegd, dat slechts zulke banden moeten aangegeven worden, die tot op 20 September niet afgeleverd werden.

Antwerpen, 15 September 1916.

Kraftfahrstelle Antwerpen.

CYCLING FOR A GOOD CAUSE

Notwithstanding the occupation, there is still quite a lot of race cycling in Belgium, even if it is confined to the velodromes. This is by no means self-evident. All bikes are confiscated by the invader, and in theory this also includes the bikes of the professional racers. At the same time, it is far from easy for both the racers and the cycling fans to get to the tracks for the meetings. To travel outside your home town or village, you need a special pass or *Reiseschein*, which the Germans are not always willing to give. Fortunately, the initial strict regime imposed by the Germans in 1914, when most forms of public pleasure and entertainment were banned, is gradually relaxed when their occupation becomes more 'normal'. In 1915 and 1916, there are cycling races to see almost every weekend.

These races are often held for a good cause. Right from the earliest days of the war, various organizations are set up to help those in need. For example, the National Committee for Food and Aid and the Society for the Assistance of the Poor and Destitute. Other groups are dedicated to helping the orphans of soldiers killed in the war or to supporting the soldiers who are being held as prisoners in Germany. It is not only the organizers of the race meetings who donate a part of their proceeds to these good causes; the racers often also donate part of any prize money they win. We have already seen that the 1915 Tour of Flanders at the stadium in Evergem was ridden for the benefit of the Prisoners of War Welfare Fund. Similarly, on 19 September 1915 a three-hour race is organized to raise funds for the Work Group for Prisoners of War in Germany. The staff of

Belgische Krijgsgevangenen. — Het Bestuur van het « Sportnieuws » en de Velodroom van Gentbrugge richtte een fietskoers in waarvan de opbrengst fr. 276.80, voor de helft werd afgedragen aan « Volksopbeuring » en « Hulp aan Krijgsgevangenen ». De renners Marcel Buysse en Cyril Josse, waren zoo edelmoedig daartoe hunne premiën af te staan. Hulde en dank aan inrichters en renners.

The announcement in *Het Vlaamsche Nieuws* on 18 October 1916.

the temporarily discontinued *Sportwereld* move heaven and earth to attract thousands of fans to the Arsenal track in Antwerp. And with success: the benefit race raises 10,000 francs for the Work Group. The *Gentenaar* newspaper describes the scene as follows: 'By half past two, all the popular places on the terraces were full with 1,500 to 1,600 spectators. The grandstand and the banks were also full. The start of the three-hour race, ridden in 12 classifications, was scheduled for seven minutes past three. And what a great race the riders made of it! Jules Dhondt and Karel Martens were the first to be lapped by Pier Van de Velde, Cocquyt and Vercautere. Saelens also fell a lap behind, as did De Jaegher. Marcel Buysse, even though clearly not in the best of form, managed to bring the whole pack back to Pier.' Even so, Van de Velde manages to hold on for the win, followed by Buysse in second place and Aloïs Persijn in third. 'First and foremost,' *De Gentenaar* continues, 'a word of thanks must be given to the organizers, who spared no effort to make this meeting a success; in particular, Mr. De Maeght, the owner of *Sportwereld*; Mr. Van den Haute, the director of *Sportwereld*; his assistants Michel and Bertin; and the announcer Arthur Duysburgh. Thanks are also due to the magnanimous donors of the prizes, the Tram Company and, last but not least, to the numerous members of the public, who helped to raise such a generous sum.'

Five thousand spectators are also present at an event held on the circuit at Laken on 24 October 1915 for the benefit of the Society for the Assistance of the Poor and Destitute. 'They must be delighted with the outcome', reports the next day's edition of *Het Vlaamsche Nieuws*. The races at this meeting are for novices and all-comers, and include '... a sprint race between Aerts and Tuytten-Van Isterdael,' as well as '... the Laken Grand Prix, a race over 50 kilometres in five categories for independent riders'. The same paper later announces in its edition for 14 July 1916 that Cyriel Van Hauwaert is also willing to ride for a good cause.

Arthur Van der Stuyft and Pier Van de Velde on the Garden City velodrome in Wilrijk.

THE VERY FIRST
SIX DAYS OF GHENT

He will '...donate his winnings to the Invalids Home and the "Child of a Soldier" organization'.

That happens in Wilrijk, where two days later the Garden City velodrome reopens its door, for the first time since the war started. The main attraction is a race between the Lion of Flanders and the popular Antwerp racer, Arthur Vanderstuyft. 'They will both strive for victory in a race behind tandems and, as they are both determined not to be beaten, it promises to be an exciting contest. The competition between Brussels and Antwerp, with Debac, Thomas, Verbist, Verheyleweghen, Van Mol, Binst, Jacobs and Schrijvers against Tyck, Redig, Pauwels, Apostel, Verberckt, Verlinden, Spiessens and Claes is also guaranteed to provide thrills and spills, in three different ways: a sprint (1,200 metres), a stayer race (half hour) and a tandem race. The races begin promptly at four o'clock. Even if it rains until half past three, the races will go ahead, since this is a track that dries out quickly.' A report of the event in the 18 October 1916 edition of the newspaper *Het Vlaamsche Nieuws* gives details of the outcome: 'There was a cycle race on the velodrome in Gentbrugge, where half of the gate receipts of 276,80 francs were donated to the 'Public Aid' and 'Help the Prisoners of War' organizations. The racers Marcel Buysse and Cyril Josse were also so generous as to donate their prize money. Praise and thanks to both the organizers and the riders!'

WIELRIJDEN.

De Zesdagen van Gent. — Het is nu vast beslist, de koers heeft plaats en wel op de volgende manier : Zondag en maandag op Evergem. Donderdag en zondag 10e op Mariakerke, Vrijdag en maandag 11 October op Gentbrugge. Den Zondag telkens om 3 ur en de weekdagen om 2 ure. De deelnam van de best uitgelezen ploegen is reeds verzekerd.

In reference books you often read that the first Six Days of Ghent took place in 1922. Yet the newspaper *Het Volk* encouraged its readers on 1 October 1915 to attend a Six Days of Ghent that was scheduled to take place that weekend. 'It has now been decided. The event will certainly go ahead and will be organized in the following way: Sunday and Monday at Evergem; Thursday and Sunday the 10th at Mariakerke; Friday and Monday 11 October at Gentbrugge. At 3 o'clock on the Sundays and at two o'clock on the weekdays. The participation of the very best teams is guaranteed.'

The 'very best teams' are nine pairs, mainly of local riders. They will complete the six-day event at three different velodromes, which is unusual and was probably stipulated by the German authorities. 'If the first races were exciting, the remaining ones promise to be nothing less', comments *Vooruit* after the opening two days in Evergem. Aloïs Persijn

The velodrome at Evergem during the First World War.

The announcement in *Het Volk* on 1 October 1915.

Pol Verstraeten, van Evergem
op TUBEN COLONIAL.

A report of the race in *Vooruit* on 7 October 1915.

from Nazareth and Avile Cocquyt from Mariakerke are leading the standings, with a three-point lead over Pol Verstraete from Evergem and Jules Van Renterghem from Ursel. 'The battle between these two teams will be fierce. (...) The riders are pumped up, and Cocquyt, the young champion from Mariakerke, has said: "So far my teammate Persijn and Pol Verstraete have taken turns to win the sprints, but in Mariakerke, on my own front doorstep, I intend to show people what I can do. If we need to, we'll take a lap lead and hold on to it!" It promises to be a great sporting spectacle!'

The newspaper also tips the duos Vermeersch-Van Waes and F. Martens-Leon Buysse as outsiders for the victory. 'Large crowds are expected, because every sport-loving man who is free is already asking all his friends: "Are you going to Mariakerke?"'

Cocquyt is unable to perform as he hopes in front of his home crowd, because after the two days of racing in Mariakerke, Verstraete and Van Rent-

erghem now lead. It will all be decided at the finale in Gentbrugge. The weather is fine both days and there is lots of public interest. On Friday, Persijn and Verstraete again share the sprints, but then Verstraete and Van Renterghem manage to get a lap ahead. On the final day, it is the team of Martens and Buysse that manages to gain a lap, but '... Persijn and Cocquyt are the heroes of the day'. But it all makes no difference to the final result: Verstraete and Van Renterghem win the first Six Days of Ghent, followed by Persijn-Cocquyt, Hudsyn-De Leener and Martens-Buysse in that order.

Pol Verstraete, the winner of the first Six Days of Ghent with Jules Van Renterghem.

VAN HAUWAERT AND VAN BEVER WIN THE SIX DAYS OF BRUSSELS

On exactly the same day as in Ghent, Sunday, 3 October 1915, the Six Days of Brussels also starts. It is the fourth edition. It was won in 1912 by the Americans Eddy Root and Fred Hill, followed a year later by the Belgian René Vandenberghe and the Frenchman Octave Lapize, with Cyriel Van Hauwaert and the Dutchman John Stol being the most recent winners in 1914. The Six Days is usually held at the 235-metre long track in the Sports Palace in Schaarbeek, near to the Josaphat Park. However, this covered winter velodrome has now been taken over for the work of the National Committee for Food and Aid, an initiative launched by Brussels bankers, industrialists and the city's burgomaster, Adolphe Max, to distribute goods received from the Commission for Relief in Belgium to the local population.

As a result, the wartime editions of the Six Days move to the Karreveld circuit. 'Here are the most important points from the rules for the Six Days that starts today', announces Sunday's *Gazet van Brussels*. 'The race will be ridden on 3, 4, 5, 6, 7 and 10 October, on Sundays at 6 o'clock and on weekdays at 4 o'clock.' In other words, like in Ghent, they do not race around the clock, which was the practice in six-day events before the war. 'The teams consist of two riders, who can take over from each other at will. At the end of each day, a results table will be drawn up. The results on the final day will count double. The team with the least number of points at the end of the sixth day will be the winners.'

The most famous name in the starting line-up is Cyriel Van Hauwaert. By now, the former winner of Bordeaux-Paris (1907), Milan-Sanremo and Paris-Roubaix (1908) is in his thirties and is starting to think more about his career after cycling than about his performances in competition. He still rides on the track, but some years ago also began selling bikes for his team sponsor, *La Française*. Van Hauwaert now decides to launch his own brand — the 'Lion of Flanders', after his own nickname — and opens a large bike showroom on the Boudewijnlaan in Brussels. The war badly upsets his plans. The materials in which he has invested — rubber, steel and his existing stock of bikes — have all been requisitioned by the Germans.

In order to survive, Van Hauwaert has to go back to racing. In 1915, he has already taken part in

meetings in Antwerp and Ghent. He now agrees to ride the Six Day of Brussels. What's more, partnered by local rider Jef Van Bever, the 1913 Belgian sprint champion, 'old Cyriel' feels he has a good chance of winning. Their main rivals are the Brussels brothers, Emile and François Aerts, who already have a grudge against Van Bever. On the fourth day, the brothers box in Van Bever and cause him to crash, breaking his collar bone. The brothers are disqualified from the race, but it seems as if the team Van Hauwaert-Van Bever has also been neutralized. Or maybe not. To everyone's amazement, Jef Van Bever appears next morning at the start. True, he can't offer much help to Van Hauwaert, but the Lion of Flanders is able to counter every attack by his rivals, so that their lead is maintained. At the end of the final ride, the team Van Hauwaert-Van Bever are still ahead of the pack and win the Six Days of Brussels, followed by René Vandenberghe and Alfons Spiessens (second) and Marcel Buysse and Pier Van de Velde (third). It is Van Hauwaert's last great victory as a rider. After the war, he returns to bike production and becomes a successful businessman.

Cyriel Van Hauwaert, seen here during a six-day event in January 1914.

85 YEARS AFTER THE BATTLE OF THE SOMME – AND STILL ALIVE!

When the First World War starts, Thomas James Robinson, born on 16 April 1897 in Encounter Bay, South Australia, is a promising young rider. Having enlisted for service abroad, on 2 June 1916 he sets off for Europe in the troopship *Kingsfaun Castle*, bound for Marseilles. After his arrival, he joins the 1st ANZAC Army Cyclist Battalion. As a Lewis gunner, he takes part in the Battle of the Somme. He survives the trenches and in 1919 returns to his native country, where he resumes his work as a bike-maker. At the same time, he also rides with the professionals. Robinson is a time trial specialist and at one time nearly all the South Australian time trial records, from the half mile to the 100 mile, are held by him. He also races on the track, where he competes against (among others) Hubert

Opperman, seven years his junior but destined to have a successful career in Europe. Opperman later enters politics and eventually becomes Minister of Labour and Immigration.

By virtue of his wartime service, Thomas Robinson is awarded the British War Medal and the Victory Medal. But this veteran warrior of the trenches also becomes something of a veteran on his bike, competing in competitions until his 66th year. In his many interviews, he always recalls his experiences during the First World War. 'I still have nightmares. In my dreams, I am back in France. I can see the shells flying, hear the machine guns. And then I attack the Germans...' In 1998, 80 years after the Armistice, Robinson wins new fame as 'the last Light Horseman' and is admitted to the French Legion of Honour. The former rider lives to be 104 and dies on 22 April 2001.

Cyclist Thomas James Robinson, '...enlisted for service abroad'.

Pier Van de Velde, winner of the second Tour of Flanders on the track.

A SECOND ERSATZ TOUR OF FLANDERS

In 1916, a second 'fake' Tour of Flanders is organized on the track. Articles in *Het Volk* and *Het Vlaamsche Nieuws* make clear that this is once again an initiative by Léon Van den Haute and several of his former associates at the now defunct *Sportwereld* newspaper. This time, the 'Tour' will take place on Sunday, 23 July, at the Arsenal velodrome in Gentbrugge. Before the race starts, Van den Haute will just have time that morning to wed his new bride, Idalie Dick.

Only 12 riders turn up to take part in the surrogate race. For many of them, it is getting harder and harder to travel to meetings. Travel by train is now irregular and unreliable, and the Germans are no longer quite so willing to issue *Reisescheinen* as they once were. As a result, the 1916 Tour is once again a race mainly for riders from the nearest provinces: East and West Flanders. It is foreseen that the 1914 winner of the Tour on the road, Marcel Buysse, will once again take part, but three days before the race he injures himself while training at the Arsenal track. According to *Het Vlaamsche Nieuws*: 'When one rider accelerated, he clipped the handlebars of another rider, causing him to fall and bringing down several others.'

As in 1915, it was decided to simulate a road race on the track, this time over a distance of 125 kilometres. Once again, the riders must repair their own bikes if anything goes wrong; accepting help from mechanics or the public will be heavily penalized. During the compulsory three-minute stop at the fixed control points, they are allowed to pick up new provisions of food and drink, spare inner tubes, etc, as well as having their control cards stamped. The race excites little enthusiasm in the press. The report in the following day's *Het Volk* is just 12 lines long. However, *Vooruit* at least publishes the full results, including the intermediary sprints. Pier Van de Velde is the overall winner, ahead of Leon Buysse, Avile Cocquyt, Jules Dhondt and Jules Van Renterghem. 'Lucien Buysse and Dhondt made a great race of it. Winning time: 3 hours and 27 minutes.'

ENRICO TOTI CYCLES AND FIGHTS ON ONE LEG

One of the most remarkable figures of the First World War is the Italian cyclist Enrico Toti. Why remarkable? Because he only has one leg. He lost the other as a result of an accident at work on 27 March 1908. Toti, a stoker for the national rail service, slips on the tracks in the station at Colleferro just at the moment when two locomotives are being coupled. One of the trains crushes his left leg, which needs to be amputated above the thigh. The unfortunate rider is only 26 years old, but adapts to his new circumstances with great courage and fortitude. After his rehabilitation, he devotes his time to all different kinds of activities. For example, he invents a number of small accessories and appliances for use with bikes, some of which can still be

Volontario Enrico Toti fights on the Isonzo against the Austro-Hungarian Army.

seen at the Historical Museum of the Bersaglieri in the Piazzale di Porta Pia in Rome.

Perhaps most amazing of all, Toti becomes a more fervent cyclist than he ever was before the accident. Riding a specially adjusted bike, in 1911 he sets off from his native village of San Giovanni, not far from Rome, with the intention of riding all the way to Paris. He then decides to cycle even further, eventually pedalling on to Lapland, via Belgium, the Netherlands, Denmark and Finland. His return journey takes him through Russia and Poland, and it is not until June 1912 that Enrico arrives back in Italy. Six months later, he undertakes a second long journey, this time heading south. From the port of Alexandria, he crosses the entire length of Egypt, finally stopping at the border of Anglo-Egyptian Sudan. He wants to carry on further, but the British authorities won't let him, because it is too dangerous.

Enrico Toti is a convinced patriot, so that when the First World War breaks out he wants to fight for his country. The 34-year-old immediately volunteers, but what on earth can the army do with a one-legged cyclist? He is rejected for service on three separate occasions, but shows the same persistence he has demonstrated ever since his accident. He buys a fake army uniform in Rome and cycles the 600 kilometres north to the Isonzo Front. He wants to reach Cervignano del Friuli, a village that was liberated from the Austro-Hungarians by the Bersaglieri on 24 May 1915. However, he is intercepted just before he enters the front zone. Perhaps this is hardly surprising. After all, a cyclist in military uniform with just one leg must look a little bit suspicious.

The military police take Toti to a nearby camp. The officers there are astonished at his determination and his desire to fight. Finally, they agree he can stay, to help out behind the front, where they can always use an extra pair of hands. But they underestimate Enrico's resolve to be recognized as a 'real' soldier. He demonstrates his skill with a bike and keeps on pestering those in authority, until at last he gets his own way. On 16 April 1916, he is made an 'unofficial member' of the battalion cyclists of the 3rd Bersaglieri Regiment. In the following months, he fights with a rifle and a crutch in the trenches, and quickly becomes a living legend at the front — for the time being.

The summer of 1916 sees the start of the Sixth Battle of the Isonzo, the sluggish river that flows through Northern Italy and part of what is now modern-day Slovenia. The Bersaglieri have been fighting the Austrians here tooth and nail for more than a year. On 6 August, Toti is wounded in an attack close to the coastal town of Monfalcone. Yet even then he refuses to give in. He struggles to his feet and on his single leg tries to throw a hand grenade, but is hit a second time. He crumples to the ground and everyone thinks he is dead. But he claws himself upright again and throws his crutch towards the enemy trenches, shouting 'Non moriro' (I will not die!). A third bullet proves him wrong.

Although Enrico Toti served as a 'civilian', he is posthumously awarded the gold military medal for bravery, a rare distinction. After the war, many streets and squares are also named in his honour. There is a memorial to him in Rome, a bronze statue in Gorizia on the Isonzo and in the 1960s the Italian navy named a submarine and a class of submarines after him. Perhaps this would have pleased him most: before he became a stoker, he served a number of years in the Italian Marine.

Toti makes the front page of *La Domenica del Corriere*, one of Italy's leading newspapers.

ALEX BENSCHECK OR THE FATAL ART OF CLEANING

While the Germans are busy fighting on several fronts, their remaining cyclists are equally busy riding at home. There are regular races in wartime Germany throughout 1915 and 1916, with editions of Berlin-Cottbus-Berlin, Dresden-Berlin-Dresden and the Hannover Street Grand Prix. There are also lots of track meetings, but no six-day events. The professionals among the *Militärradfahrer* — military cyclists — are often given protected status by the High Command. Sprinter Franz Krupkat is initially sent to fight in the Westhoek, but his superiors soon recognize that he can better serve the fatherland on a bike than in a trench. He is sent back to Germany, retrains as a stayer and wins the 1917 national championships. After the war, he becomes a successful six-day racer.

Fritz Finn, another sprinter but also a six-day specialist, is less fortunate. Until March 1915, he takes part in several track meetings in the Berlin Sports Palace, but later that year is sent to the front in German-occupied Lithuania, where he dies on 16 September. Equally unlucky is Erich Bäumler. This professional stayer is mobilized in August 1914 as a motorbike rider in a reserve division of the German air arm, but after three years of service is allowed to resume his cycling career. This turns out to be a tragic mistake. During a meeting at the Treptower track in Berlin on 26 August 1917, he catches the back wheel of his pace bike and crashes to the ground. He is rushed to hospital but dies of his injuries the next day.

Even more ironic — if that is the right word — is the death of Alex Benscheck. Before the war as an amateur, he is third on two occasions in the German team time trial championships. He is also third in the national sprint championship and in 1913 reaches the semi-finals of the world championship. As a conscript, he serves with the *Kraftradfahrer-Abteilung*, a motorbike unit. In 1916, his superiors decide that he can take several weeks leave and he uses this opportunity to ride at a number of track meetings. On 6 August, he even wins the kilometre race at the Prussian War Championships. Ten days later, he is back at the front, living the life of a soldier. Sadly, while cleaning his rifle on 16 August he forgets that there is a bullet in the chamber and accidentally shoots himself in the chest. The wound is fatal.

Alex Benscheck accidentally shoots himself in the chest on 16 August 1916.

A SPRINT CHAMPION DIES
IN A MOTORBIKE ACCIDENT

At the start of the 20th century, track racing is hugely popular and the sprint is the queen of the track events. Meetings with riders like Thorvald Ellegaard, Willy Arend, Walter Rütt, Gabriel Poulain, Harie Meijers, Frank Kramer and Henri Mayer attract crowds of several thousand spectators to velodromes across Europe. Then there is Emile Friol, famed for his 'finishing jump' at the end of a race. Or as Georges Matthys describes the French sprinter in his excellent book *Galerij der Wielerkampioenen* (Gallery of Cycling Champions): 'Before Scherens, he was probably the rider with the best finishing burst there has ever been; it was truly like lightning.'

Friol is born in Lyon on 9 March 1881 and grows up in the small town of Tain-l'Hermitage in a wine-growing region of the Rhone valley. The young Emile helps out in the local cycle repair shop but initially has little enthusiasm for the sport. This all changes when he goes to Paris to complete his military service. He attends a number of the spectacular winter races on the capital's covered tracks and can hardly believe his eyes. He is immediately bitten by the cycling bug. After his time in the army, he decides not to return to Tain, but to stay in Paris. He looks for work in the cycling world — after all, repairing cycles is his profession — and eventually finds his way to the Vel' d'Hiv circuit,

Emile Friol, three-time world sprint champion, tries to catch the legendary Major Taylor during the 1908 Grand Prix de la République.

where he becomes friends with the German sprinter, Henry Mayer. Such good friends, in fact, that he soon become Mayer's permanent mechanic.

When he is not working, Friol also tries his hand on the track. It is soon clear that he is a natural talent. Mayer encourages the young Frenchman to turn professional. Less than two years later, in 1904, he wins his first national title in the sprint. Writing in the *L'Echo* newspaper, Géo Lefèvre describes his victory in the following glowing terms: 'The best German, Danish or American sprinter could not have won with more style, with greater suppleness or such remarkable speed.' His words are prophetic. Friol soon fears no-one on the international sprinting scene. Three years later, he is world champion. In the final, he beats... his friend and mentor, Henry Mayer. Friol's list of career victories is truly impressive. He wins two more world championships (1909, 1910), two European championships (1907, 1910) and four national titles (1906, 1907, 1910, 1913). In total, he wins 31 major sprint tournaments. He might even have won much more, but he only rides seldom outside of France.

In 1914, Friol — by then 33 years old — wins the Grand Prix de France and is runner-up in the national championship. But then the war breaks out. Like many former racers, he serves as an officer's orderly, carrying messages from one place to another just behind the front, usually by motorbike. On 16 November 1916, he is riding towards Amiens. Near the village of Dury, he suddenly sees a lorry approaching from the opposite direction. He notices that it is an American make, so there is no need to worry: there won't be any Germans on board! Suddenly, however, the lorry begins to swerve violently across the road. It is impossible for Friol to avoid a crash and he hits the lorry head on. He is killed instantly. It is later discovered that the driver of the lorry was dead behind the wheel. He had been hit by a stray bullet, which explains why he lost control with such dramatic consequences. In the village of Tain-l'Hermitage, Emile Friol lives on through a street that was later named in his memory. The local cycling club also honours him in the same way.

A CYCLIST BECOMES THE HERO OF THE CONGO DEFENCE FORCE

The First World War is not only fought along the IJzer and on the Somme. There is also fighting in darkest Africa. At the end of the 19th century, the Germans acquire a number of colonies there, including German East Africa, an area that roughly covers the modern-day countries of Burundi, Rwanda and Tanzania. However, they also have their greedy eye on the Congo, a colony that provides Belgium with many scarce and valuable natural resources. At more or less the same moment that the Germans cross the Belgian frontier to open the war in Europe, they also sink the *Alexandre Delcommune*, the only Belgian warship on Lake Tanganyika, which forms the border between German East Africa and the Congo. They are convinced that they will win the European war and that this will allow them to seize the French and Belgian colonies as well. But things turn out differently.

In April 1915, the Belgian Minister for the Colonies, Jules Renkin, decides to fight back. He aims at nothing less than the recapture of Burundi and Rwanda. This, however, will take some careful logistical planning. It will require the attack force of some 18,000 soldiers to be provided with food and ammunition, carried exclusively by bearers through harsh and unforgiving bush country. In addition to their permanent complement of 20,000 bearers, they recruit an additional 260,000 men and women for the *Force Publique*, otherwise known as the Congo Defence Force. In total, Belgium will commit a total of 297,833 people, including native bearers, to the fighting in the African continent. This is almost the same number as on the IJzer Front, where it is estimated between 267,000 and 360,000 Belgian soldiers are engaged in the course of the war.

One of the key figures in the Belgian military effort in Africa is Aimé Behaeghe, who in the years before the war was an amateur racer of modest ability. Born in Kachtem on 17 November 1890, he grows up in the (then) West Flanders village of Herzeeuw (now Herseaux), where he turns out to be a bright lad. In the college in nearby Moeskroen he follows the 'modern' syllabus, which in those days is by no means evident for the twelfth child of a poor tailor. University is sadly beyond his reach, and so he starts helping his younger brother, Joseph, to construct bikes. The business does well, and it is possible to see Behaeghe bikes in the Moeskroen region until well after the Second World War.

To promote their brand, Aimé decides to do some racing. He turns out to be quite good (but not outstanding), and puts together a creditable string of results in the classics as an amateur, including an eighth place in Liege-Bastogne-Liege and ninth in Antwerp-Menen. But his most promising success is in the 1909 edition of the Star of Charleroi race, a four-day stage race in and around the city. Behaeghe wins the third stage and is second in the overall standings behind Paul Deman, who four years later will be the first winner of the Tour of Flanders for professionals.

In 1910, the West Fleming confirms his talent for stage racing on the road. In that year's Tour of Belgium over a difficult course he finishes in the top ten in four out of the five stages and ends fifth in the overall standings. But then Aimé decides he has suddenly had enough of cycling. Like his brother, Joseph, he becomes fascinated by the newest and most exciting discoveries of the age: the motor car and the aeroplane. Enthralled by the exploits of men like Louis Blériot and Alberto Santos-Dumont, both Behaeghes now want to become car mechanics and plane builders. They set about realizing their dream and in that same year design their first biplane with a 25 horsepower engine. A year later, it is ready to take to the air — but the first test flights are a failure.

Undeterred, Aimé and Joseph refuse to give up. Neither of them was educated as an engineer, but they have plenty of practical knowledge and, above all, pioneering spirit. They build more planes. In 1912, they even get the chance to demonstrate one of their designs to the Belgian Army at Casteau, but the officers present are not convinced. Perhaps they will have more success abroad? Inspired by stories about the great South American flyer Santos-Dumont and the Frenchman Roland Garros, who both give demonstration flights in Brazil, around New Year 1913 the brothers set off for Rio de Janeiro and take one of their aeroplanes with them. Aviation in this part of the world is still in its infancy, even more so than in Europe. As yet, the Brazilian Army does not yet have a single plane, but there is interest. Aimé demonstrates their model, but once again they fail to win a contract. These self-taught entrepreneurs are finally starting to realize that launching your own plane is much more difficult than launching your own bike. To make matters worse, several countries are now starting to produce planes on an industrial scale. Unless they can find extra financial support, the brothers will be unable to compete. Yet even in failure, what the amateur racer has been able to achieve together with his sibling between his 16th and 24th year is illustrative of huge determination and a deep affinity with all matters technological.

When the Germans invade Belgium, Aimé and Joseph Behaeghe return to Europe and offer their services to the Belgian Army. Aimé becomes a pilot in the air arm 'for the duration of the conflict'. He achieves rapid promotion through the ranks: corporal on 23 November 1914 (after completing his training at the flying school); sergeant on 17 April 1915; first sergeant on 2 May; adjutant on 30 May; and sub-lieutenant on 22 November. Between 15 April and 8 December of that year, he takes off 143 times from the aerodrome at Kerkepanne (opposite the present-day air base in Coxyde) to fly missions over the IJzer Front. His task is initially limited to spotting for the artillery and monitoring the movements of German troops. Even so, he is involved in aerial dogfights no fewer than 17 times.

On 12 December 1915, Aimé Behaeghe is seconded to the Ministry for the Colonies, which soon leads to his transfer to the *Force Publique* in the Belgian Congo. His African adventure can begin! The most important objective of the Congo Defence Force is to reopen the free movement of shipping on Lake Tanganyika. The long and narrow lake in the middle of the map of Africa is more than just a boundary between the Belgian Congo and German East Africa; it is also a 673-kilometre long transport artery in the heart of the continent's otherwise inaccessible central highlands. Whoever controls the lake has control over a huge area around it, including the province of Katanga in the southern part of Congo, a crucial mining area with rich stores of copper, cobalt, iron and diamonds. Understandably, the Germans are anxious to get their hands on this wealth of natural resources.

Since November 1914, German gunboats have dominated the lake. The most powerful and most feared is the *Götzen*, armed with a large cannon in the bow and two machine guns astern. It can transport up to 800 soldiers, so that the Germans can carry out large-scale landings anywhere around the lake. For Belgium, the message is clear: sink the *Götzen*! The best way to do this is by aerial attack while the boat is moored in the harbour at Kigoma. But to date, no aircraft has ever flown in Central

Africa, never mind bombed something. In fact, the British — and many Belgians too — doubt if a plane will even be able to take off in the tropical climate at an altitude of 800 metres, where the air is so thin.

What's more, the target is anchored at a distance of over 100 kilometres from the nearest available air base, much further than any bombing raid flown so far on the IJzer Front. Equally discouraging, the *Götzen* would need to be attacked with slow-flying seaplanes that are only capable of speeds of 100 kilometres per hour and have open cockpits with no windshields. This makes them an easy target for the ship's defensive arsenal of machine guns. Retaliation is out of the question, since the planes carry no armaments and even the bombs have to be dropped over the side of the fuselage by hand. In short, it is almost a suicide mission. There is only one man in all Africa convinced that it can work: Aimé Behaeghe — and he persuades his commanders to let him try.

It is a key turning point in the war in German East Africa — and Behaeghe is its main protagonist. On 14 May 1916, he starts his first long-range flying tests. For everyone watching — both Europeans and local people — it is a remarkable and somewhat frightening spectacle. Most of them have never seen a plane before. The tests are good, but then poor weather delays the mission. However, by 10 June everything is ready. Behaeghe coaxes his plane into the air, with enough petrol for four hours' flying, two 30 kilogram bombs and a bomb-aimer named Collignon, who will throw the projectiles over the side. By some miracle, the mission succeeds. The *Götzen* is hit and put out of action. Behaeghe and Collignon return safely, although their plane is peppered with machine gun bullets.

Aimé Behaeghe's attack on the *Götzen* completely changes the course of the war on and around Lake Tanganyika, tipping the balance firmly in the Allies favour. It breaks the German stranglehold on Katanga and frees the lake for the transport of Allied troops and materials. It is a crucial moment. The Belgian air arm also plays an important role in the capture of Kigoma. Together with a second plane, Behaeghe repeatedly bombs the city on the German shore of the lake between 17 and 23 July 1916. When the *Force Publique* advances to the attack, the badly shaken Germans withdraw and Kigoma falls without a fight. This opens the way for a campaign that in six months' time will overrun Rwanda and Burundi. After that, the Allies turn southwards towards Tabora, the capital of German East Africa. A year later, in

October 1917, working in concert with the British, the Belgian Defence Force pushes on to the harbour town of Kilwa, driving the remnants of the last German units over the border into Mozambique. The battle for Central Africa has been won.

The Belgians have captured a territory five times bigger than their own country. After the war, the Belgian government is happy with its 'reward' of Rwanda and Burundi as Belgian mandates. Germany loses German East Africa, as well as its other colonies in the continent: Cameroon and Namibia. Victory in the campaign is attributed by its commanders in large measure to the success of Aimé Behaeghe's daring raid. He is made a knight in the Order of the African Star, the highest decoration that the *Force Publique* can bestow. King Albert awards him the War Cross with Palm, one of the lowest ranking officers to receive this distinction (usually reserved for generals) throughout the war.

On 1 November 1916, Aimé Behaeghe sends a postcard from Albertville on the western shore of Lake Tanganyika to his brother Joseph, languishing in the trenches on the IJzer Front. The message reads: 'Will be home around mid-January 1917. See you soon.' It is the middle of January before Joseph receives the card, but sadly Aimé never makes it home. He falls ill and dies in a hospital at Niemba in Katanga. The circumstances surrounding his death are shrouded in mystery. Some say he dies of malaria; others of dysentery. His obituary card says he dies on 3 December 1916, but that is also far from certain. What is certain is that he is buried in Niemba and a headstone is erected over his grave. This grave is now lost, but his memory lives on. In 2004, the street in Kachtem (Izegem) where he was born is renamed the Aimé Behaeghestraat. And in 2016, exactly 100 years after his famous raid, the cyclist-pilot is commemorated on a Belgian postage stamp.

Cyclist-pilot Aimé Behaeghe (right) was a key figure in the war against German East Africa.

The Belgian Army finally opts for a one-piece frame. Officers note during exercises that the soldiers can cross rough terrain quicker and more easily on foot if the bike doesn't have to be folded, but can be lifted directly on to their backs.

BAD LUCK FOR AN OLYMPIC CHAMPION

On 2 January 1917, Léon Flameng, a brave pilot in the French air force, is given the honour of testing the latest model of a new biplane. Sadly, the plane breaks into large pieces above the village of Ève. The 39-year-old Flameng, a former Olympic cycling champion, tries to jump to safety, but his parachute fails to open...

Flameng won his Olympic title back in 1896, during the first Games of the modern era held in Athens. The track racing takes place at the newly built 333-metre long Neo Phaliron velodrome. The 19-year-old Parisian takes part in four events and wins three medals: gold in the 100 kilometres, silver in the 10 kilometres and bronze in the 2,000 metres. It is his victory over the longer distance that most captures the public's imagination. The race was watched by 20,000 spectators, including the Greek royal family. Flameng completes the 100 kilometres in 3 hours and 18 minutes. This includes a stop during the race to help repair the bike of his Greek rival, Yeoryios Kolettis. Even so, he still wins the race by 14 laps.

Flameng makes his professional debut two years later. Everyone predicts a great future for him, but he is unable to live up to these expectations. After completing his military service in the 8th Artillery Regiment, he decides to give up cycling and turns instead to writing. But his short stories and novellas are equally unsuccessful. Only one of his books sells well — and that is a plant manual intended for use in agricultural colleges. In the meantime, the ex-rider — like so many of his

contemporaries — becomes fascinated by flying. He follows the necessary training courses and is awarded his license.

During the war, Flameng flies for the 2nd Aviation Group as a pilot on observation missions. On 21 June 1916, his plane is hit in the skies above Verdun. His fellow crew member is killed instantly and Flameng is badly injured in the face. With blood pouring from his wounds, he manages to land his aircraft safely and is rushed to the field hospital at Vadelaincourt. The surgeons operate and against all odds he survives. Remarkably, just three months later he is back flying over the front. He is promoted to sergeant and takes part in air raids on Thionville and Hayange. On New Years' Day 1917, his superiors ask him if he would like to test a new biplane the following morning. He accepts, but what seems like a routine task turns into a tragedy. It is sheer bad luck; a design fault that has nothing to do with the vagaries of war. The Olympic champion is posthumously awarded the Croix de Guerre and is buried in Ermenonville, close to the village of Ève where he crashed. His name is mentioned on a commemorative plaque in the military plot.

The same plaque also mentions the name of another cyclist-pilot: Emile Hervé. Born in 1885, Hervé rides mainly on the track in meetings close to his home town of Tours. He becomes a professional in 1911 and occasionally wins a speed event, but is no match for the real kings of sprinting like Thorvald Ellegaard and Louis Grogna. However, Hervé is a versatile sportsman. He also excels at table tennis and sometimes takes part in motorbike races. At the velodrome in Angers on 17 April 1911, he is second in a one-hour tandem cycle race with Maxime Hardy, before hours later winning two races for *motocyclettes* at the same meeting.

During the early part of the war, Hervé is a driver in the air force, but his ambition is to fly. He follows the necessary training and obtains his pilot's license at the end of 1915. Posted to the 2nd Aviation Group, he achieves two quick promotions to corporal and sergeant. Just weeks after this second promotion, on 21 September 1917, he collides with the plane of his lieutenant, Louis Mathey, in the sky above Lagny-le-Sec. Both men are killed.

Olympic champion Léon Flameng (right), next to his compatriot Paul Masson.

FROM VELODROME TO... FIREWOOD!

The occupation in Belgium begins to weigh more heavily on the population. Freedom of movement is restricted, there are frequent identity checks on the streets, food is scarce, bureaucracy is rampant and requisitioning is commonplace. In 1916, the number of these regulations increases dramatically. Anything of military or economic value is confiscated by the Germans. The seizure of industrial and agricultural goods is bad enough, but even worse for people at a personal level is the introduction of a scheme for compulsory labour. In contravention of the Geneva Convention, the Germans start to force both men and women to work for them behind the front and in Germany — the so-called *Zivilarbeiters* (civilian workers). At the same time, the financial burden on the occupied parts of the country increases. Initially, the Germans demanded a levy of 40 million francs per province per month. At the end of 1916, this is raised to 50 million and at the start of 1917 to 60 million. This requires taxation at a level that is double the rate applicable in Belgium in 1913.

With all these rules and regulations, the occupier has one simple objective: to bleed the country dry. This also has consequences for cycling. While quite a lot of cycling takes place in the summer of 1916, by the end of the year it is becoming ever more difficult to organize meetings. Because the Germans have requisitioned all rubber, the racers have exhausted their supply of tyres. The practice of recent years to smuggle in tyres from the Netherlands has also become too dangerous, as a result of tighter security along the border.

The event organizers are also finding things harder, since the Germans have imposed severe taxes on all public events, including track meetings. These meetings are no longer profitable — in fact, they lose money, even when the races are well attended — and the velodromes are forced to close. Sometimes, they even need to be sold and demolished to pay off debts. Of the 42 velodromes registered with the Belgian Cycling Federation in 1914, only nine are still active by the end of 1916. The Belgian public can expect to see very little cycling in 1917.

It is the wooden velodromes that are most severely affected by this lack of racing. They need more maintenance and quickly fall into disrepair when they don't get it. The wood is then sold... or stolen. One of the first velodromes to disappear is

Aalst. 'Demolition Day' announces a newspaper advertisement in *De Volkstem*: 'At the velodrome in Aalst, from Monday 7 February onwards, each morning from 9 o'clock to midday. Sale of firewood and building materials.' In the same month, the same fate befalls the circuit at Mariakerke, where the first Tour of Flanders had such an exciting finish in 1913. On 16 February 1916, *Het Volk* informs its readers that '...new and old wood, sawn in all shapes and sizes, (...) is available for private purchase every day, except Sundays and public holidays. This includes elm planks and maple planks, in all widths and thicknesses, spars, laths, slats, battens, pivots, seating, flooring and firewood.'

The resulting outcome is reported some weeks later in *Vooruit*: 'Our town had a velodrome that was well known and attracted many people to the Gentsesteenweg throughout the summer. That velodrome is now gone, which must be a great disappointment for all lovers of sport. Be that as it may, the ground has now been levelled by unemployed workers and will be divided up as allotments. The derelict land will be converted by the municipality, so that at least 500 families can be given their own garden free of charge. Good work!'

In Antwerp, the Zurenborg velodrome manages to hang on for longer than most, but in June 1917 the axes finally fall. Even the Karreveld track in Brussels, where (like Zurenborg) the weekly meetings were once watched by thousands of enthusiastic fans, finally falls victim to the demolition team's saws and hammers. The ground is rented by a successful local football team, Daring Club de Bruxelles, the forerunner of the RWDM fusion club, which will later install football pitches, tennis courts and an athletics track on the site (and also become football champions of Belgium in 1975). But this all lies in the future. During that final winter of the war, the wood from the famous track disappeared as smoke up many Brussels chimneys...

Velodroom Mariakerke.

Alle dagen uit ter hand te koopen, uitgezonderd de zon- en feestdagen :
Alle slach van oud en nieuw gezaagd hout, zooals OLMEN PLANKEN en KANADAPLANKEN, op alle dikte en breedte, BATTERS, KEPERS, SCHALIEBERD, PANLATTEN, MEDRIERS, BOOMSPILLEN in olm en kanada; eene partij ZITBANKEN, PLANCHER, BRANDHOUT en eene volledige GARAGE, gansch in hout. Eene partij ZOUT en eene RESSORTKAR van 2000 kilo draagvermogen. Zich te bevragen op het werk.   (1494)

A newspaper advertisement in *Het Volk*, 16 February 1916.

Like in Germany, 'normal' cycle races continue in the neutral Netherlands throughout the war, albeit on a reduced scale. In terms of organizers, numbers of racers, sponsors and a specialized sporting press — in other words, the complete cycling infrastructure — the Dutch still lag a long way behind other countries. But the Hollanders are fast learners, and during the war years they perhaps learn most of all from Belgian refugees and internees who have built cycle tracks at their camps in Harderwijk and Uden, where they organize competitions of an almost professional standard. On 2 October 1916, some 2,500 local people gape in near amazement at the Grand Prix La Belgique, held at the Harderwijk camp. The programme includes both a one-hour race and an 'American-style' relay. To mark the patron saint's day of King Albert on 26 November, the camp authorities even allow the Belgians to organize a road race through the countryside of the neighbouring Veluwe district.

To begin with, Urbain Anseeuw and Jan Somers are the big stars on the 'Belgian track' in Harderwijk, but from 1917 onwards the name of Alfons Spiessens also starts to appear more frequently in the results. This is surprising, to say the least. Not that Spiessens is not a good racer. On the contrary. He was a top-ten rider in the Tour de France in both 1913 and 1914, and in September 1915 won the Six Days of Brussels with René Vandenberghe. But how does a rider from occupied Belgium find a way to take part in races in the Netherlands, when the frontier between the two countries is closed by an electrified fence?

Spiessens and Anseeuw — later a decent professional rider in his own right — help to make cycling popular 'north of the border'. As 1917 progresses, more and more sprint meetings are organized at Harderwijk. On 12 July of that year, there is even a Grand Fête Cycliste, to which all the locals are invited. The response is phenomenal and large crowds thrill to a whole day of racing. Partly as a result, the decision is taken to convert the original — and provisional — track into a proper velodrome. Interned military engineers from the Belgian Army complete the task in just two weeks. The new track is 400 metres long, making it the longest in the Netherlands, and the inaugural event is held on 19 August.

By now, the local population is cycling-mad, not least because a number of their own Dutch riders start competing against the Belgians. Well-known names like Klaas van Nek, the 1916 national road champion, and Cor Blekemolen, a world stayer champion at amateur level, are seen with increasing frequency at Harderwijk and Uden. Above all, it is the budding new talents of Dutch cycling who come to the Belgian tracks, where they hope to learn their trade from their more experienced southern neighbours. Here they can meet and compete with interned Belgian soldiers, who until August 1914 lived and worked as professional

The 'Belgian track' at the internment camp in Harderwijk is of great significance for the development of professional cycling in the Netherlands.

racers. One of these young Dutch hopefuls is Jorinus van der Wiel, who will later become national road champion in 1915, 1917, 1918, 1921 and 1925 (which is still a record for the total number of victories). Frits Wiersma, another three-time road champion, is also a regular visitor to the Harderwijk track and after the war will end fourth in the 1919 Tour of Flanders.

Like most Dutch riders, Piet Moeskops — who becomes national sprint champion for the first time in 1914 — is unable to ride in international competitions and so decides to maintain his competitive fitness in meetings on the tracks at Harderwijk and Uden. He listens to the tips he gets from the Belgian racers and applies them in practice. As a result, he is soon winning a number of races. After the Armistice, he turns professional and is five-time world champion at the sprint between 1921 and 1926. As the historian Nico Oudhof once put it: 'During the war, Belgium gave a great boost to Dutch cycling.'

In fact, it is hard to underestimate the impact of Harderwijk on the sport of bike racing in the Netherlands. Another of the talents it nurtures is Piet van Kempen. As in so many other cases, the First World War puts a break on his ambitions. Travelling abroad to race is out of the question. What's more, he also has to do his own Dutch national service. Fortunately for him, he can arrange to be posted as a motorcycle rider to the barracks in Harderwijk. He is not a natural soldier and only enjoys himself on his free days, when he can cycle on the track in the internment camp. It is there that he learns his love for the sport. The Belgian riders immediately recognize his ability and advise him to come and cycle in their country after the war.

Piet — his official name is Dingeman — cannot wait for the Armistice. On 9 November 1918, he deserts from the Dutch Army and cycles to Belgium. He immediately contacts all the organizers of

race meetings, both great and small, and wherever he rides, he wins. He even takes part in six-day meetings — a discipline with which he is unfamiliar — and in 1920 finishes fifth in the Six Days of Brussels with Léon Vanderstuyft. The Swiss champion Oscar Egg is impressed with the way he rides and tells him that the really big money can be earned in the United States. He takes his advice and at Madison Square Garden in March 1921 the 'European super team' — van Kempen and Egg — wins the Six Days of New York. For van Kempen, it is the first step in a phenomenal career — a career that begins in 1918, when he wins the Dutch championship — ridden *nota bene* on the 'Belgian track' in Harderwijk — for the first time. It is, however, one of the last big events at Harderwijk, since the end of the war is now approaching.

Van Kempen continues to be the most successful six-day racer in the world until well into the 1930s. In Europe he is known as 'the Flying Dutchman'. And because he not only impresses male cycling fans, but also has the allures of a film star, in America he is referred to as 'the Rudolf Valentino of the track'. He wins no fewer than 32 six-day events and heads the all-time world rankings until the early years of the 1940s.

On 16 May 1918, the Dutchman Klaas van Nek and the Belgian Florent Luyckx win the team race in Harderwijk over 50 kilometres.

The talent of Piet van Kempen first becomes evident on the Belgian track in Harderwijk.

For the Belgian racers fighting in the Great War, the world of cycling seems a long way away. Behind the front, racing for them is difficult, if not impossible. When in 1915 the High Command introduces a system of licensed leave, some riders make use of their free days to keep their physical condition more or less in order. From the summer of 1916 onwards, occasional races are also organized in the unoccupied zone, mostly in connection with some kind of military celebration or as part of local fairs to improve public morale, where cycling might share the programme with high jumping, boxing or even sack racing. As the war progresses, some senior army officers encourage more cycle racing. On 27 September 1917, *De Legerbode* — an army newspaper — gives an account of a large-scale sporting event involving, among other things, '... a football match, a jousting competition for the cycling company and a cycle race over 40 kilometres'. Cyclists are fortunate: they are more often given permission by the military authorities to practice their sport — often at some distance from their units — than the practitioners of other sports.

Henri Vanlerberghe is one of the lucky few who is allowed to travel to France to compete. With Jules Masselis, he finishes third in a team event over 100 kilometres in Paris. When the spectators ask him afterwards how he maintains his race fitness in the army, his answer leaves no room for doubt: 'It's easy to keep fit at the front. I'm with the cyclists, and when you are trying to avoid falling shells, you soon learn how to ride fast!' During the spring of 1917, Vanlerberghe is even given the opportunity to travel to London, to take part in the Military Sports Carnival Event, held in and around Stamford Bridge, the home of Chelsea Football Club. The event is organized by the Molinari Athletics Club, but in addition to athletics there is also a cycle race on the programme. The proceeds from the ticket sales will be donated to help Italian prisoners of war and other victims of the conflict. Among others, Vanlerberghe rides against Eugène Degrendele and Emiel Aalman, but the winner of the 5-mile Molinari Cup is Jules Van Hevel from Ichtegem, a gunner in the 1st Artillery Regiment. He is followed over the line by Hills, Berger and Storms.

In January 1918, Vanlerberghe is transferred to the 15th Artillery Regiment. His new commanding officer soon gives him the chance to cross the Channel again, to take part in the 1918 edition of the Molinari Cup. Once again, Van Hevel wins and Hills is second. Just months later, Vanlerberghe is back in London for a third time, but this time as a patient in the King Albert Hospital. The precise reason for his admission to the hospital is not known, but he was probably wounded when his unit was involved in heavy fighting around Merkem on 17 April.

As the end of the war approaches in the autumn of 1918, there is no longer any question of cycling. Every man is needed at the front to at last drive the Germans out of Belgium. On 21 and 22 September, Vanlerberghe and his unit are in positions to the south of Houthulst Forest and take part in the bombardment that precedes the Victory Offensive. Once the wood has been captured, he moves forward with the guns to Staden hill. The Germans continue to retreat and the 15th Artillery Regiment supports the British as they advance towards the rivers Leie and Schelde. When the war ends on 11 November, Henri Vanlerberghe is in the village of Semmerzake.

Henri Vanlerberghe posing in his army uniform.

VAN HEVEL, CYCLIST AND ARTILLERYMAN

Jules Van Hevel, whose superiors allow him twice to travel to Stamford Bridge in 1917 and 1918, and who twice rewards them with victory in the Molinari Cup, is four years younger than Henri Vandenlerghe but universally recognized as a great cycling talent of the future. He has already proved this before the war even starts. In the novices' category, he wins an impressive 42 races and in the spring of 1914 as an independent rider was the best in the Tour of the Coast, the Grand Prix Franco-Belge and Evergem-Ostend-Evergem. These top-class performances do not escape the attention of Karel Van Wijnendaele. This is hardly surprising. Van Hevel grows up in the hamlet of Den Engel near Ichtegem and the journalist takes the name of the castle at Wijnendaele as his pseudonym. The castle is part of the municipality of Torhout, Van Wijnendaele's home town, and the neighbouring municipality is... Ichtegem. In other words, the journalist and the young racer are almost neighbours. In fact, it was largely at Van Wijnendaele's insistence that Van Hevel — who initially works as a stoker on trams in Wallonia — becomes a professional. 'I am not afraid to describe him as a future champion, if he puts his mind to it', writes Van Wijnendaele in 1919, the year in which Van Hevel wins the Championship of Flanders, after an impressive solo of 80 kilometres.

But before he can fulfil his potential, Van Hevel first has another matter to deal with: the First World War. Like for so many others, the conflict delays his further progress for four long years. On 21 July 1914, he triumphs in the Grand Prix Karel Verbist, a road race that finishes on the Zurenborg velodrome, but two weeks later all his cycling ambitions are forgotten. When the Germans invade, his father — a mill builder — is working at Meaux, 40 kilometres east of Paris. In the circumstances, his wife and daughters need him home quickly, but in the chaos of war their letters remain unanswered. Jules, just 19 years old and the only son in the family, decides to cycle the 300 kilometres to France, to search for the pater familias. When he reaches Meaux, he finds that father Alfons has left the day before, hoping to make his way back to West Flanders. But in early September the Germans break through to the River Marne and the route north to Flanders is cut. Alfons eventually

makes his way to the Channel port of Le Havre, but can get no further. Jules is also unable to get back to Ichtegem — which in the meantime has been occupied by the Germans — and is forced to stay in northern France. The family will remain separated for the next four years.

To earn a living, Jules works temporarily in a chicory factory. Three months later, he decides to move on to Calais. There he is picked up by Belgian police and forced to work for the Belgian Army, which has a large camp just outside the city. Because the strategically vital harbour is regularly bombed by Zeppelins at night, Van Hevel and his fellow labourers sleep in damp cellars under the city ramparts. As a result, he falls ill and needs to be treated in a military hospital for several weeks.

In the meantime, a decree passed by the Belgian government in exile on 1 March 1915 requires all Belgian men between the ages of 18 and 25 years, who live behind the line of the River IJzer and are not yet under arms, to report immediately for service with the army. Since he was born in 1895,

Henri Vanlerberghe and Jules Van Hevel travel together as soldiers to London and later to New York, where they ride the Six Days.

this means that Jules Van Hevel will also necessarily become a member of what will be known as the Special Contingent of 1915. On 28 July of that year he is sent for training; first to an infantry camp near the Normandy town of Valognes and later to an artillery school at Eu, in the Seine-Maritime department. On 1 July 1916, the man from Ichtegem is deemed fit for active service and is posted as a cyclist to the 1st Artillery Regiment.

Van Hevel's unit is involved in heavy fighting at the front, mainly in the Noordschote sector (near the Ieperlee Canal) and at Nieuwkapelle (on the River IJzer). At the end of 1916, he is transferred first to the 7th Artillery Regiment and then, the following spring, to the 13th Artillery Regiment. 'He served his unit well, in recognition whereof his superiors gave him the opportunity to compete in three races abroad. These were also opportunities to distinguish himself', writes Arthur Soetens in a brief biographical sketch of the racer after the war. Two of these three races are in the Molinari Cup on the track at Stamford Bridge. And he does indeed distinguish himself, winning on both occasions. He also makes a deep impression on Esther Slabbinck, a young refugee from Ostend who he meets in London and will eventually marry on 15 October 1921. Van Hevel also wins the third of his three races abroad, a 100-kilometre event on 8 September 1918 at Gravelines, not far from Dunkirk. He destroys the rest of the field and arrives at the finish with a lead of six minutes over Henri Stockelynck.

Immediately after his victory, Van Hevel must rejoin his unit, which is preparing for the final offensive of the war. Twenty days later, the Belgian Army, together with the British 2nd Army and a French corps, launch a massive new attack to break through the German lines. In a single day, the entire Ieper Salient is recaptured. On 16 October, the German defences on the IJzer Front also start to give way. The Belgian troops are reinforced by the French 30th Corps and four American divisions. Under the command of King Albert, this combined force sweeps up the Belgian North Sea coast and liberates Bruges. Van Hevel is present when his home town of Ichtegem is also liberated. 'Thank God, like his father, [he came] home safe, sound and in good health from the world's greatest ever disaster, where to his relief he found them all fit, well and in one piece. True, his mother had aged a lot and the youngest sisters grown so much that Jules could hardly recognize them and their brother. Even so, a boundless joy reigned in their reunited family circle.'

THYS NOW STARTS WINNING CLASSICS AS WELL

During the First World War, cycle racing in France comes almost to a standstill. It is only in 1916 that a limited number of track meetings are again organized and in 1917 the French authorities also give the green light for a number of road races to go ahead. Roubaix is in German hands, so that is obviously out of the question. But Paris-Tours is a possibility. On 6 May, three years after the previous edition, a sizeable field sets off in the direction of the city on the Loire. Philip Thys, still serving as a mechanic at the Belgian aviation school in Etampes, is among them. The two-time winner of the Tour de France, now a sergeant, has kept himself in good condition. He dominates the race and wins by some distance. Only 19 riders reach the finish, the last of them almost two hours after Thys.

Following this success, his superiors also give the man from Brussels permission to ride in Italy. On 4 November, the annual Tour of Lombardy race will take place as usual — the only one of the great classic races not affected by the war. With Costante Girardengo, Leopoldo Torricelli, Gaetano Belloni and Henri Pélissier among the starters, it is a strong line-up. But perhaps the most remarkable starter of all is Alfonsina Strada, a 26-year-old woman. She manages to complete the gruelling course, more than 200 kilometres long, but is never a serious contender for victory. The main players in this 13th edition of the race are two Belgians: Charles Juseret and, again, Philippe Thys. Together with the Italians Lucotti and Torricelli and the Frenchman Pélissier, they enter the final stages with a lead of three minutes over the pack. The Tour ends with a tumultuous sprint at the velodrome in Milan. The five riders collide and all slide over the line together in a tangled heap. But the judges decide that Thys is the winner. He has added two classics to his list of victories in just six months' time.

In 1918, the Belgian flying school exchanges the barracks at Etampes for the airfield at Juvisy, not far from the site of the present-day Orly airport. At first, it seems like it is going to be an unlucky sporting year for Thys. On 9 May, he is disqualified as the winner of the Champion of Champions race held over 100 kilometres on the Parc des Princes circuit, supposedly because he had illegally changed bikes. The victory is awarded to the

Frenchman Charles Mantelet. Ten days later, the same Mantelet triumphs in that year's edition of Paris-Tours, in large part because Thys is unable to defend his title: a delayed train means that he doesn't even make the start. His luck finally changes on 9 June, when he wins the reverse race: Tours-Paris. It is, however, a low-calibre field. Following their third offensive in as many months, the Germans have broken through the French lines on the Chemin des Dames and are once again within 70 miles of Paris. The French Army cancels all military leave, so that only 27 riders line up at the start in Tours. But a win is a win: Thys sprints faster than Charles Mantelet and Georges Sérès to crosses the line first at the Parc des Princes.

After the Armistice, Philippe Thys is not able to return home immediately. He first needs to help dismantle the Belgian camp at Juvisy. It is only at the end of January 1919 that he is sent on indefinite leave. In many ways, his was an uneventful war. He will not be awarded any medals or campaign stripes. He never flew and never saw a trench. But none of this bothers the imperturbable Thys: he prefers to win his stripes on his bike, not the battle-field. He certainly gets off to a good post-war start: at the beginning of April 1919, he wins the Six Days

of Brussels, riding with the French sprint champion Marcel Dupuy. Two weeks later, Henri Pélissier is the only rider better than him in Paris-Roubaix. He is not much interested in the 1919 Tour de France. *L'Auto* is not really organizationally prepared for the event, the weather and the roads are atrocious, and there is little money to be earned. However, all this has changed by the time the 1920 edition is ready to start and Thys now looks forward to the race with renewed enthusiasm. He wins four stages and heads the overall standings from the second day onwards. By the time he arrives in Paris, he has a lead of a massive 57 minutes over his fellow coun-tryman Hector Heusghem. In fact, that year the first seven places are all occupied by Belgians.

This victory means that Philippe Thys is the only rider to win cycling's greatest race both before and after the First World War (1913, 1914 and 1920). It could perhaps have been more. As he once said: 'How sad that the world conflagration so disrupted cycling. No Tour de France for four years. And those were four of my best years.' Although he never said as much himself, there are many who think that Thys could have won five or maybe even six Tours — a record that not even Anquetil, Merckx, Hinault and Indurain would have beaten.

The start of Paris-Tours in 1917. The eventual winner — Philippe Thys — is on the right.

NEW ZEALAND CYCLISTS
AND THE GREAT MINE BATTLE OF MESSINES

During the First World War, 98,950 New Zealanders serve overseas in Europe and elsewhere. In total, there are well over 100,000 men in uniform, a remarkable 10% of the country's entire population at that time. The 'Kiwis' fight as part of ANZAC — the Australian and New Zealand Army Corps. Following a boat trip that can take anything up to six weeks, they land in England, before being sent to the battlefields of France and Flanders. They take part in the fighting on the Somme and at Ieper, often suffering heavy losses but also winning great victories. There are also cyclists among their ranks. In contrast to the Australians, who have cycling units in each of their five divisions, the New Zealanders have a single Cyclist Corps.

The ANZACs will play an important role in the Battle of Messines in June 1917. The plan is to blow the Germans off the Messines-Wijtschate Ridge by planting 25 large mines under their positions. In great secrecy, 6,000 British tunnellers and miners begin digging tunnels towards the enemy lines. From April 1917 onwards, the New Zealand cyclists are also involved in the preparations for the battle. The battalion digs some 37 kilometres of trenches, varying in depth from 1.8 to 3 metres, and strong enough to withstand the shock that will be caused by the mine explosions. Much of this work is carried out at night, without light and exposed to enemy fire if they are seen. It is back-breaking and dangerous work, made even more difficult by the appalling nature of the shell-cratered ground. Below the surface, the British tunnels are making good progress. From Hill 60 in the north to Ploegsteert in the south, the mine chambers under the German trenches are packed with high explosive. All is ready for the offensive to begin.

On the day of the battle, the task of the cyclists is to lay a new track, 1,800 metres long, to allow the

Men of the 2nd Australian Tunnelling Company at work near Nieuwpoort, November 1917.

men and horses of the Otago Mounted Rifles to move forward to attack the retreating Germans. The track needs to be laid out in the open and there will probably be some German shellfire to endure. At a quarter past two on the morning before the battle, 13 officers and 291 men of the 2nd ANZAC Corps Cycling Battalion leave their camp at Steenwerck and cycle 13 kilometres north-east, until they reach Hill 63 near Ploegsteert. There is a huge network of tunnels under the hill, constructed by the 1st Australian Tunnelling Company, where the assault units are able to shelter before the attack. As the cyclists approach the front, German gas shells start to fall all around them, so they need to cycle in their gas masks.

At Zero Hour — ten past three in the morning (English time) on 7 June 1917 — 19 of the 25 mines explode as planned. The combined effects of more than 500,000 kilograms of explosive are devastating. Great mushrooms of earth and debris shoot into the air, while the shock waves created by the blast feel like an earthquake. The Germans defenders are quite literally blown 'sky-high'. It is the largest explosion of the war — in fact, the largest man-made explosion of all time, before the nuclear bomb — and could even be felt as far away as London.

The few Germans who survive the initial blast are too stunned to put up much resistance. In most cases they are quickly taken prisoner. An hour after the explosions, the New Zealand Cyclists are already out in no-man's-land to lay the new track through the captured German lines towards Middle Farm, a position just north of Messines village (now Mesen). They fill in shell craters, cut barbed wire, and throw bridges over trenches and ditches. Soon they come under German shelling but they carry on with their task. Four cyclists are killed and 22 wounded. Towards late afternoon, the rough track is complete and the Australian and New Zealand cavalry can advance over the ridge with comparative ease. By the end of the day, the Allies have retaken both Messines and Wijtschate and pushed forward their front line by 7 kilometres — a huge distance by First World War standards. For his role in this success, Major Charles Evans, commander of the New Zealand Cyclists, is awarded the Distinguished Service Order.

Tour winner Octave Lapize's fascination for flying proves fatal.

14 JULY — NO JOUR DE GLOIRE FOR OCTAVE LAPIZE

During the Great War, many sportsmen try to set a good example for their fellow countrymen to follow. Sometimes this means taking part in propaganda campaigns. Sometimes it means volunteering for the armed forces. But the Great Game (as some people initially refer to the war) is anything but a game and the toll on human life is high, even among sportsmen. This is something that Octave Lapize, winner of the 1910 Tour de France, finds to his cost.

Born in Montrouge in the Hauts-de-Seine department on 24 October 1887, Lapize is probably the best of all the pre-war racers. He first makes the headlines as an amateur in 1907, when he triumphs in both the national road and cyclo-cross championships. During the 1908 Olympic Games in London he wins a bronze medal in the 100-kilometre track race. He turns professional in 1909 and is the best in Paris-Roubaix on three consecutive

occasions — a record that will not be broken for many years. In 1911, he is victorious in Paris-Tours, followed in 1912 by the Six Days of Brussels (teamed with René Vandenberghe). He also claims the French national road title and wins Paris-Brussels for three years in a row: 1911, 1912 and 1913. But his biggest success comes in 1910, when he wins four stages and the final classification in that year's Tour de France. It is the first Tour to ride over the Pyrenees and Lapize demonstrates his versatility both on the flat and in the mountains.

Another first that year is the organization of a flying demonstration to coincide with the arrival of the penultimate stage in Caen. In 1910, planes are still a new and fascinating novelty, and as leader in the race Lapize is given the privilege of making a brief flight with Léon Morane, one of the great pioneers of early French aviation. During the flight, Lapize is metaphorically (and almost literally) on cloud nine. He has never experienced anything like it and is immediately bitten by the flying bug. A short time later, Morane sets a new height record and the aviation magazine *La Vie en Grand Air* publishes a photo taken at Caen in which the cyclist and the flyer pose together.

1914 is not such a good season for Octave, who is universally known as *Le Frisé* because of his rich head of curly hair. True, he is second in the Six Days of Brussels and wins the Tour stage from Perpignan to Marseilles, but that is a modest haul by his high standards. Then, suddenly, the world is at war. Lapize is exempt from military service but his huge popularity in France makes it almost impossible to remain on the sidelines in his country's hour of need. A few weeks after the finish of the Tour, he volunteers for the army. *Vive la France!*

He is initially posted to the motor section of the 19th Squadron. Just three days after he takes up this posting, his wife, Juliette, gives birth to a daughter, Yvonne. Fortunately, the barracks are near their home, so that the ex-racer can see mother and child almost every day. Lapize is an exemplary soldier, but after his aerial 'baptism' in Caen he has never given up his dream of one day learning to fly. Pilots like Blériot and Morane: they are the real heroes in the war. And then there is Georges Guynemer. Not only is he France's ace of aces, but after a famous aerial duel with the German Ernst Udet, he acquires an almost legendary status. During their dogfight, the Frenchman sees that Udet's guns have jammed, but gallantly refuses to fire on his defenceless enemy.

The two men salute each other and fly back to their respective bases. However, Guynemer himself has no such luck on 11 September 1917, when his Spad is shot down over the village of Poelkapelle in the Ieper Salient. After the war, a monument is erected in the village to the memory of the great flyer. It is topped by a stork, which is a reference to the nickname of his squadron: *Escadrille de Cicognes*. Tradition has it that in later years Udet and some of his fellow comrades visit the memorial to lay flowers as a mark of respect to their former adversary.

It is stories like this that persuades Octave Lapize to apply for a transfer to the air force in 1916 — or at least in part. There is also another reason. He wants to see his daughter grow up and pilots are given much more leave than soldiers in other units. For his training, the former racer is sent to an aviation school at Avord. By November, he has mastered the art of flying and presses to be posted to the front. First, however, he is sent to the air base at Cazaux to be trained as an air-gunner. Later, he is transferred again, this time to the military school in Pau, where he learns flying in formation and aerial tactics. It is not until February 1917 that he is deemed to be a fully-fledged combat pilot. Now, at last, he is ready for battle. He is first sent to N504 and N203 Squadrons, with their base at Bar-le-Duc, before finally being moved on to N90 Squadron in Toul. These five different bases are in five different French departments: it almost seems as though Octave is doing a new Tour de France, only this time by air.

Lapize, who by now is almost 30 years old, flies under the command of Lieutenant Pierre Weiss. Octave's plane is No.4 and like all the squadron's planes in Toul it is painted with a crowing cockerel emblem. He writes home that he is proud to be serving as a pilot in the great French Army. However, this patriotism is soon to cost him his life. During a routine flight on 14 July — *quatorze juillet*, the French national day! — he is surprised in the skies over Flirey, north-west of Nancy, by a pack of four German Fokkers. Outnumbered and alone, he has no chance and his plane is soon shot down. Badly wounded in the crash, he is rushed to the military hospital in Toul, but dies soon after. In November 1917, his remains are transferred at his family's request for reburial in his home town of Villiers-sur-Marne.

GENERAL REHEARSAL ON THE KOPPENBERG

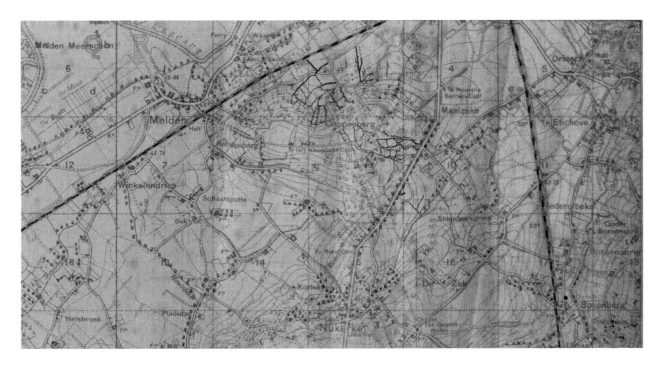

Today, the Koppenberg hill is famous as being one of the toughest climbs in the Tour of Flanders. During the First World War, it is one of the places where German stormtroopers are trained for battle. The stormtroopers are hand-picked men who it is hoped will break through the Allied lines, using new weapons and tactics. Initially, the occupying authorities regard the Koppenberg — like most parts of the *Etappengebiet* — as just another area to be exploited for anything that can be useful to the German war effort. In the Koppenberg's case, this means wood. From August 1915 to the end of January 1916, hundreds of trees are cut down on the *Bult van Melden* (as the hill is also known) to provide wooden reinforcing for their trenches at the front. This woodland actually belongs to the local Commission for Civil Hospices, but they never receive a single franc or mark as payment for the theft of their property.

However, from 1917 onwards the Germans find another use for the Koppenberg. The remaining woods and the surrounding fields become a training ground for *4. Sturmbataljon*. The cream of the German Army — its best officers and men — are brought together to learn and rehearse the revolutionary new infiltration tactics that must change the course of the war. Fighting on the Somme and at

Passendale has shown that broad, large-scale bombardments are no longer effective. From now on, the Germans want to concentrate their artillery on specific targets, so that their fast-moving stormtroops, armed with flamethrowers, hand grenades and light machine guns, can seek out and infiltrate the weak points in the enemy's defences. To employ these tactics each division in the German Army is instructed to raise its own elite storm battalion. These are the troops who will train at the Koppenberg. The ground, like the troops, has also been specially chosen, because it resembles the strategically important ridges where the storm battalions will be employed, such as Polygon Wood in Zonnebeke and the wooded slopes of northern France.

Nowadays, there is little on the Koppenberg to suggest that it was once the setting for such scenes of frenzied military activity. After the war, the woods were replanted and the fields returned to agriculture. It is only on the northern fringes of the hill — towards the Onderbos and the Maria van der Gheynstraat — that it is still possible to find traces of bomb-craters and the zig-zag pattern of practice trenches, although these features, a century later, are now little more than shallow depressions in the peaceful landscape.

An original German map marked with the practice trenches dug at the Koppenberg.

Kemmel. — Drève sur la Montagne.

Another hill that has become famous in modern-day cycling is destined to play an even more important strategic role in the war than the Koppenberg: this is the Kemmelberg, known to the English as Mount Kemmel. When the front to the south of Ieper grinds to a halt in November 1914, the hill that now-adays is crucial for deciding the winner of the an-nual Ghent-Wevelgem bike race becomes crucial for another reason: as a vital observation position for the Allied armies. In this part of the front, running from Sint-Eloi to Ploegsteert, the Germans hold nearly all the high ground, and in particular the formidable Messines-Wijtschate ridge. To counter this, the Allies have to rely exclusively on Mount Kemmel to keep a careful watch on their enemies across no-man's-land. Many of the British units on the hill are stationed on the Lettenburg, a spur jutting out from the western flank of the Kemmel-berg, where a complex of underground bunkers from the war years can still be visited today.

With the exception of Wijtschate, the villages of the Flemish hill country — Heuvelland — remain in British hands for most of the war. This changes, however, when the Germans launch their great Spring Offensive in 1918. On 9 April, they break through the Allied front line. A week later, they capture Dranouter and Kemmel and push on to the foot of the famous hill. On 25 April, the hill itself is captured. Fighting continues until the end of June and tens of thousands of troops on both sides are

killed. In the so-called Battle of Mount Kemmel alone the French lose more than 5,000 men. One of the soldiers on the German side later describes his experiences during this battle is his book *Der Tod am Kemmel* (Death in Kemmel). This phase is now part of the modern Belgian cycling vocabulary, used to describe a rider who cracks during the double ascent of the Kemmelberg in Ghent-Wevelgem.

It is not until 5 September that the Allies, with the help of American troops, are able to retake Mount Kemmel. At the foot of the slope where today's racers climb the steepest side of the hill (a gradient of 23%!), there is a military cemetery and ossuary containing the remains of 5,294 officers and other ranks of the French Army. At the top of the slope, there is a 17-metre high monument to the memory of French 32nd Division, which fought here in 1918. Crowned by a statue of the goddess of victory, with her wings spread wide, the monument is known locally as *Den Engel*: The Angel.

It is not just the cemeteries and memorials along the modern-day Ghent-Wevelgem course that remind us of the First World War. Between 1947 and 1960, the finish for the spring classic was situated on the local airfield. This was first con-structed by the Germans in 1916 at the insistence of the famous German ace Manfred von Richthofen, better known as the Red Baron. With his red-painted Albatros D.III biplane and his Fokker Dr.1 triplane he shoots down no fewer than 80 enemy planes, a 'score' unequalled by any other aviator during the war.

Von Richthofen wants a base closer to the Ieper Salient and the High Command is willing to listen. They chose a location on the boundary between Bissegem and Wevelgem, close to the River Leie and the Kortrijk-Menen railway. *Zivielarbeiter* are con-scripted from the surrounding villages to level the site, construct its buildings and lay a second railway line. By July 1917, the new base is ready for use, just in time to play a role in the Third Battle of Ieper, more commonly known as Passchendaele. The first operational unit to serve there is *Jagdstaffel 6*, with a total of 18 planes. After the war, the airfield becomes a training base for the Belgian air force. From 1947 onwards, its 2-kilometre long runway is used as the finishing straight for Ghent-Wevelgem. The first rider to triumph here is Maurice Desimpelaere,

A peaceful scene in pre-war Kemmel, a place where thousands will die in 1918.

A RECORD-BREAKING ATTEMPT

One of the very few cycling races to be organized in Flanders in 1917 — and an extraordinary one, at that — is held on Sunday, 1 July at the Arsenal circuit in Gentbrugge, one of the last velodromes still operating. If the *Vooruit* newspaper can be believed, it is '...one of the hardest and fastest races ever ridden'. The reason for this is that the race '...is an attempt to break the local record for the distance of 80 kilometres. A wager of 500 francs that they can better the record has been accepted by the top favourites Leon Buysse and César Debaets. Colonial Rubber has also promised a bonus of 100 francs to any team that breaks the record.' The warm-up programme for this main event includes an Australian race in teams and an elimination race for novices. In addition to the challengers Buysse-Debaets, the other professional teams include Van de Velde-Maertens, De Muynck-Cocquyt, Mathys-Josse, Vermeersch-Goetgebuer, Van Renterghem-Bauwens and Van Hecke-Devrieze. 'The team that crosses the finishing line in first place most times wins the race. This means that whoever sacrifices their own chances of victory for the record and thereby makes the race a memorable one, has as much chance to be well rewarded as the record breakers. It also means that teams have a chance of winning without sprinting.'

followed in later years by Valeer Ollivier, Marcel Kint, André Rosseel, Rolf Graf, Noël Foré and Léon Vandaele. Three of the great names of Belgian cycling — Raymond Impanis, Rik Van Looy and the legendary Briek Schotte — even manage to win twice on 'the German airstrip'. To amuse the crowd while they wait for the arrival of the big race, a number of criterium races, sprints and derny competitions are organized, which also regularly attract big names in these disciplines, like Jef ('Poeske') Scherens, Arie van Vliet, Rik Van Steenbergen, Theo Middelkamp, Wim van Est, Gerrit Schulte and Hugo Koblet.

At the insistence of Manfred von Richthofen, the Red Baron, the Germans build an airfield at Wevelgem.

An announcement in Vooruit on 30 June 1917

UNKNOWN HEROES OF CYCLING, GREAT HEROES OF THE WAR

Before the First World War, Alfons Landuyt, born on 4 April 1893 in Niel, is one of the most promising young riders in Belgian cycling. He rides mainly on the circuit nearby Boom, but in 1913 he also wins in Aartselaar as an independent. Landuyt is called up to serve at the front as a Private Second Class in the 17th Line Regiment. For his courageous behaviour in the trenches he is awarded the War Cross on 16 June 1916. During one of his brief periods of leave, on 7 July 1916 he marries his sweetheart Elisa Trooster in the church at Pollinkhove, just behind the lines. A year later, on 5 August 1917, he is wounded by a German shell in Oudekapelle as he is driving back to his unit on his motorbike. He is evacuated to the field hospital at Hoogstade, but later dies of his injuries, on the same day that his baby daughter Germaine is born. The ex-racer now lies buried in the military cemetery at Oeren.

The amateur cyclist Gustaaf Van Uytvanck grows up in Kieldrecht and in 1916 volunteers to serve in the Belgian Army. As a Private Second Class, the 24-year-old is posted to the 12th Artillery Regiment. On 15 October 1917, at Sint-Jacobs-kapelle in the IJzer Front, he is hit by an aerial torpedo and dies of his wounds. He is buried by his comrades two days later in Hoogstade.

During the final year of the war, three other Belgian cyclists are fated to meet their end. On 1 June 1918, it is the turn of Frans De Vogelaere. On the same day that he hears of his promotion to sergeant, he is hit in the head by a shell splinter at Kaaskerke, close to the notorious 'Trench of Death', and dies instantly. De Vogelaere is a member of a famous racing family from Bachte-Maria-Leerne. His older brothers Guido and Abel are both professionals, with the latter winning the Championship of Flanders at Koolskamp in 1912. Even so, the experts think that 'little' Frans has more talent than both of them. When he cruises to victory in the Championship of Flanders for novices at Aalst in June 1914, *Sportwereld* describes him as '... a second Cyriel Van Hauwaert'. A bright sporting future awaits him but two months later this future is put on ice. War has broken out and Frans De Vogelaere is called up to serve with the 8th Company of the 2nd Line Regiment. A German shell at Kaaskerke ensures that this future will never be realized. Like Alfons Landuyt, Frans is buried in the military plot

at Oeren. His name is also listed on the war memorial in Bachte-Maria-Leerne.

The second cycling victim of 1918 is Jean De Blauwe, who dies on the IJzer Front at Diksmuide on 29 September that year. Born in Mechelen on 30 September 1889 and a professional racer since 1909, he rides mainly on the velodrome in Leuven. However, he also races on the road and in 1912 is a creditable fourth in the Autumn Prize. His final competition before the war is Brussels-Anseremme on 19 July 1914. Just days later, he is mobilized as a Private Second Class in the 5th Line Regiment. Although originally buried in Diksmuide, his remains are transferred to the civil cemetery in Sint-Jans-Molenbeek on 23 March 1922.

The last Belgian racer to die in the war is probably Jules Van Eysendyck, less than a month before the Armistice. A native of Borgerhout and a member of the Royal Antwerp Bicycle Club, he turns professional in 1914 and rides mostly on the track. While serving as a Private Second Class in the 16th Artillery Regiment, he is seriously wounded on 8 October 1918. He dies of his injuries four days later at the military hospital in the French town of Guemps. The remains of the 30-year-old Van Eysendyck are later brought back to Borgerhout for burial in the civil cemetery.

Amateur cyclist Gustaaf Van Uytvanck is killed on the IJzer on 15 October 1917.

THOMAS GASCOYNE, A NAME ON THE MENIN GATE

The Menin Gate in Ieper is engraved with the names of 54,896 officers and other ranks of the British Empire who died during the First World War but have no known grave. One of them — whose name is listed on panel 93 — is Thomas Gascoyne, who was a successful track racer between 1893 and 1911.

Born in Whittington on 17 August 1876, Gascoyne grows up in the Derbyshire town of Chesterfield. He begins cycling in his spare time when he is 17 years old. Not that he has much spare time. He is employed as a stoker on the railways, a hard and unhealthy profession. Not that it seems to affect him. Three years later, he breaks the world 25-mile record. He completes the distance (roughly 40 kilometres) on a cinder track in 57 minutes and 18 seconds, which is 1 minute and 53 seconds faster than the previous record holder, the Belgian Hubert Schaeffer.

Gascoyne is both a sprinter and a pursuit rider. In 1900, he travels to Paris for the UVF (*l'Union Vélocipédique de France* or French Cycling Union) Grand Prix, a renowned sprint competition that has been organized since 1894 and attracts the big names of the day, like August Zimmerman and Georges Banker. Gascoyne progresses comfortably through the heats and in the final comes up against the Frenchman Léon Domain, who beats him in a close race. Undismayed, he continues his quest for new records. In 1901, riding with Sidney Jenkins, the British record holder for 2 miles (2 minutes and 5 seconds), he sets a new best time of 25 seconds for the quarter mile with flying start at the track in Crystal Palace.

Later that same year, he sets sail from Southampton with his tandem partner Jenkins on the SS *Kaiserin Maria Theresa*, bound for New York. Such is his renown that the *New York Times* reports his arrival on 5 June 1901. The newspaper also comments on his unique riding style: 'Grimly determined, with his head bent forward over his front

British rider Thomas Gascoyne is reported as missing in action during the Battle of Passendale.

wheel and a high pedal rotation, he leaves his rivals trailing hopelessly in his wake.' The British pair takes part in several tandem races in the famous Madison Square Garden, before moving on to Boston. There, on 20 July, Gascoyne twice manages to beat the 'Flying Negro' Major Taylor, the world sprint champion of 1899. The very next day he races again, this time on the velodrome at Vailsburg in Newark, where he wins the half mile against John Bedell. Just minutes later, and with little time for recuperation, he is back on the start line to take part in an Australian pursuit event. After three miles he is caught by William Fenn. It is Gascoyne's first ever defeat in a pursuit race.

After the turn of the 20th century, British track racing goes into something of a decline. As a result, it does not allow Gascoyne to earn the money he was hoping to gain from his sport. Disillusioned, he decides to leave Europe to find a better life in Australia. With his wife Linda, he initially settles in Newcastle, New South Wales, before later moving to Preston, a suburb of Melbourne. Gascoyne takes all different kinds of jobs to make ends meet, but also carries on racing, quickly making a name for himself on the local tracks. He starts to focus more on six-day events, often partnered by Alan Lloyd. He becomes a popular racer, especially in Sydney after he wins the famous Five Mile Scratch Race there in 1907. He also rides his last race in Sydney, in December 1911. The 35-year-old Gascoyne ends 11th with Lloyd in the Six Days.

When the First World War starts three years later, Australia rushes to the aid of the British motherland. Throughout the war, some 416,000 Australians from a total population of just 4.7 million serve in the armed forces as volunteers. Some 60,000 of them are killed, 45,000 on the Western Front. In February 1916, Thomas Gascoyne also enlists in the army. After a period of training at Broadmeadows, Victoria, he is posted to the 20th Battalion and sent to Europe. His first experience of the war's brutality is on the Somme. In a desperate attempt to capture the ridge at Pozières, the Australians suffer 23,000 casualties in just six weeks — more than in the entire eight-month Gallipoli campaign. The Australian historian Charles Bean will later comment: 'Pozières ridge is more densely sown with Australian sacrifice than any other place on earth.'

Gascoyne is one of the lucky few who survive this bloodbath. But things do not get much better for him and his Australian comrades. In April and May 1917, they take part in another disastrous attack, this time at Bullecourt, near Arras. The four Australian divisions involved lose another 10,000 men, in large part as a result of serious errors made by the British High Command. This creates bad blood between the two nations for the rest of the war.

The heavy losses make a degree of reorganization necessary in the Australian Imperial Force. Gascoyne is transferred from the 20th to the 21st Battalion and is also promoted to corporal. But the worst is yet to come: the Australians are now sent to the dreaded Ieper Salient. The British commander-in-chief, Douglas Haig, hopes to bring the Germans to their knees by a massive new offensive over a wide front. This offensive — the Third Battle of Ieper — starts on 31 July 1917. In pouring rain, the British attack towards Pilkem, Polygon Wood and Passendale. By the next day, it is clear that the hoped-for breakthrough will not be achieved. Even so, Haig insists on pressing forward with renewed attacks in the most appalling conditions, irrespective of the mounting toll of dead, wounded and missing. In total, the 100-day campaign results in British losses amounting to 400,000 men, and this for a territorial gain of just a few kilometres. In later years, the name of Passchendaele (Passendale) — the village where the offensive finally grinds to a bloody halt — becomes synonymous with the futility and brutality of war at its very worst.

The Australians are inevitably involved in this massacre. Between 4 and 9 October, they attack the ridges beyond Zonnebeke, where Tyne Cot Cemetery now stands. The torrential rain makes the ground almost impassable but the attack is not called off. The result is a predictable shambles. The men are cut down in droves the moment they leave their positions, adding new corpses to the thousands who already lay there. Wounded soldiers sink into the thick mud and are drowned, never to be seen again. It is in this hell on earth that Thomas Gascoyne also disappears. The exact details of what happens to him are not known and his body is never found. All that now remains of him is a name, engraved on the walls of the Menin Gate Memorial, inaugurated in 1927 to commemorate the countless thousands of missing soldiers of the British Empire who fell somewhere in the Ieper Salient.

New Zealand cyclists on the road to Passendale. For many of them, it would be the road to their deaths.

THE ROAD TO PASSCHENDAELE

On the 's Gravenstafelstaat in the West Flemish village of Passendale stands Passchendaele New British Cemetery. It contains the graves of 1,026 British, 292 Australian, 654 Canadian, 126 New Zealand and 3 South African soldiers of the First World War. Only 501 of these 2,101 graves — less than a quarter — are identified. One of them is Matthew Herbert Austin, an amateur cyclist from Australia.

Born in Clifton, a coastal town between Sydney and Wollongong in New South Wales, Austin works in the mines at Kurri Kurri from an early age. In his spare time, he likes to cycle. He rides mainly on the track and scores victories at various amateur meetings. In 1914, he marries Elizabeth Roberts. On 15 December 1915, the couple's first son, Donald Hugh, is born. Just 15 days later, Matthew reports as a volunteer at the barracks in nearby Newcastle and enlists in the 35th Battalion of the Australian infantry. On 1 May 1916, he sets off from Sydney in the troop ship HMAT *Benalia*, bound for Europe. After a two-month voyage, he completes his training at Lark Hill camp in England.

Together with his mates in the 35th Battalion, he finally reaches the front on 21 November 1916. He fights first in France but later also takes part in the great mine battle at Messines on 7 June 1917, where he is wounded. After some weeks in a field hospital, he is found to be 'fit for service' and is sent back to his unit. By now, the Third Battle of Ieper — better known as Passendale or Passchendaele — is raging with full fury. Austin is told to report to Line 64 — and he knows exactly what this means. Line 64 is the pre-war railway line between Ieper and Roeselare. Today, it has been transformed into a pleasant cycle path, but in the autumn of 1917 it is a highway to hell for thousands of British, Australian and Canadian troops. This is the 'road to Passchendaele', taking them to the heart of the battlefield from where many would never return.

It also turns out to be a one-way journey for the ex-track racer from Clifton. His battalion suffers heavy losses during the Passendale offensive and Austin is one of those reported missing on 12 October 1917. It is only after the war that his body is found and a certificate is issued confirming his death. His son, Donald Hugh, follows in his father's footsteps and becomes a successful amateur racer in the 1930s. It takes until 1975 before he makes the long trip to Flanders fields and can finally stand in front of the headstone in Passchendaele New British Cemetery, which reads: '707 Private M.H. Austin, 35th Bn. Australian Inf., 12 October 1917, Age 24'.

FROM TASMAN BAY TO HELL ON EARTH

Bike racing 'down under': the start of the Timaru to Christchurch race on 2 September 1905.

The date of 12 October 1917 is engraved in black letters in the national consciousness of the people of New Zealand. It is the bloodiest date in their history, the date on which the most New Zealanders ever die in a single day. That day, on the other side of the world from their homes, the New Zealand Division is preparing to take part in an attack on the Bellevue spur, one of the pieces of high ground in front of the village of Passendale. But the attack is a costly and bloody failure. Very bloody. For a gain of just 400 metres of mud, the New Zealanders lose 2,700 men in just four hours. Eight hundred and forty-six die the same day; many others later succumb to their injuries in field hospitals behind the lines. Since then, the name 'Passendale' has become synonymous with 'hell on earth' for the Kiwi nation. It sums up everything that was most terrible about the First World War.

One of those killed is a cyclist: James Leslie — 'Les' — Green. The 26-year-old second lieutenant grows up on a sheep farm in Pokororo, not far from Tasman Bay in the northern part of New Zealand's South Island. In the nearby towns of Richmond and Nelson he comes into contact with a new sport: bike racing. There are regular races to watch and Les is soon bitten by the cycling bug. He wants to have a go himself and it soon becomes clear he has some talent. Like all the other young riders in his region, his dream is to win the season-long competition sponsored by the Dunlop Pneumatic Tyre Company. This involves a series of races over a number of months, in which the riders can win points. The rider with the most points at the end of the season is the overall winner. But the real bonus is that this winner is then allowed to ride in the Timaru to Christchurch race, the most important event organized each year by the New Zealand League of Wheelmen. A good performance here often opens the door to the lucrative Australian circuit.

In July 1914, Green wins the race from Nelson to Belgrove and back again, securing his place in that year's Timaru-Christchurch. But he never gets to ride it. Instead, he enlists with the 12th (Nelson & Marlborough) Infantry Regiment. On 16 October 1914, he is one of the first group of volunteers to leave Wellington for Europe on the troopship *Athenic*. Les takes part in the Gallipoli campaign, where he is seriously wounded. He is evacuated to Taplow, not far from London, where the Canadian Red Cross has set up a hospital on the estate of the wealthy Astor family. It takes a year before he is ready to resume duty, following which he is sent as an instructor to Sling Camp in Bulford (a military base north of Salisbury, which still exists today). Here he trains wounded soldiers from the 4th New Zealand Brigade, trying to get them fit for a return to the front.

At Bulford, Green quickly reveals his excellent leadership qualities. He is promoted first to sergeant, and then to sergeant-major. He is given the opportunity to go back to New Zealand, but decides instead to go back to the front in France, where he is given the officer rank of second lieutenant. In the summer of 1917, the New Zealand Division moves north to Flanders to take part in the great British offensive in the Ieper Salient. Instead of the victory they were no doubt hoping for, the young man from Tasman Bay and his comrades soon find themselves in the 'hell on earth' that is the Bellevue spur on 12 October 1917. James Leslie Green is one of the victims of that terrible day and his name is now commemorated on the semi-circular memorial to the missing in Tyne Cot Cemetery in Passendale. He is similarly honoured on war memorials in Motueka and Ngatimoti in his native country.

AND WHAT ABOUT THE BELGIAN MILITARY CYCLISTS?

While all this carnage is taking place in the Ieper Salient, the Belgian Carabineer Cyclists continue to be active on the IJzer Front. At the end of October 1917, they distinguish themselves by taking part in a French attack in the flooded fields around the village of Merkem, during which the Luigem 'peninsula' is recaptured: the first piece of Belgian territory to be regained by Belgian troops from the invader. In January 1918, the High Command carries out yet another re-organization. With further offensive action in mind, each Belgian division now receives a 'light brigade'. From now on, the cyclists can rely on the support of two squadrons of cavalry and a motorized detachment of three armoured cars.

Two months later, the 2nd Cyclist Battalion is sent into action at the Reigersvliet in Oud-Stuivekenskerke, where, together with the 5th Lancers, they beat off a German attack. The two cycling battalions also play an important role in the final offensive of the war, when they fully justify their reputation for speed and determination in pursuit of the retreating Germans. On 16 October 1918, they knock out a German machine gun position near the town of Lichtervelde and take its survivors prisoner. Next day, they push on to Torhout and by the same evening reach the outskirts of Bruges. Another day later, they liberate Knesselare. In Maldegem, they take part in a fire-fight along the Schipdonk Canal. With the wind in their sails and courage in their hearts, they race at top speed through the liberated countryside, finally fulfilling the role for which they were created before the war. On 3 November, the 2nd Battalion drives the enemy out of Wippelgem. By the time the Armistice is signed on 11 November, they have pushed as far forward as Eeklo.

The Carabineer Cyclists or 'Black Devils' are still remembered at Onze-Lieve-Vrouw-Hoekje (Our Lady's Corner) in Oud-Stuivekenskerke. Since 1928, a stone pillar at the site bears the inscription *Aux morts des 1er et 2e Bons de Carabiniers Cyclistes* (To the dead of the 1st and 2nd Bns. of the Carabineer Cyclists). Beneath the text there is a carved emblem that epitomizes their fighting spirit: a devil riding on a wheel, with a trident in his hand...

Lucien Petit-Breton wins the Tour de France in 1907 and 1908.

LUCIEN PETIT-BRETON: A STUPID ACCIDENT

Lucien Mazan — born on 18 October 1882 in Plessé — is only eight years old when he emigrates with his family to Argentina. His father makes a living in the capital city, Buenos Aires, as a goldsmith and watchmaker. He hopes that his son will follow him into the family business but Lucien has other ideas. He wins a bike by chance in a lottery and soon loves nothing more than practicing sprints on the local track. By the time he is 16, he wants to become a professional. His father is appalled. He has no time for 'common cyclists' and forbids his son to visit the local velodrome. Undeterred, Lucien decides to apply for a professional license under a pseudonym. He first thinks of calling himself 'Lucien Breton', in honour of the part of France where he was born. But there is already a rider with this name and so he later adds a 'Petit' to reflect his own short stature. And so he becomes Lucien Petit-Breton. Under this

name, he wins the Argentine national title on the track just months later.

In 1902, Louis 'Petit-Breton' Mazan returns to France to complete his national service in the army. He is soon demonstrating the same cycling talent he showed in Argentina. He immediately claims second place in that year's prestigious 24-hour Bol d'Or race, an event he will go on to win in 1904. It is the start of a highly successful cycling career. On 24 August 1905, he even breaks the world hour record on the Buffalo velodrome in Paris. His new distance is 41.110 kilometres, comfortably beating the American Willie Hamilton's 40.781 kilometres, set seven years before in Denver.

The French 'Argentine' wins races in all disciplines. He now also rides on the road and is an impressive fifth in his very first Tour de France in 1905. The following year he wins Paris-Tours, but his greatest triumphs are still to come. In 1907, he is the best in Milan-Sanremo. In 1908, he outclasses the field in both Paris-Brussels and the Tour of Belgium. However, he reaches new heights of success when he wins the Tour de France in two successive years. His 1907 victory has a touch of fortune, since he actually finishes the race behind Emile Georget, who is later disqualified. But in 1908 his dominance is complete. He wins five stages outright, as well as recording three seconds, four thirds, a fourth and a tenth place in the other stages.

Tour organizer Henri Desgrange is full of praise for France's new cycling hero: 'There is much more to Petit-Breton than hard pedalling and an ability to take pain. He is a rider who embodies all the different qualities you need to win the Tour. He has limitless energy and determination, but always remains calm whatever the circumstances and never panics.' The double Tour winner is, indeed, a rider ahead of his time. He is one of the few who investigates the course in advance. And with his white cap, sky-blue jersey and carefully trimmed moustache, he always looks the model of a professional cycler. What's more, he is a material freak: in hotels, he sleeps with his freshly polished bike alongside his bed. All these things make Petit-Breton extremely popular with the public, as does his habit of announcing in advance where he plans to attack. This inevitably draws the fans in their thousands to the locations he indicates.

Even during his career, Lucien begins writing articles for the newspapers and his book *How I ride* is also well received. Perhaps he is already thinking about the future, because after 1908 his career gradually moves into decline. True, he still wins a stage in the 1911 Giro and is third in the 1912 edition of Paris-Tours, but this is modest in the extreme for a rider of his calibre. In 1914, he starts in the Tour but pulls out during the stage to Nice on 14 July, when he learns that his mother has died.

During the war, Lucien Petit-Breton serves with the 11th Army Corps. He fights at the front and is wounded on more than one occasion. Sadly, he does not live to see the Armistice. However, his death is not caused by a German bullet or shell, but by a stupid traffic accident more than 20 kilometres behind the lines. By now, the ex-Tour winner is acting as an orderly, driving senior officer or taking messages from place to place. It is this role as a courier that finds him in the vicinity of Troyes on the late afternoon of 20 December 1917. Suddenly, in the twilight he sees a horse and cart approaching on the wrong side of the road. He sounds his horn and instinctively pulls away to the left. Unfortunately, the horse is panicked by the noise and shies away to the right. A frontal collision is unavoidable.

The 35-year-old racer is thrown violently against the steering wheel and dashboard of his vehicle. Passers-by rush to his aid and pull him from the wreck. He doesn't have a mark on his body, but the crash has killed him instantly.

Tour winner Lucien Petit-Breton dies as a courier in a road accident behind the front.

GHENT-WEVELGEM HONOURS THE NEW ZEALAND CYCLIST CORPS

Following their involvement in the great mine battle at Messines on 7 June 1917, the New Zealand cyclists are sent north to take part in the Third Battle of Ieper and the assault on Passendale. On 12 October, they are close behind the front opposite 's Gravenstafel and the Bellevue spur, waiting to run out new telephone cables behind the advancing New Zealand infantry. But the attack is a disaster. The division is repulsed with heavy losses and is pulled out of the line for rest and reorganization on 17 October. Most of the winter of 1917-1918 is spent in the sector around Polygon Wood. When the five Australian divisions are amalgamated into an independent Australian Corps in January 1918, the New Zealand Division becomes part of the British XXII Corps. On 12 February, Sergeant W.H. Thomas and Corporal Foulds are rewarded for their bravery in the face of the enemy with the award of the Belgian War Cross. In April, the cyclists are involved in the defence of the strategically important Mount Kemmel and also fight at Vierstraat, a hamlet near Wijtschate. Nineteen cyclists are killed in action that spring, nine of them with no known grave.

Later in the year, the cyclists put up stout resistance against German attacks on the River Leie and in July/August provide support for a new Allied offensive during the Second Battle of the Marne. Throughout the course of the war, the New Zealanders send a total of 708 cyclists to serve at the front. This is more than the Australians and their losses are greater as a result. Sixty-three soldiers of the New Zealand Cyclist Corps lose their lives, with a further 259 wounded. The Australian cyclists suffer 27 fatalities, 37 gas cases and 55 wounded.

To honour the sacrifices made by the New Zealand Cyclist Corps during the Great War, in 2017 — exactly 100 years after the mine battle — the organizers of Ghent-Wevelgem decide to create a new trophy. Because of the special significance of Mount Kemmel, both for today's modern cyclists and for the New Zealand cyclists during the war, a cobble from the road leading up to the summit of the hill is removed during a ceremony attended by the daughter of one of the New Zealanders who fought there. This cobblestone is then mounted on a piece of wood removed from the First World War bunker that still exists under Zonnebeke church and the resulting trophy is handed over to the New Zealand racers Sam Bewley (of the Orica-Scott team) and Jack Bauer (of the Quick Step team), with the intention that they should take it back to their native country, where it will be awarded each year to the winner of the national Under-23 championships — the same age category as most of the men who fought and died between 1914 and 1918. In this way, the memory of the New Zealand Cyclist Corps will be kept alive among a younger generation of cyclists.

Some members of the No.1 New Zealand Cyclist Company. The commanding officer, Major Charles Hellier Evans, is seated in the middle of the front row.

One of the seven New Zealand cyclists who die in defence of Mount Kemmel in April 1918 is Private Albert William Hunter. His is a remarkable story. Not simply because he is a well-known racer in his day, but because before he joins the New Zealand Cyclist Corps he spends 12 years... serving on a submarine! Hunter comes from Christchurch, the largest city on New Zealand's South Island. After he completes his education at the West High School, he travels to the United Kingdom and enlists in the British Royal Navy. He is posted to serve in the submarines, which requires a special kind of mentality: not everyone can adjust to the cramped and claustrophobic atmosphere of a life under water. Perhaps this explains why, when war breaks out, Hunter returns to his native country and volunteers for the Cyclist Corps: the contrast between cycling along the open road and being trapped within the steel hull of a submarine could hardly be greater.

In 1917, Hunter is part of the Cyclist Battalion attached to the New Zealand Division which storms the Messines-Wijtschate ridge during the great mine battle. However, the Germans refuse to accept that their loss of the ridge is permanent and start making plans for its recapture. The excellent observation it offers over Ploegsteert and Armentieres in the south and the villages of Nieuwkerke and Kemmel in the west is too strategically important to be given up without a fight.

This fight starts again in earnest when the Germans launch their Spring Offensive — the *Kaiserschlacht* — in the early months of 1918. Both sides know that this will be the year of decision on the Western Front. By launching unrestricted submarine warfare in an attempt to break the crippling British naval blockade, the Germans have brought America into the war on the Allied side. However, it will be many months before the Americans can make their presence felt in Europe. In

Private Albert William Hunter, one of the 840 names on the Messines Ridge Memorial to the Missing.

contrast, the withdrawal of Russia from the war following the Bolshevik Revolution means that the Germans now have a million men on the former Eastern Front who are instantly available for use in the west. Their choice of strategy is therefore a simple one: they must use these men to beat the British and French before the Americans can arrive. And one of the units trying to prevent them will be the New Zealand Cyclist Corps.

The first thrust of the offensive falls in France on the sector between Arras and St. Quentin, but on 9 April the fighting moves north to the hills and ridges of Flanders. Armentieres and Messines are threatened, as are the villages of Ploegsteert and Hollebeke. Several New Zealand units, including the cyclists, are attached to a British brigade and rushed forward to try and plug the holes in the defence. One of these holes is at Mount Kemmel and it is there that Albert Hunter and his comrades lie in wait for the advancing Germans. The battle is fierce, but the New Zealanders resistance is stubborn. The Germans are held, but part of the price for this victory is the life of the former submariner from Christchurch, who is killed just ten days after his 38th birthday.

Albert is buried in a field grave, but this is lost in subsequent fighting around the hill, which lasts until 29 April. But his sacrifice and the sacrifice of thousands like him is not in vain. The *Kaiserschlacht* fails and Germany's last chance to win the war has gone. Denied any hope of victory, discipline and the will to fight slowly breaks down in the Germany Army. It is the beginning of the end, although it will take until 11 November before that end is reached. But the Armistice comes too late for Albert Hunter. Together with 839 of his fellow New Zealanders, he is commemorated by name on the New Zealand Memorial to the Missing in Messines Ridge British Cemetery.

A NEW ZEALAND RACER ON THE SOMME

Even though he is a professional cyclist, John — 'Jack' — Arnst does not serve with the Cyclist Corps during the war. Instead, he fights with the infantry as a member of the Canterbury Regiment. Born on 3 February 1882, he grows up at Tai Tapu near Christchurch. His brothers Richard, Herman and Bill are also cyclists, both on track and road. Jack makes his professional debut in 1902 and finishes third in the Timaru to Christchurch race, one place ahead of Richard. In 1903, the brothers travel across the Tasman Sea to take part in a number of races in Australia. Jack wins the Melbourne to Warrnambool Classic, a race over 266 kilometres that doubles as the national 'long distance' championship. The brothers return again to Australia during the following two seasons and Jack once more scores a number of good top-ten results, including in the Goulburn to Sydney race.

On 14 April 1909, Jack sets a new best time for the ride between Christchurch and Dunedin. He covers the distance of 240 kilometres over rough gravel paths and across streams and rivers in a time of 12 hours and 31 minutes. However, the record is not officially accepted, because his team forgets to notify observers from the League of Wheelmen.

As a private in the Canterbury Regiment, he soon finds himself serving at the front in France and Flanders. He comes through several fights but his luck finally runs out on 25 August 1918, when he is killed on the Somme during the Second Battle of Bapaume. He is buried in the British military cemetery at Grévillers, but is also commemorated on three memorials in New Zealand at Takapau (Hawkes Bay), Spotswood (North Canterbury) and the Honours Board at Ladbrooks Community Hall.

Jack Arnst crossing the line first in a 2-mile scratch race somewhere 'down under'.

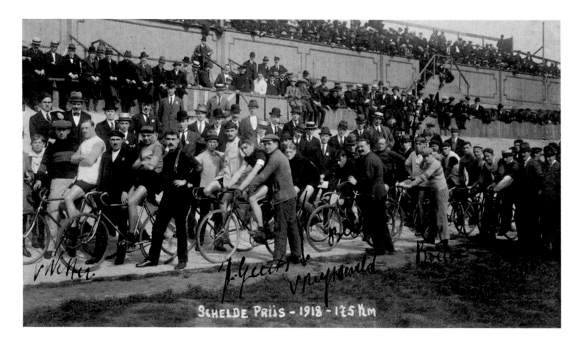

29 September 1918: the start of the Schelde Prize on the
Garden City velodrome in the Elsdonk district of Wilrijk.

On Sunday, 29 September 1918, the day after the
Allies launch the final offensive that will win the
war, the Schelde Prize — one of Belgium's classic
cycle races — is ridden 'as normal'. Well, perhaps not
exactly as normal. Like the Tour of Flanders in
Ghent and the Tour of Belgium in Brussels earlier in
the war, this is an 'ersatz' version of the race, which
is fabricated on the track of the Garden City velodrome on the Sterrenlaan in Wilrijk. The newspaper
Het Vlaamsche Nieuws describes it as a competition
over '... 175 kilometres without the help of assistants
between the following riders: De Graeve, Aerts
(winner of Brussels-Spa, the 500 kilometre race, the
Brussels Grand Prix, the Brussels Championship,
seventh in Paris-Roubaix), Geers, Van Ruyssevelt,
Van Wetter (double winner of the Schelde Prize in
1912 and 1913 and also of various other races), Block,
Tyck, Bouw, Maes, Tubbax, Van Hyneghem, Van den
Bosch, Roeckaert. Opening: 11 o'clock by the tower
clock. Start: 12 o'clock by the tower clock.' That
Sunday, none of the many spectators will yet be
aware of the heavy fighting that is taking place in
West Flanders, nor that the Germans are falling back
with heavy losses. All they know is that Block wins
the race ahead of Bouw. It is announced at the end
of the day that they will both be back at the velodrome next Sunday for a new meeting, almost as

though nothing of significance is happening 100
kilometres further westward in the Ieper Salient and
among the shattered trees of Houthulst Forest.

The 1918 edition is not the first Schelde Prize
of the wartime years. A similar surrogate race is
organized in 1916, held on Sunday, 14 May at the
Hemiksem velodrome. It is a team race over
100 kilometres and the *Geïllustreerde Zondagsgazet*
lists the starters as including '...De Graeve-Tyck,
J. Machiels-Beths, Scampaert-Van Heyneghem, De
Belder-Van Camp, Verberckt-Maes'. No results are
published in the following day's press, so it is not
certain that the race takes place. The last Schelde
Prize before the war — ridden 'as normal' on the
road — is exclusively for independent riders and
takes place on Sunday, 19 July 1914, just two weeks
before the German invasion. This is already the
eighth edition of the race, which was first contested in 1907 at the initiative of Alfred Martougin,
a local chocolate manufacturer and chairman of the
Antwerp Section of the Belgian Cycling Federation.
Victory in 1914 goes to Jacques Octave. Like so
many others, however, the racer from Sint-
Genesius-Rode will not live to see the end of the
war. He dies on 19 July 1918 as a prisoner of the
Germans in Sint-Gillis, although the reason for his
imprisonment is not known.

PARENT SURVIVES VERDUN, BUT NOT THE SPANISH FLU

The Frenchman George Parent has only been a professional for two years when he wins the world championship for stayers in Copenhagen. This victory should normally guarantee him lucrative contracts on the German tracks where this kind of racing is so popular. But in contrast to other French riders like Louis Darragon, Henri Contenet, Jules Miquel and Paul Guignard, Parent is not welcome. Born on 15 September 1885 at Tresserve in Savoy, he has the reputation of being a difficult character. Apparently, the track organizers feel their meetings are better off without him, and even when he wins the French national championship three times running between 1908 and 1910 the lucrative international contracts continue to elude him. As a result, one of the best stayers of his generation has to content himself with riding at local meetings in France, Belgium and Luxembourg. To make ends meet, he also works as a waiter in a coffee bar.

On 19 July 1914, Parent is second in the national championships at the Parc des Princes in Paris. Sixteen days later, his country is at war. The former racer now becomes an infantryman and in 1916 he takes part in the Battle of Verdun. This is one of the worst battles of the entire war. The fighting continues uninterrupted for ten months from February to December and results in a combined total of 700,000 dead, wounded and missing for both sides. Verdun becomes for the French what Passchendaele will be for the British: a symbol of the horror and futility of war. Georges Parent is mentioned in dispatches four times and is awarded several decorations for bravery. He meets his end on 22 October 1918, just three weeks before the Armistice. He does not fall victim to the Germans, but to the epidemic of Spanish flu that is sweeping through Europe. Aged just 33, he succumbs to his illness at a military hospital in Saint-Germain-en-Laye, just east of Paris.

Stayer Georges Parent, here seen in 1906, dies just three weeks before the Armistice.

PAUL DEMAN: SAVED AT THE ELEVENTH HOUR

As the war draws to a close in 1918, Paul Deman is still working as a wartime spy. He has ridden 14 times through the *Etappengebiet* to deliver messages for the resistance movement to their contacts in the Netherlands and so far he has always been able to avoid the German checkpoints and patrols. But at the end of September 1918, things go wrong. He is picked up by the Germans and searched. The real nature of his 'business' soon becomes clear to them.

Espionage carries the severest penalty: death by firing squad. While he is waiting in prison for his 'show trial' (the verdict is a foregone conclusion) and for the date of his execution, he is interrogated to find out what he knows. This 'interrogation' is often brutal. He is kicked and beaten each day to try and force him to reveal the names of other people in his network, but he never says a word. He has no intention of betraying his comrades. He wins time by inventing stories that it will take the Germans a long time to check. And that is what saves his life. Just weeks after his arrest, the Allies finally break through the German lines. For him, the Armistice comes just in time. He is almost literally 'saved at the eleventh hour' — the time when the ceasefire comes into effect and all hostilities end. He is liberated from his cell in Leuven prison by the Americans and allowed to return to his home village of Outrijve, where his wife — and his bike — are waiting for him.

Four years of war, four years of deprivation and four years of no training mean that the post-war peloton is very different from what it was in 1914. Hundreds of cyclists, including Tour winners Lucien Petit-Breton, Octave Lapize and François Faber, have been killed at the front. Good riders like René Anno and René Vandenberghe, but also champions like Cyrille Van Hauwaert and Louis Trousselier, have survived the conflict but are broken both mentally and physically. Initially, Paul Deman also finds it difficult to pick up the threads of his career. He only recovers slowly from his imprisonment and by now is also 30 years of age — not young for a cyclist. He misses the 1919 edition of the Tour of Flanders, but a few months later starts in the Tour of the Three Twinned Cities. It is not a success.

Little by little, he manages to regain his competition rhythm. He decides to take part in the 1920 edition of Paris-Roubaix, ridden on 4 April. His expectations are low: the field includes top riders like French champion Henri Pélissier, Italian champion Costante Girardengo, Gaetano Belloni (winner of that year's Milan-Sanremo) and Jules Van Hevel (winner of that year's Tour of Flanders).

This 21st Paris-Roubaix takes place over 'roads' that have been devastated by the war. Belloni is quickly forced to retire with technical problems. In Lens, Girardengo's bike is also damaged beyond repair and Van Hevel likewise drops out. Four riders are still in contention in the final stages, but Pélissier gets a flat tyre and Honoré Barthélémy and Lucien Buysse are having problems with their chains. Almost without realizing it, Paul Deman finds himself with a lead. He doesn't think twice but puts his head down and pedals for all he is worth. He enters the velodrome in Roubaix alone and wins the race by a huge margin: a fine reward for his courage and determination, six years after his last classic win in Bordeaux-Paris. Since the war, he has been awarded medals from the British Intelligence Service, the French government and the Societé Royale des Sauvateurs de Belgique, but one suspects that this victory means more to him than all his medals put together.

In 1923, Paul Deman also wins Paris-Tours but that is his last major triumph. He dies on 31 July 1961 and is buried in Outrijve. His headstone not only reads 'former cycling champion' but also 'spy during the 14-18 war'.

11 November 1918 comes just in time for Paul Deman.

PART III
RACING
ON EMPTY

After 11 November 1918

AFTER 1,568 DAYS OF WAR, THE GUNS FINALLY FALL SILENT

The final offensive of the war — the so-called Liberation Offensive — begins on 28 September 1918. The Allies attack along the full length of the Western Front. It is now or never. In West Flanders, Belgian infantry divisions recapture Langemark, Poelkapelle, Passendale, Zonnebeke and Broodseinde. British divisions push forward as far as Beselare and Geluveld. In a second phase at the start of October, the offensive makes progress in the direction of the Komen Canal, Wervik and the River Leie. Along the coast, a thrust is made towards Bruges, which is liberated on 17 October. The Germans offer fierce resistance along the Leie and the Schipdonk Canal, but the Allied momentum cannot be halted. By 11 November, they have advanced to the line Terneuzen-Ghent-Bergen-Mézières-Sedan. The Germans have had enough and sue for peace. At five o'clock in the morning, in a train wagon at Rethondes in the Forest of Compiègne, the act of capitulation is signed by a German delegation and Field Marshal Foch, supreme commander of the Allied armies.

Because it takes time to notify the units at the front on both sides, the ceasefire is scheduled to take effect at 11 o'clock. During those last six hours, men continue to fight and die. But once the clock strikes 11, the guns finally fall silent. After 1,568 days of brutal conflict, a strange peace descends over the Western Front. But at what a price! Four years of madness have cost an estimated nine and a half million human lives. The casualties are mostly soldiers, young men aged between 16 and 30 years old. The German and Russian Empires — which have ceased to exist — both lose roughly 1.7 million people; the Austro-Hungarian Empire — which has likewise ceased to exist — 1.2 million; and the British Empire 900,000. France has also suffered grievously, with more than 1.3 million fatalities, equivalent to one out of every six soldiers who served. In Belgium, 41,000 soldiers and 25,000 civilians lose their lives — or these at least are the best estimates, since no precise figures were kept. The same applies for the millions who were forced to flee their homes as refugees or were wounded and often maimed for life.

In addition to this sorry human toll, the war also has huge political, economic and social consequences. Trade and industry are in a state of complete dislocation. Countries like Italy and Great Britain are now burdened with a huge weight of debt. The political map of Europe and colonial Africa is radically redrawn. The Communists now rule in Russia, Austria-Hungary has been split up into smaller states and in Germany the Kaiser has been replaced by the Weimar Republic.

Like every other sector of society, the cycling community is also badly hit by the Great War. Some riders never return from the battlefield. Once again, there are no precise figures but it seems likely that at least 375 and possibly as many as 400 cyclists and ex-cyclists died between 1914 and 1918. As already mentioned, this includes some famous names: Tour winners Lucien Petit-Breton, Octave Lapize and François Faber; Giro winner Carlo Oriani; triple stayer world champion Georges Parent; and Léon Flameng, winner of the 100-kilometre Olympic title. Many lesser cycling gods are also killed at the front or die of other causes. Perhaps inevitably, it is France, the home of modern cycle racing, which suffers most: at least 222 of its cyclists, from great professionals to modest amateurs, do not live to see the Armistice.

Four years of madness finally come to an end.

THE BICYCLE, 'A SYMBOL OF FREEDOM RESTORED'

To prevent their valuable possessions from being plundered or requisitioned by the German occupiers, most Belgian families have hiding places where they can keep these things safe throughout the war. During the final offensive, many homes in the occupied zone are damaged by shelling — sometimes with unfortunate consequences for these hiding places. 'It was painful but also comical to see how among the ruins, from behind shell-blasted walls and bits of plastering, in the cavities between blown-in ceilings and roofs now open to the sky, strands of wool hang everywhere and copper items of all kinds roll around the attics that were once their secret sanctuaries', writes Stijn Streuvels, not without a touch of irony, in his *Herinneringen uit het Verleden* (Memories of the Past).

One of the many things hidden in this manner are bicycles and it is not long after the Armistice before they make their welcome reappearance on Belgian streets and roads. 'Thousands of them, as if by magic!' Streuvels asks himself how it was possible to hide so many without the Germans finding them. Where did people put them? 'These bikes were kept safe throughout the entire occupation and because we hadn't seen them for such a long time, they now seemed something of a novelty. The bicycle was once again our means to travel quickly and freely across our roads and fields. It was symbol of freedom restored, a sign that the violence and misery of war had subsided.'

The war is over and people can once again cycle wherever they like!

ABRAHAM HANS, CYCLING WAR REPORTER

Stijn Streuvels is not the only writer who likes cycling and is interested to learn more about the events of the war taking place around him. Abraham Hans shares both these same passions. In contrast to Streuvels, however, who lives in occupied Belgium, this Flemish writer and journalist, who also has a Dutch family background, spends the war is his second — and conveniently neutral — homeland. From the border towns of Sluis and later Vlissingen, he files regular reports for the Amsterdam newspaper *De Telegraaf* about events at the IJzer Front and the situation elsewhere in Belgium. He also sets up a service to help prisoners of war in Germany, works with Anna De Vos and her 'wartime godmothers' scheme (*Het Werk der Vlaamsche Oorlogsmaters*), and writes theatre plays for performance in the refugee camps.

Even before the Armistice, but after the liberation of Bruges on 17 October 1918, he crosses the frontier and cycles through West Flanders. The things he sees form the subject for a series of articles in *De Telegraaf* and in *Het Laatste Nieuws*. 'I rode by bike from Bruges to Ghent. There were Belgian soldiers in every village (...) I had several letters from soldiers with me for their families. In spite of the lateness of the hour, I wanted to deliver them before finding a bed for the night. I first called at the house of a lonely old man, who lived by himself on the quayside. He had had no news of his son for four years. And now I arrived out of the blue with a letter. The father naturally wanted to read the letter, but tears blinded his eyes and trickled down his cheeks on to the fragile paper. The news seemed too good to be true...'

After 11 November, Hans cycles further into the province, eventually reaching the Westhoek, where the worst of the fighting has taken place. He is shocked by what he sees. So too are many of the people who read his series of articles in *Het Laatste Nieuws*. He describes the Westhoek as *'de verwoeste gewesten'* (the devastated areas) and writes that a campaign should be started to help speed up the region's recovery.

There is a fine fictionalized account of Hans' travels through West Flanders in the excellent book *De Sluiswachter van de IJzer* (The Lock-keeper of the IJzer) by Benedict Wydooghe. He describes how the journalist, cycling towards Nieuwpoort, sees the landscape gradually change from green pastures to a muddy wasteland. He reaches a place that his map tells him should be Mannekensvere, but there is nothing to be seen. The village has disappeared. Sint-Joris is also nothing more than a pile of rubble. Hans asks for directions from the few people he finds standing next to their ruined homes. He eventually arrives in Nieuwpoort, but the town is deserted. Everything has been levelled to the ground. It is even difficult to see where the roads once were. Nevertheless, he decides to press on. 'His bike becomes difficult to control. The wheels keep getting stuck in the clay. He tries to keep the damned thing moving, however slowly, but has to give up when confronted with barbed wire and a muddy ditch, into which he almost falls headfirst. Hans knocks the clay from his gaiters and surveys the scene. There is no other option: the bike will have to go on his shoulders. He steps forward, slips, starts again, and finally he manages to scramble across the ditch.'

Abraham Hans does indeed succeed in reaching Nieuwpoort — or what little is left of it. He takes photographs and records the testimonies of the few people he meets. In the course of his travels, he becomes fascinated by the figure of Karel Cogge, the man who helped to flood the IJzer valley in 1914. Later, he reworks all this information into a series of historical books and novels: *Roeselare in den Oorlog* (1919), *Het bloedig IJzerland* (1920), *De dood in Vlaanderen* (1921), *De Groote Oorlog* (1921), *Gabrielle Petit, onze nationale heldin* (1921), *Een Vlaamse jongen in oorlogstijd* (1921) and *Het Woud van Houthulst of de Duitsers in Vlaanderen* (1923). As these titles suggest, Hans is a prolific writer. In his lifetime he publishes 170 popular novels and in 1922 he starts writing children's books. These are the so-called *Hansjes* and he eventually pens an astonishing 745 of them, which are equally as successful as the legendary *Vlaamse Filmpjes* series (which still exists today). The seventh of his *Hansjes* is entitled *De overstroming van de IJzer* (The flooding of the IJzer) and tells the story of Karel Cogge.

FAREWELL TO THE DAYS OF FAT CONTRACTS!

The young but already popular sport of cycling does not come out of the war unscathed. Many of its most talented racers lie buried in the cemeteries that dot the Western Front. Others have been maimed for life. Those who survived have not been able to train for the past four years. Some have also suffered from malnutrition and are now only a shadow of their former physical selves. Those who were taken prisoner still carry the scars, mental and otherwise, of the beatings and the hard labour to which they were subjected. After this long and difficult period of inactivity, it is by no means easy to resume a physically demanding sport like cycling. There are also organizational and technical problems that need to be overcome. Good bikes are in short supply. Most of the available models date from before the war and are barely rideable, certainly for competition purposes. Rubber tyres are even harder to find, having all been seized by the Germans during the occupation. Worst of all, most of the velodromes have disappeared, forced out of business by the restrictions on cycling during the war years. The few tracks that are still open are nearly all in a poor state of repair... Bearing in mind all these things, it is a miracle that there is any cycling in Belgium in 1919. Even so, the first events are soon organized and the sport recovers at a rate that no-one imagined possible. The track owners and event organizers know that after four years of misery, people want a return to happier times and to the popular pastimes of the pre-war era.

But from the point of view of the riders, the days when it was possible to earn not only fame but also fortune with your bike are gone for good. The big-money contracts for riding at the German circuits are a thing of the past, and many riders who rode there before the war and often deposited their winnings in German bank accounts have lost everything. Even when racing resumes in France and Belgium, the number of races is much fewer than in the past. And if the outlook is far from bright for the riders, it is even gloomier for the bike manufacturers who sponsor the sport. Companies like Alcyon, Automoto, La Française and Peugeot have not only suffered serious loss through wartime damage to their factories and machines, but are also struggling to replace both their riders and their skilled workforce, most of whom are now dead on the field of battle. What's

more, the damage caused by the war to the economy in general means that people are struggling to make ends meet. In these circumstances, buying a bike — the reason why the manufacturers sponsor the sport — is not everyone's highest priority.

As a result of these factors, none of the bike manufacturers, who were all so successful before the war, now has the resources to sponsor a cycling team of their own. The only solution is to form a cartel. The idea is that the riders still under contract will no longer promote specific brands, but will promote the bike in general under the name 'La Sportive'. Some manufacturers still persist with the 'own team' idea, but more than half the manufacturers back the La Sportive initiative. This includes the three biggest brands — Alcyon, Automoto and Peugeot — as well as smaller firms like Hurtu, Labor and Liberators. The companies discuss with each other how much they are willing and able to invest in the sport and, with this in mind, also agree to keep the salaries of the riders artificially low. From now on, a new contract means no more than a new bike, a jersey and perhaps a small allowance to cover travel expenses to and from meetings. However, as soon as the economy in general and bike production in particular start to pick up, cracks soon appear in the cartel's solidarity. Peugeot is the first of the 'big three' to relaunch its

own team, although it also continues to provide riders for La Sportive. This ambivalent situation persists until the 1921 Tour de France, won by the Belgian Léon Scieur, but after that the cartel breaks up and La Sportive ceases to exit.

Obviously, the riders are not happy with this situation, but there is not a great deal they can do about it. To make matters worse, it is not only the manufacturers who turn off the money tap. The race organizers do much the same thing and for much the same reasons: they are short of cash. Whereas the winner of the Tour in 1914 took home a princely 26,000 francs, in 1919 this is reduced to 6,000 francs — and devalued francs at that! It is inevitable that at some point the riders will protest. They are expected to ride as far and as fast as ever, but for a fraction of the money they once earned. In 1919, Philippe Thys withdraws from the Tour halfway through as a protest against the low prize money. The Buysse brothers decide to accept new contracts in Italy, which has suffered less from the war and where good money can still be earned. Léon rides for Legnano-Pirelli and Marcel for Bianchi. Following their example, Henri Pélissier also bids farewell to La Sportive and accepts a much better offer from Bianchi. The landscape of European cycling has changed forever.

Alcyon takes part in the 'La Sportive' initiative, a consortium of bike manufacturers and cycling sponsors.

THE LAST RACER TO DIE...

INTERRUPTED, BUT NOT ENDED

Georges Tribouillard is also one of the racers who takes part in the last pre-war Tour de France in 1914. Even though he is relatively old at the age of 31 and has been a professional for six seasons, it is his first ride in *La Grande Boucle*. He is actually more of a specialist in the classic one-day races and has achieved third place finishes in Paris-Roubaix (1911), the Tour of Lombardy (also 1911) and Paris-Tours (1913). In contrast, stage races have never been his forte and in the 1914 Tour he pulls out after just two days.

He shows more determination during the war, where he serves as a corporal in the 21st Colonial Infantry Regiment, but is badly injured in a flying accident in 1918. He has the doubtful distinction of being the last cyclist to die as a result of his participation in *La Grande Guerre,* succumbing to his injuries on 16 March 1919 in Paris, a full four months after the Armistice was signed.

The first official cycle race to be organized in Belgium in 1919 is the Mechelen Grand Prix, held on 16 March. It goes without saying that a mere 125 days after the Armistice the country has not yet recovered from the ravages of four years of war. The Germans took everything of value during their occupation, so that the Belgian state, although free once more, is now on the verge of bankruptcy. The refugees returning from the Netherlands, France and the United Kingdom find a nation in chaos. There is an acute shortage of almost everything, especially food, clothing and coal. In an attempt to correct the situation, taxes are eight times higher than they were before the war.

To distract people's attention from all this misery, the local authorities in many towns and cities decide to organize popular entertainments. In the present circumstances, however, these entertainments need to be cheap and cheerful. And so they spend their limited funds on the local football club, the local brass band, the local theatre group and, of course, on local cycling — one of the most popular of all entertainments before 1914. Mechelen is the first municipality to give this a try, organizing a race of 80 kilometres through and around the city. It is still not easy for potential competitors to travel. True, the German restrictions have been lifted, but before they left they blew up many bridges and stretches of railway line, so that the train service is still neither complete nor punctual. Even so, an impressive 61 riders line up at the start. 'Once they were ten kilometres outside the city, Van Hevel and Roelens broke away from the pack. No-one could follow. As the race progressed, they increased their lead. Following a burst tyre and a broken wheel, Roelens dropped out of contention. But his lack of support did not prevent Van Hevel from building his lead to an impressive ten minutes, winning from Tyck, Destombes, Claessens, De Jonghe, De Loo, Laureyssens, Verbeuwen, Van Heughten, Frans Spiessens, etc.' The winner has just returned from 30 months service at the front and is still officially part of the military garrison at Ghent. He will not be demobilized until 14 October 1919, although his officers give him plenty of free time to train in the interim.

A successful rider in the 'independent' category before the war, Jules Van Hevel is now at last able to pursue his cycling career at the age of 24. 'The war

Georges Tribouillard dies in the spring of 1919 as a result of wounds he incurs at the front.

interrupted his glittering career, but has not ended it', says Constant Cleiren, writing about the talented rider from West Flanders in the newly resurrected *Sportwereld*. His journalistic colleague Karel Van Wijnendaele is equally impressed. He encourages the rider — who lives in Van Wijnendaele's neighbouring village — to turn professional as quickly as possible. Van Hevel doesn't need telling twice. A week later, he has his professional license and joins the line-up for that year's Tour of Flanders. He is no match for Henri Vanlerberghe, who wins the race with a massive 14-minute advantage, but Van Hevel is involved in the sprint for second place on the velodrome in Gentbrugge and is only pipped to the line by the speedy Leon Buysse. Even so, it is an impressive debut.

A year later, he does even better. The fourth road edition of the Tour of Flanders takes place over 248 kilometres on 21 March 1920. The decisive moment of the race occurs almost literally in front of Van Hevel's own front door, in his home village of Ichtegem. 'A fierce battle was fought on a small hill in Ichtegem. Berten De Jonghe broke away, followed by Fons Van Hecke, with Jules Van Hevel close behind. The three leaders worked well together and kept the chasing pack at a distance, no matter how hard they tried to close the gap.' There is a long way to go, through Kortrijk, Ronse, Ninove and Aalst, but the trio still has a lead of 11 minutes when they enter the velodrome in Ghent. Van Hevel is the best sprinter of the three and wins comfortably. 'Flanders' finest' is a race that suits him. He is second in 1921, fourth in 1923, and fifth in 1924.

Van Hevel also wins the Belgian national championship on the road in two successive years, in 1920 and 1921, on both occasions in La Hulpe. He similarly achieves back-to-back wins in the prestigious Aces Trophy, ridden on the circuit at Longchamps near Paris. 'Van Hevel's victory was fully merited, to the point of being indisputable,' comments a Paris newspaper on his second triumph in 1924. 'It does great credit to this formidable athlete, for whom the limits of average men do not apply.' For good measure, he also wins Paris-Roubaix in the same year, beating Maurice Ville, Félix Sellier, Nicolas Frantz and Henri Pélissier.

On the track, he also makes a name for himself as one of the so-called 'Flandriens', a group of

Flemish hard riders from the stable of manager Mac Bolle (alias Karel Van Wijnendaele). He is often teamed with Henri Vanlerberghe, who lives not far from Van Hevel in Lichtervelde. Van Wijnendaele takes this pairing, together with Dossche-Vandevelde and Debaets-Persijn, to the Six Days of New York in 1920. On this occasion, they don't win, but Van Hevel later wins both the Six Days of Brussels (1923) and the Six Days of Ghent (1925) in a new partnership with César Debaets. Track racing undergoes something of a renaissance in the 1920s and the man from Ichtegem keeps on turning out fast laps — and earning good money — until well past his 40th birthday. Of 391 victories in his long and successful career, 312 are won on the track.

Jules Van Hevel lives to the ripe old age of 74. He dies of a heart attack in the Sacred Heart Hospital in Ostend on 21 July 1969. The news hardly makes the press. The passing of one of Flanders' best ever cyclists is overshadowed by an event of much greater historic importance: man's first landing on the moon. 'One small step for a man, a giant leap for mankind...' And if the moon landing dominates the front pages of the newspapers, the back pages are dominated by Eddy Merckx, who the day before wins his first Tour de France. *Sic transit gloria mundi.*

As a neo-professional, Jules Van Hevel (right) finishes third in his first Tour of Flanders.

'YOU MIGHT AS WELL ALL GO HOME NOW!'

As soon as the Armistice is signed, Léon Van den Haute is keen to pick up where he left off with the Tour of Flanders. He immediately starts with preparations for a 1919 edition. It will be the fifth in total, but only the third raced on the road. This goes against the advice of his partner, Karel Van Wijnendaele. He lives close to the front region in West Flanders and knows how hard the province has been hit by the ravages of war. Fifty-nine towns and villages have been wiped off the map. Thirty-two others have been badly damaged. The roads are also in a terrible condition and, perhaps most problematic of all, there are almost no good bikes available: the materials to make new ones are unaffordable. Organizing a major cycling race in these circumstances seems like folly, according to Van Wijnendaele.

But Léon Van den Haute is nothing if not persistent. He ignores his partner's advice and presses on with his planning. As a result, on Sunday, 23 March 1919 47 riders line up in Ghent for the start of their 203-kilometre long trek through the Flemish countryside. Wisely, the route avoids the regions around Ieper and Diksmuide, but leads via Bruges and Roeselare directly to Kortrijk, before returning via Ronse and Aalst to Gentbrugge. For the first time, the riders have to tackle the steep slope of the Kwaremont, which is warm work on this glorious spring day.

One of the riders in this year's race is Henri Vanlerberghe, who was second in the 1914 edition. He has almost literally come straight from the front to take part. Four months after the Armistice, he has not yet been demobilized and is still officially a soldier. It will not be until 26 September 1919 that the army finally releases him. As a result of his time in the war, he is the holder of four 'front' stripes (one for each year), the Active Service Medal (awarded to those who came under enemy fire), the Victory Medal and the 14-18 Remembrance Medal. But the distinctions that 'Riet'n' really wants to win are those he can win on his bike. As a serving soldier, he needs the goodwill of his superiors to be able to carry on training. Fortunately, they are sympathetic, so that when Vanlerberghe arrives in Ghent for the start he is once again ready to 'ride 'em all dead!'

The man from Lichtervelde is a no-nonsense racer. He is the prototype of the 'Flandrien', the kind of rider who is not interested in the tactical niceties of racing, but simply wants to destroy the field through his own pure strength. On the atrocious cobbles of the rising road between Vichte and Ingooigem, he makes one of his typically impulsive decisions. Even though the wind is against him and there are still 120 kilometres to go, he attacks. 'With powerful thrusts of his pedals', he manages to break away from the pack. Between Ninove and Hekelgem, he finds the road blocked by a broken-down train at a level crossing. No problem for Henri. With his bike on his shoulder, he opens the carriage door on one side, works his way through the astonished passengers, and jumps out of the door on the other side, before cycling on his way as though nothing has happened. He reaches the finish in Gentbrugge with a lead of 14 minutes, a record victory that will never be beaten. Leon Buysse later wins the sprint for second place.

His winning margin might have been even bigger. According to cycling folklore, before Vanlerberghe entered the velodrome in Gentbrugge, he threw his bike against the wall of a nearby tavern, went inside for a beer, and only then rode on to the track to claim his first (and last) Tour of Flanders victory. Is it true? Probably not. But it was the kind of thing a man like Henri might have done and people were more than willing to believe it. And so the legend was born. What we do know for certain is that after crossing the line he celebrates his victory with a lap of honour, waving to the crowd and shouting: 'You might as well all go home now! I'm half a day ahead of the rest!' The crowd are delighted, but so is Henri Vanlerberghe. At last, he has won the race that in Flanders guarantees you everlasting cycling fame and glory. He has achieved his greatest ambition: he has become a part of the epic that is the Tour of Flanders.

When Henri Vanlerberghe wins the Tour of Flanders in 1919, he is still officially a soldier.

THE HELL OF THE NORTH

By the time the Armistice is signed on 11 November 1918, the north of France, like the Westhoek in Flanders, is little more than a wasteland. Whole villages have been wiped off the map. Major towns and cities are in ruins. In this industrial region, nearly all the mines and textile factories have been destroyed. Of the 107 pitheads that existed before the war, only four are still standing. Even though peace has returned, the people living the Nord department will remain cut off from the rest of France for several months to come. All the roads, railways and locks have been seriously damaged. At least 1,500 kilometres of rail track needs to be relaid. The entire front zone, often 30 kilometres wide, is a confused tangle of abandoned trenches and water-filled shell craters. Entire woods have been obliterated and what were once fertile fields are now strewn with more than 6,000 concrete bunkers, millions of tons of unexploded ammunition and the countless rotting corpses of the dead of both sides. It is in this sombre setting that on Sunday, 20 April 1919 the Paris-Roubaix race will be ridden 'as normal'.

The desire to resume racing is huge in France, the 'birthplace' of modern cycling. It is one of the ways to show that things are returning to normal, that the French nation can rise above the disasters of the war years. Even so, the 1919 Paris-Roubaix promises to be a difficult one. *'C'est l'enfer!'* (It's hell!), writes Victor Breyer, a special correspondent for the *L'Auto* newspaper, when he inspects the final section of the course a week before the race. It is a name that sticks. From now on, the race will always be known as 'the Hell of the North'. The level of devastation in the war zone makes a deep impression on Breyer. 'All you can see are tracks of beaten earth, deeply rutted by passing wagons. In some places, these paths are broken by large craters. The woods have been annihilated and the fields ploughed up by the explosions of thousands of shells.' It is clear that the pre-war Paris-Roubaix course will need to be amended; the old trajectory is simply impassable. Once the riders reach Doullens, they will no longer race via Arras and Lens, but will reach Roubaix via Saint-Pol-de-Ternoise and Bethune. Since the old velodrome in the city was also destroyed during the war, the new finish will be in the Allée des Villas in Parc Barbieux.

Henri Vanlerberghe / Henri Pélissier.

The 20th edition of Paris-Roubaix is announced in the press on 29 January 1919.

For this first post-war edition of the race, 130 riders line up at the start — considerably more than for the Tour of Flanders, ridden just a few weeks earlier. The starters include 'old favourites' like Philippe Thys, Eugène Christophe, Odiel Defraeye, Louis Mottiat, Oscar Egg, Henri Vanlerberghe, Charles Deruyter, Jean Rossius, Louis Heusghem, Léon Scieur, Maurice Brocco, Emile Masson and Henri Pélissier, accompanied for the first time by his younger brother, Francis, who has just obtained his professional license. Another Frenchman tipped for success by both journalists and supporters is Honoré Barthélémy, who was national champion in the independent category before the war. Having said that, people are generally cautious with their predictions: no-one knows what their wartime experiences will have done to even the best of riders. Will they still be as good as they once were?

This 20th riding of Paris-Roubaix begins with an emotional one minute's silence for the many cyclists who failed to make it through the war alive, including former race winners Octave Lapize and François Faber. The sombre atmosphere is matched by the weather: it is raining and there is a cold wind, blowing strongly from the north. The race only breaks open when the pack reaches La Bassée, more than three-quarters of the way through the 280-kilometre course. The Pélissier brothers launch an attack. In no time at all, they build up a two-minute lead over a chasing group that is finding it harder and harder to cope with the cold. However, the younger Pélissier soon falls back: he has three flat tyres and is unable to replenish his energy levels, because it is almost impossible to eat anything on the bumpy roads around Habourdin, Loos and Lille. If you take your hands of the handlebars for just a few seconds, you are almost certain to fall.

Deprived of his brother's support, Henri Pélissier decides to wait for double Tour de France winner Philippe Thys, who has now also managed to escape from the pack. This duo is held up by a closed level crossing, which allows Honoré Barthélémy to catch them up. The three of them sprint for victory on the Allée des Villas. Pélissier is the fastest, just ahead of a deeply disappointed Philippe Thys. Five other Belgians finish in the top ten: Louis Heusghem, Alexis Michiels, Jean Rossius, Emile Masson and Alfred Steux.

Henri Pélissier is the strongest in the 1919 'Hell of the North'.

THE TOUR OF THE BATTLEFIELDS

If there was a prize for the most bizarre cycle race ever held, the Tour of the Battlefields, ridden in the spring of 1919, would be a strong contender for the title. The race is held in stages over seven days and the course passes through all the most war-ravaged zones in West Flanders and northern France. Although the event is motivated by the idea of 'peace restored', for the riders it will be an ordeal that almost matches the trials of the war itself. It is a near miracle that any of the participants reach the finish and it is no surprise that there is little enthusiasm to organize further editions.

Le Circuit des Champs de Bataille is announced in the press on 19 December 1918, scarcely a month after the Armistice is signed. Under the motto 'A sporting Easter. For Alsace! For Lorraine! For the youth of France!' the newspaper *Le Petit Journal* unveils its plans to organize a number of sporting events to honour 'glorious episodes' from the First World War, in which it hopes many of the soldiers fresh from the trenches will take part. One of these events is a cycle race across the battlefields. Perhaps not unsurprisingly, the start is in Strasbourg. This is the capital city of the Alsace region, which, together with the province of Lorraine, was ceded to Germany following France's defeat in the Franco-Prussian War of 1870-1871. The first stage, some 275 kilometres in length and ending in Luxembourg, winds its way through the entire length of this much disputed border zone, which is of huge emotional significance for the French riders in the race. Revenge for the humiliation of 1871 and the 'liberation' of the 'lost' provinces has dominated French national life for the past half century and has now, at long last, been achieved.

The following stages take the riders from Luxembourg to Brussels (301 kilometres), Brussels to Amiens (323 kilometres), Amiens to Paris (277 kilometres), Paris to Bar-le-Duc (333 kilometres), Bar-le-Duc to Belfort (313 kilometres) and Belfort back to Strasbourg (163 kilometres). There is a rest day between each stage, and even two in Paris. *Le Petit Journal* makes no secret of the fact that the Tour of the Battlefields will be a major sporting challenge. Not so much because of the total distance — which is 'only' 1,895 kilometres, in comparison with the 5,560 kilometres of the Tour de France later that same year — but more as a result

Berten De Jonghe, leader of the Tour of the Battlefields after the first two stages.

of the appalling state of the roads over which the race will be ridden. Many of these roads have been badly damaged, so that they are barely passable, not to mention the many bridges that were blown up by the retreating Germans during the final months of the war. The race is also an organizational nightmare for its initiators. Where can they find overnight accommodation in shell-blasted towns? How can they set up control points in the wastelands of no-man's-land? In the interests of their readers — in other words, in the interests of the newspaper and its sales figures — they must succeed! It is a symbol of the new optimism that will see France rise from the ashes of the war!

Equipped only with out-of-date pre-war bikes, the riders struggle through a landscape of shattered villages and desolate ruins, littered with thousands of unexploded shells and all the other waste materials of war. The newspaper encourages the cyclists to be 'careful', but adds that it cannot be held responsible for any accidents that occur. The racers also have to cover their own costs, which are likely to be high, since the risk of flat tyres, broken wheels, cracked frames, etc on the region's war-torn roads is considerable.

The only thing that makes the Tour of the Battlefields attractive to racers is the size of the prize money. *Le Petit Journal* guarantees 6,000 French francs to the winner, 4,000 francs to the second, 3,000 francs to the third, and so on. There is also 3,000 francs on offer in each of the seven stages. As an extra incentive, several of the towns and cities along the route offer bonus prizes, as do the cycling manufacturers, a number of local sponsors and even the President of the Republic, Raymond Poincaré. This is enough to ensure a decent field of participants, especially as all riders — both amateur and professional — are eligible to take part (except Germans, Austrians and Hungarians).

By the close of registration on 1 February 1919, 138 riders have applied to take part. However, only 87 of them turn up at the starting-line in Strasbourg on Monday, 28 April. The main reason is that travel to Alsace is still extremely difficult, so that many fail to arrive in time or give up en route. Even so, the organizers are happy with the turnout. Along with Henri Vanlerberghe, the winner of the previous month's Tour of Flanders, many of the great names of French and Belgian cycling are present: Paul Duboc, Jean Alavoine, Maurice Brocco, Charles Deruyter, Pier Van de Velde and Aloïs Verstraeten. There are also rising stars like Lucien Buysse, Jules Van Hevel, Berten De Jonghe and José Pelletier. The Tunisian Ali Neffati, three Luxembourgers and three Swiss riders add a cosmopolitan touch to the field.

It is one of the Swiss — Oscar Egg — who triumphs in the first stage. This is not really a surprise. He is world record-holder for the hour, won Paris-Tours in 1914 and was best in two stages of the Tour de France that year. During the war, he was able to keep himself in top physical condition by riding in Italian road races and six-day events in America. Egg arrives in Luxembourg with a lead of seven minutes over a group with Jules Van Hevel, Lucien Buysse, Basiel Matthys, Hector Heusghem and Wies Verstraeten. The strong winds and heavy rains mean that only 72 of the 87 competitors reach the finish. The last of them collapses across the line some fourteen and a half hours after Egg. This is the deaf-mute racer André Perrès, who has to walk the last 23 kilometres with his broken bike. Perhaps unsurprisingly, he fails to start the next day.

The second stage takes the riders to what *Le Petit Journal* calls 'our beloved and recently liberated regions of the north'. It is snowing when the race begins in Luxembourg. The route leads from the duchy to Liege, via Bastogne, Stavelot and Spa, and then on to Brussels via Tongeren, Tienen and Leuven. 'It rains, it pours, and water sluices from the riders, who look like little more than mud-spattered rags', writes Karel Van Wijnendaele in *Sportwereld*. Notwithstanding the dreadful weather, the roads around Liege are lined with enthusiastic spectators. Lucien Buysse builds up a good lead, but the East Fleming is then plagued by bad luck, first with his chain and then with a flat tyre. He is caught and passed by Berten De Jonghe, who sets off on a solo ride to victory. Buysse is later joined by Hector Heusghem, but they make little impact on De Jonghe's lead.

What they see when they ride into Leuven after more than ten hours of cycling defies all description. The once proud university city has been reduced to ruins by four years of war and deprivation. But De Jonghe has little time to muse on such things. He presses on and an hour later he crosses the finishing line in the park at Laken. Eleven minutes behind him, Buysse comes in second, followed after a further seven minutes by Urbain Anseeuw. The racers are frozen to the bone. In the case of Oscar Egg, almost literally. He falls from his bike and cannot continue. He is not alone. Thirty-six of the 87 starters have now given up. And the worst stages are yet to come…

BEYOND ABSURDITY

On Friday, 2 May 1919 the third stage is held between Brussels and Amiens. After passing through Ghent and Bruges, the riders finally reach the 'real' front region, the sectors where the heaviest fighting took place. They ride first across the valley of the IJzer, before turning south toward the Belgian towns that will forever be most closely associated with the First World War: Diksmuide and Ieper. Then it is over the border and into France, taking in Bapaume and Albert on the old battlefield of the Somme, before heading east to the finishing line in the cathedral city of Amiens.

The conditions for what is supposed to be a 'sporting' event are almost unimaginably hard. The riders struggle their way between abandoned trenches and craters. The roads are hardly roads at all. Many are still half blocked with the ruins of houses and the debris of war. And as if that is not bad enough, the weather is also at it harshest. Like so often during the war, the heavens open at the worst possible moment, driven into the faces of the riders by a fierce west wind. 'Those who didn't pedal hard enough risked being blown from their bikes', reports *Sportwereld*.

As the riders approach the Westhoek, the whole atmosphere of the race changes. So far, there have always been people along the side of the road to cheer the peloton on its way. But nobody lives in the Westhoek now. The local population was forced to flee during the war and very few have yet returned. What's more, the landscape has been blasted out of all recognition by the constant bombardments and

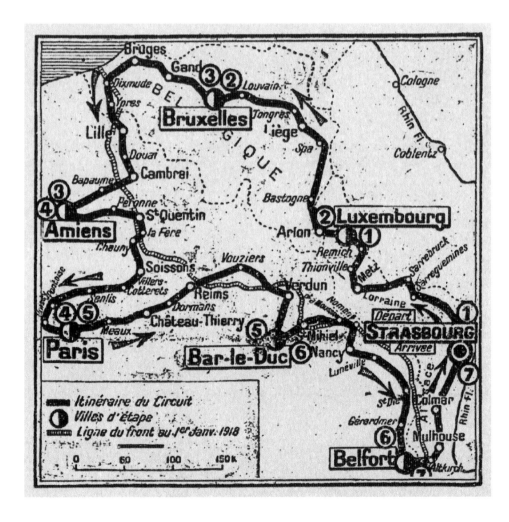

The course for the Tour of the Battlefields is designed to include symbolic places from the war years, like Ieper and Verdun.

large areas are still flooded. In some places, the riders have no idea where they are supposed to go and need the help of race commissioners to point them in the right direction. Kaaskerke, Oudekapelle, Woesten and Elverdinge have all become ghost villages. Ieper has been reduced to rubble. Amidst the ruins of the great Market Square there is a control post, from where the riders need to ride through the Menin Gate and out on to the Menin Road. But some of them cannot find it: what was once a road is now a muddy track running through the middle of a surreal moonscape of craters, barbed wire and bunkers. It is only when the racers finally reach Menin (now Menen) itself that they start to see supporters again. The people of Lille, also badly hit by the war, likewise brave the appalling weather to watch the spectacle pass by. Amidst the ruins of the city centre, some riders again lose their way. But Charles Deruyter is from these parts and knows how to find the road to Douai. Aloïs Verstraeten and Urbain Anseeuw follow in his wake. Berten De Jonghe, the overall race leader, is hard on their heels, but in Ennetières he is involved in a crash. His bike is damaged beyond repair. Because reserve bikes are not allowed, he is forced to give up. In the meantime, the rain continues to pelt down. At many points, the riders wade rather than ride through the deepening mud. This is no longer a race, it is nightmare. All that counts is survival.

At crossroads, the direction boards are also covered with mud, so that they become unreadable. The riders need to dismount and wipe them clean before they know which way to go. In Aubigny-au-Bac, they discover that the bridge over the River Sensée has collapsed, requiring them to make a long detour. By now, Anseeuw and Verstraeten have had enough. They seek out the shelter of a nearby house, where they try to get warm. A short time later, they are joined by Henri Vanlerberghe. 'They had probably taken a different road to me, and a much longer one. As a result, I was able to make good 20 minutes on them in just 15 kilometres', recalled Vanlerberghe in a series of interviews he gave to the *Oude Thorhoutenaar* in 1966, shortly before his death. 'We then set off together, but soon found ourselves in a camp full of wild-looking soldiers, French colonial troops. At first, we thought they were going to eat us!'

Karel Van Wijnendaele encourages the riders not to give up. In the meantime, Deruyter is well out in the lead and arrives in Bapaume. The small town was devastated during the First Battle of the Somme in 1916 and, as in Diksmuide and Ieper, there is not a soul to be seen. The same story is repeated in Albert, another sea of ruins. The French authorities are still debating whether or not to rebuild the town, because it contains so many unexploded shells. One wonders what goes through the minds of race organizers who dare to send their riders through conditions as absurd as this. In fact, it is beyond absurdity. But it doesn't seem to worry Charles Deruyter, who presses on bravely, ignoring both the conditions and the danger. By now, the wind has blown his jersey to tatters and his wheels are so clogged with mud that they hardly turn any more. It takes him seven hours to complete the final 90 kilometres, but at last he struggles over the finishing line in Amiens. By now, it is 11 o'clock at night and he has been in the saddle for eighteen and a half hours...

It is long past midnight before the second rider reaches the cathedral city, with the rain still teeming down. It is Paul Deboc, who finally finds his way on to the Boulevard de Beauville more by touch than by sight. The 35-year-old Frenchman has always been one of the peloton's 'hard men', but this has tested even his legendary endurance to its limits. Forty-five minutes later, Vanlerberghe and Anseeuw arrive, safe but completely exhausted. It is then another seven hours (!) before the fifth rider, Theo Wynsdau, can be seen approaching, at roughly half past eight on the Saturday morning. A further hour sees Jean Alavoine complete the top six. Of the 42 riders who left Brussels, 30 will eventually finish the stage, the last of them more than 20 hours after the winner. Many take shelter for the night, before continuing the next day. Wynsdau spends an uncomfortable few hours sleeping in a trench near Bapaume. Hector Heusghem and Henri Henlet got lost in Aubigny and ride an extra 60 kilometres as a result. A frustrated Arsène Pain hitches a lift part of the way on a lorry and receives a time penalty of one hour. Jules Van Hevel wrecks his bike and makes his way to the nearest station to find a train home. Of Pier Van de Velde there is no sign at all...

THE NEW BOY AND THE OLD HAND

The fact that Urbain Anseeuw performs so well in the Tour of the Battlefields is something of a surprise. True, both as an amateur and as an independent rider he achieves a series of promising results, but the war cuts off a possible professional career before it has even started. On 28 July 1914, he is called up to serve in the Belgian Army. Following the fall of Antwerp on 10 October, he is forced to flee, like so many of his comrades in arms, across the border into the neutral Netherlands. During his time in the internment camp at Harderwijk, he trains hard to keep in good condition and regularly wins races on the camp's 'home-made' track. On 14 December 1918, he is finally allowed to return home. He turns professional and rides his first elite race in the Tour of Flanders on 23 March 1919, finishing in a creditable 15th place. Even so, there is nothing to suggest that he will be among the leaders in the Tour of the Battlefields. He even finds it hard to believe himself. He is second in the overall standings, but fears he will lose his position. After the stage to Amiens, he confides to Karel Van Wijnendaele: 'They are all such great racers. Just look at the names! Deruyter and Riet'n, and Smedten, and Alavoine, and Heusghem, who simply flies up mountains as though they are nothing. What can I possible do against the likes of them?' Yet in spite of this lack of self-confidence, Anseeuw holds on to his second position and finishes the race in Strasbourg as runner-up. Sadly, however, he never makes the really big breakthrough he hopes for. He starts twice in the Tour de France, but fails to reach Paris on either occasion. In 1923, he gives up professional cycling and opens a bike shop in Aalter. His son, Frans, later takes over the family business, which still exists today.

In contrast to Urbain Anseeuw, Charles Deruyter, the race leader, is already an experienced professional. Born as a Belgian in 1890 in the Café Au Coin Fleur in the French border village of Wattrelos, sandwiched between the larger towns of Moeskroen, Tourcoing and Roubaix, Deruyter has built up a reputation as a versatile rider, who has success on both the road and the track. Before the war, he is something of a 'nearly-man', finishing second in Paris-Menen (1911), Paris-Tours (1912) and Paris-Roubaix (1913). In the 1912 Tour de France, won by Odiel Defraeye, he finishes a distant 16th. In 1915, he joins the Belgian Army, but, like Philippe

Thys, he becomes a mechanic working on military aeroplanes, so that he does not serve at the front. Again like Thys, his superiors give him permission to train and race during the war. As a result, in 1916 he wins Paris-Orleans and a criterium race in Lyon. A year later, he is also the best in Paris-Tours. After his success in the Tour of the Battlefields, he will later go on to triumph in the 1921 edition of the Six Days of Brussels with Marcel Berthet. In 1922, now partnering Maurice Brocco, he is third in the Six Days of New York and in 1923 comes second in the Tour of Flanders behind the Swiss rider Heinrich 'Heiri' Suter. After his career, Deruyter moves to Saint-Servais in the Belgian province of Namur, where he opens a bike shop on the Chaussée de Waterloo. Together with Armand Marlair, he helps to launch the 'Splendor' make of bike. He also serves as pace-man for stayers like Stan Ockers, Dolf Verscheuren and Wim van Est. Charles Deruyter dies at his home in Saint-Servais on 24 January 1955.

Urbain Anseeuw, once an internee in the camp at Harderwijk, is second in the Tour of the Battlefields.

'THE TRIUMPH OF THE IMPOSSIBLE'

Although several of the competitors in the Tour of the Battlefields have served at the front, so that they are used to having things tough, the stage from Brussels to Amiens will be remembered as the one of the hardest trials — and certainly the hardest sporting trial — of their lives. 'In the history of cycling, riders have never before been asked to undertake such a difficult task', writes *L'Auto*. Indeed, the riders have never experienced anything like it and hope never to experience it again. One consolation is that the weather during the next day's ride from Amiens to Paris is fine. But the roads are still treacherous and the surroundings are equally depressing. Villages like Mons-en-Chaussée and Poeuilly have been shelled flat. The once proud basilica of St. Quentin is in ruins. And even when they leave the Somme behind, they pass into new areas devastated by other battles, like the Aisne and the Marne. The countryside between Soissons and Senlis is also a wasteland of destruction. It is only as the racers approach Paris that things get better. In the city itself, the damage is only slight: it almost seems like the Paris of old. Charles Deruyter is first to enter the velodrome at the Parc des Princes, again followed by Paul Duboc, but this time with a lead of just four minutes.

By the time the fifth stage to Bar-le-Duc starts, there are only 22 riders left in the race. Via Meaux and the ruins of Rheims, they make their way towards the scene of one of the bloodiest battles of the entire war: Verdun. For Deruyter and his colleagues this means an obstacle-strewn course along the valleys of the Marne and Meuse, passing ruined vineyards, ravaged woods and villages that have been razed to the ground. Once again, the weather is glorious, but this brings new problems of a different kind. Instead of the mud and rain of the first three stages, the riders are now plagued by dust and a blistering sun. On the way to Bar-le-Duc, the route takes the race along the *Voie Sacrée* (Sacred Way), which was the main supply line to the hard-pressed front at Verdun. This is a tribute to the two million soldiers who passed along this road during the great battle of 1916, in many cases never to return. The victory in Bar-le-Duc goes to Jean Alavoine, with Hector Heusghem second and Albert Desmedt third.

Charles Deruyter still heads the overall standings and his lead is starting to look unassailable. After this fifth stage, the worst is behind the riders and from now on the roads are generally good. But this does not mean there are no natural obstacles. The sixth stage to Belfort takes them over the Ballon d'Alsace, a difficult 9-kilometre climb reaching an altitude of 1,247 metres. At this height, the rain of the previous days has fallen as snow, which covers the ground to a depth of a metre in some places. The cars of the race commissioners get stuck near the summit, but the bikes are able to force a way through. Heusghem is the best climber and reaches the top with a lead of three minutes over Deruyter and Vanlerberghe. It is enough to ensure him victory in Belfort.

The 21 riders who set off for Strasbourg on the seventh and final stage have achieved what *Le Petit Journal* describes as 'the triumph of the impossible'. Just completing this monster of a race is indeed a triumph. It is almost a miracle that they — and their bikes — have survived. But the organizers also emerge from the race covered with glory. They, too, have managed to achieve something that no-one thought was possible: the organization of a stage race through the parts of France worst affected by the war just six months after the Armistice.

The last 163 kilometres take the riders through the largely unspoilt countryside of the 'liberated' province of Alsace. As a race, it has little to offer, but in terms of symbolism it is perhaps the most important stage of all. As the riders approach Strasbourg, the crowds begin to grow. In the city itself, they ride for kilometre after kilometre through a double row of cheering supporters. At the finish in the Tivoli Square there are thousands of people and a military band. It is a huge outpouring of French national emotion. Charles Deruyter wins his third stage and confirms his victory in the overall standings, taking his total prize money for the event to 8,600 French francs, a small fortune. Urbain Anseeuw holds on to second place, with Henri Vanlerberghe in third. They, too, return home with well-filled pockets.

Charles Deruyter, here at the start of Paris-Roubaix in 1914, is the winner of the Tour of the Battlefields.

Ottavio Bottecchia learns to cycle during the war and just years later wins the Tour de France.

For most people the war is a disaster. But for a few it is a cloud with a silver lining. One of the latter is unquestionably Ottavio Bottecchia. In 1914, he is just another Italian soldier, called up to serve at the front. Even though he has never ridden a bike in his life — he comes from a poor family in the Veneto region, which has no money for such luxuries — he is posted to the Bersaglieri. There he is obliged to learn how to ride a two-wheeler. It is destined to be the turning point in his life. But first he needs to survive the war.

Ottavio is sent with his unit to the Trentino to fight against the Austro-Hungarians. Although he is a novice on a bike, it soon becomes clear that he can pedal extremely hard. To his own amazement, he can cycle up the steep slopes of the Dolomite mountains with comparative ease. His officers are equally amazed. One of them tells him: 'You're not a soldier, you're a cyclist!' Bottecchia is taken prisoner three times during the war, but on each occasion he escapes because he can cycle faster than his captors. By now, everyone in the Bersaglieri Division is convinced that after the war he must turn professional.

But Ottavio is not immediately convinced. When the Armistice comes, he resumes his pre-war job as a bricklayer. But the long hours of back-breaking work for poor pay slowly force him to think again. Perhaps his officers were right, after all? And what does he have to lose? Using his hard-earned savings, he buys himself a modest bike and at the age of 25 becomes a racer. It isn't long before he is winning races and just a year later he joins the ranks of the professionals. That year he finishes eighth in the Tour of Lombardy. In 1923, he is fifth in the Giro d'Italia. This brings him a contract with the famous Automoto team, which enters him just two months later for the Tour de France. As a debutant, he immediately wins the second stage, and proves himself to be a good climber in both the Alps and the Pyrenees. Against all expectations, he finishes in Paris as runner-up in the overall standings, behind his teammate Henri Pélissier.

The following year Ottavio does even better. He wears the leader's yellow jersey from the first day of the race until the last and so becomes the first Italian to win the Tour de France. He repeats his triumph in 1925, again winning four stages and bringing his total to nine. While Ottavio is riding from victory to victory on French roads, members of his family who still work in the construction industry as bricklayers and stonecutters have moved to Ieper, to help with the city's rebuilding after the war. There are not enough local craftsmen to complete a task of this scale, so workmen from abroad — often from Italy — are recruited to make good the shortfall. There are still Bottecchias living in Ieper today.

Having survived the dangers of the war, Ottavio Bottecchia ultimately comes to a tragic end. One day, he fails to return from a training ride. A farmer's wife finds him unconscious at the side of the isolated road to Osoppo. His bike is leaning undamaged against a tree. He dies nine days later on 14 June 1927 in the hospital at Gemona, without ever regaining consciousness. The precise cause of his death remains shrouded in mystery. Some think he was killed by the mafia; others believe he was assassinated by the Mussolini regime, which disliked his anti-fascist politics. Then there is the story that he was accidentally killed by a farmer who threw a rock at him because he had stopped to pick some of the farmer's cherries... At the end of the day, it all makes little difference: Italy's first double Tour winner was dead and buried at the age of just 32.

WHEN YOU ARE IN LOVE, YOU ARE ALWAYS TWENTY

War can do strange and unpredictable things to people. Just look at the story of Ottavio Bottecchia! Equally remarkable — but with a happier ending — is the story of André Perchicot. After four years of misery at the front, his life also changes in a way he could never have imagined. Before the war, he was a cyclist. After it, he becomes... a brilliant singer. To a large extent, the decision to quit cycling is forced upon him. He survives a plane crash, but his injuries are so severe that a further professional career as a cyclist is out of the question. This is a huge disappointment: between 1910 and 1914 he was undoubtedly one of the best sprinters in Europe.

Born in Bayonne on 9 August 1888, André Perchicot might just as easily have become a successful engineer. But during his studies he takes up cycling. His passion for his new 'hobby' soon decides that the young man will try to make his living on two wheels. He graduates as planned, but from 1909 onwards he concentrates fully on professional track racing. Three years later, he becomes the French national sprint champion in the Parc des Princes, a title he extends in 1913. That same year he also wins the European title. With such goods results, Perchicot naturally receives invitations to ride at top events in Brussels, Copenhagen and Leipzig. He is even seen on tracks in Toronto and New York. In addition, he twice wins a bronze medal in the world championships: in 1912 in Newark (behind the American Frank Kramer and the Australian Alfred Grenda) and in 1913 in Berlin (behind the German Walter Rütt and the Dane Thorvald Ellegaard).

The 1914 season also begins promisingly for Perchicot. Together with Oscar Egg, he finishes third in the Six Days of Paris. But then the war intervenes. He volunteers for the air wing of the French Army and becomes a fighter pilot. It is a dangerous choice and in 1916 his plane is shot down. By some miracle Perchicot survives the crash, but has serious injuries to his legs, back and pelvis. During his long period of rehabilitation it becomes clear that cycling at the top level is no longer a possibility. But the Frenchman refuses to be downhearted by this setback. Ever the optimist, he even tries to cheer up his fellow patients in the military hospital by singing songs to them. His songs are well received and before long he is invited to perform in

other nearby hospitals. He also organizes cycling competitions for the benefit of the Red Cross.

Now that André has discovered his artistic talents, he decides to make further use of them after the Armistice. He makes his debut as a professional singer at the casino in Toulon, but soon receives offers to give café concerts in Paris. His strong and melodious voice makes a powerful impression on his growing number of listeners. His popularity blossoms throughout the 1920s, a decade in which he also makes his first long-playing record (he will go on to make 26 others). His most famous song is *When you are in love, you are always twenty*, released in 1923. But he never forgets that cycling was his first love and his other hits include *Les Tours de France* and *Sur le Vélo*. From 1930 onwards, he becomes a celebrated music hall artist and tours Europe, North Africa and the Middle East with his stage show *La Tournée Perchicot*. He also appears in three motion pictures.

Such is his success that he is able to buy a number of villas in and around Paris, as well as owning two yachts, several cars and a bus company in his native city of Bayonne, where a street is also named after him. André Perchicot dies on 3 May 1950 at the age of 62.

The remarkable life of André Perchicot is the subject of a book with the appropriate title *De la piste à la scène* (From the track to the stage).

FINALE

In 2004, 90 years after the outbreak of the First World War, there is just one veteran from the conflict still alive in Belgium. What's more, he is — or was — a cyclist. His name is Emile Brichard and he is 104 years young. He was not a champion; far from it, in fact. But he did race in his youth. Even so, his name is almost completely unknown, both to cycle fans and pub quizzers alike. Not that there is anything wrong with that. Emile's cycling career, like the man himself, was modest. He never won a single race and he would probably have died in anonymity was it not for the fact that he suddenly became famous as the last survivor of the 14-18 War. This also brought to light that the man from Wallonia was the oldest surviving participant in the Tour de France. Coincidentally, the 2004 Tour is also scheduled to start in Wallonia, with the first four stages taking place on Belgian soil between 3 and 6 July. 'Since the Tour is passing within 5 kilometres of his front door, the very least that should be done is to honour Emile Brichard one last time', writes Guy Crasset, editor of the *Coups de Pédales* cycling magazine. Sadly, Tour boss Jean-Marie Leblanc sees it differently. The race passes by with hardly a thought for the sprightly centenarian.

Emile Brichard is born on 20 December 1899 in Arsimont, not far from Sambreville. Before his first birthday, he moves with his parents, brothers and sisters to Ham-sur-Sambre, which is today part of the municipality of Jemeppe-sur-Sambre. During the early weeks of the war, the Brichard family is shocked and frightened to learn of the massacre of civilians in nearby Tamines. On 21 and 22 August 1914, the Germans burn down all the houses in the village and kill 384 innocent men, women and children. Like so many others, the Brichards decide to flee across the River Sambre, eventually arriving at the Flemish town of Eeklo, before later being shipped across the English Channel to settle in the Midlands city of Wolverhampton.

The 15-year-old Emile is immediately set to work in a factory making soldiers' boots. Less than a year later, he is called up by the Belgian Army to return for service in the war effort. At first, he works in a munitions plant in northern France, but in July 1915 he is reassigned to the 4th Medical Corps. This means moving up to the front, where his task will be a simple but nonetheless dangerous one: to act as a stretcher-bearer taking wounded soldiers from the battlefield back to the aid posts and hospitals behind the lines. During the final months of the war, he finds himself at the famous L'Océan Hospital in De Panne, where he meets Queen Elisabeth.

By now, he is 'nurse' Brichard, even though he has no training other than what he has picked up during the war. 'Not that we had to do much nursing', he later recalls in an interview. 'Most days we were just picking up corpses. We brought out very few who were still alive or had a chance of survival...' Even though he never takes part in any actual fighting, he sees as much of the horror of war as any front-line soldier. 'All the houses had been shelled flat. The hospital was just a series of tents. There was mud everywhere. We earned 25 centimes a day, shared one loaf with four other soldiers, occasionally got something that was supposed to be soup, and had to sleep on straw. Those six or seven months were hell! And do you know what? The older you get, the more the memories start coming back to haunt you...' Even after the Armistice, Emile's misery is not immediately at an end. It is months before the army discharges him and in the meantime he has to serve with the Army of Occupation in Germany. It is only in the autumn of 1919 that he is allowed to go on indefinite leave.

Back in Belgium, the 20-year-old Emile Brichard now needs to find a job. But what? In his home region, the answer is easy to find. The huge losses in young men during the war means that there is a shortage of labour to work in the region's coal mines, which are now more crucial to the economy than ever. Emile therefore spends much of the next ten years of his life underground. During the summer months, he also crosses the border to work in the brick kilns of northern France, where they also need all the help they can get.

These are both physically demanding jobs, but Emile is a strong young man and a hard worker. And as if this were not enough, in his free time he also takes up the equally challenging sport of cycling. What starts off as a hobby soon becomes a way to earn a little extra money. In fact, he can often earn as much in a couple of hours racing as in a whole week down a mine. He is a good rider, but not an outstanding talent. He never wins a single race and is happy if he can keep up with names like Louis Mottiat, Firmin Lambot, Hector Tiberghein, Léon Scieur, the brothers Fernand and Félix Sellier and Hector and Louis Heusghem, all of whom he meets in the local races he rides in the provinces of Namur and Hainaut.

His 'breakthrough' comes in 1926, when another Walloon rider, Adelin Benoît, recommends him to the Alcyon team. 'Such a contract didn't mean much. There was no money. All you got was a bike and some clothing. But Benoît, who won a stage in the 1925 Tour de France, thought I might be useful to him as a personal helper.'

When Benoît pleases his team bosses again in 1926 with a victory in Bordeaux-Paris, he is able to persuade them to take his helper along to that year's Tour. Emile Brichard — an occasional rider straight from the mines, with the coal dust still in his lungs — is going to start in *La Grande Boucle*! It promises to be a serious challenge. With a distance of 5,745 kilometres, spread over 17 stages, the 1926 Tour will be the longest in history. Together with Adelin Benoît and Félix Sellier, Emile proudly rides to the headquarters of *L'Auto* in Paris. There he shakes the hand of Tour organizer Henri Desgrange, before setting off to the Champs-Élysées for the parade and the presentation of the riders. To his dismay, he there discovers that the Alcyon-Dunlop team intends to start with the sextet Nicolas Franz, Bartolomeo Aimo, Jan Debusschère, Félix Sellier, Adelin Benoît and Raymond Englebert. There is no place for André Brichard. Clearly, Benoît does not have as much influence with his French bosses as he thinks.

All André can now do is take part in the race as an *isolé*, an unsupported rider. This means that in contrast to the team riders, who will be well looked after by their squad of helpers, he will be forced to do everything for himself, even down to finding (and paying for) his own food, drink and overnight accommodation. But at least he is not alone. That year no fewer than 82 *isolés* are scheduled to take part in the Tour. Most of them are Frenchmen or Italians, but there is one other Belgian — Henri Beirnaert — and with Kisso Kawamuro even a rider from Japan!

The same day, all 126 starters are taken by train to Evian-les-Bains. For the first time in its history, the Tour will not start in Paris. The first stage is from the spa town to Mulhouse, over a distance of 373 kilometres. Emile Brichard, wearing number 143, has never ridden such a distance before in a single day. Even more daunting, he has never ridden in the mountains before, never mind trying to race up them. That 20 June 1926 is tropically warm and the riders' first big test is the steep slopes of the Jura, including the Col de la Faucille, a 14-kilometre

long climb up to an altitude of 1,323 metres. 'The road surface was terrible. There were rocks as big as melons. And potholes. Deep potholes. You raced as fast as you could through the dust and over the sharp gravel. I soon had a flat. And again. And again. Because I only had two spares with me, I had to sew up my tubes with coarse thread. That cost me a lot of time.' As if that is not bad enough, Ottavio Bottecchia, winner of the Tour in 1924 and 1925, decides to launch an early attack. The head of the peloton starts to pull away, leaving Brichard further and further behind. Bottecchia pays for his impulsiveness, running out of steam long before the finish. He ends in 16th place, 36 minutes behind his teammate at Automoto-Hutchinson, Jules Buysse. The rider from East Flanders — the younger brother of Lucien Buysse, who three weeks later will win the race — completes the 373 kilometres in 14 hours and 12 minutes. This gives him a lead of 17 minutes over a group with Van de Casteele, Debusschère, Benoît and Van Slembrouck. While Buysse is receiving the victor's bouquet on the podium in Mulhouse, Brichard still has another five hours of cycling to go. Although 'cycling' is perhaps something of an exaggeration. His bike is clearly not up to the challenge of this kind of attritional race and he is constantly plagued by technical problems. And as an *isolé*, he is completely on his own. 'My tubes were cut to ribbons, I was riding on my rims. It was hopeless.' Dejected and dismayed, ten kilometres from the finishing line he climbs off his bike and withdraws from the race. His Tour adventure is over even before the end of the first day. Once again, however, he is not alone. Another 12 *isolés* have similar troubles and retire either during or after the stage, including Beirnaert and Kawamuro.

André Brichard walks disconsolately into Mulhouse. He doesn't dare to go home and he gives up all his cycling aspirations on the spot. 'I had hoped to complete a few stages, at least those in northern France. I eventually took the train back to Charleroi and for the first few days stayed indoors. I didn't want to be seen. Giving up in the Tour was a disgrace, not just for me but for the family as well. No-one went outside that first week. Since then, I have never talked much about my Tour escapades. For a long time, I just wanted to forget about it, because I was so ashamed. I never took part in another major race after that, not even the Tour of Belgium.'

Not surprisingly, Alcyon are not impressed by André's 'performance' in the Tour. As a result, his professional contract is not renewed in 1927.

1926 remains his one and only participation in the world's greatest cycle race — and a short one at that. He goes back down the mine, but carries on riding independently at local fairs and events in his own region for another three years, before finally hanging up his bike for good. He also says farewell to the miner's life, using his savings to open a wine and liqueur store in Chatelinau.

From then on, he lives a quiet but healthy life. 'I never drank the stuff I sold. I tasted it, to see if it was good, but then spat it out.' He outlives three wives and also his two sons. He spends the last 30 years of his life in Villers-Poterie, a village in the municipality of Gerpinnes. He is still driving a car at the age of 96, until his insurance company withdraws his cover. Nobody knows that the retired liqueur salesman was once a racer and he no longer has an archive of his own to remind them. This is the 'fault' of his first wife. Following their divorce, she takes everything in the house with her, including all his medals and photographs from the First World War and from his time as a cyclist...

Brichard slips quietly into anonymity, spending his old age with his cat, Poupousse. In fact, the only reason his name eventually appears in the paper (and today even has its own Wikipedia page) is because he lives for so long. When all his other comrades have gone, he becomes the last surviving Belgian combatant of the Great War. His *moment de gloire* — or 15 minutes of fame, if you prefer — comes in 2004. The Tour de France is in Wallonia. Fabian Cancellara wins the prologue in Liege. The next day, Jaan Kirsipuu wins the sprint in Charleroi. Some of the journalists pick up a rumour that the oldest surviving Tour participant lives nearby.

One of them, Jean Nelissen of the Dutch NOS television station, decides it might be interesting to drive down to Villers-Poterie and interview the ageing Brichard. Not so much the portrait of a cycling hero, but more as a kind of curiosity piece. After all, the statistics don't lie: he was no great shakes as a racer. Even so, at the august age of 104 years André Brichard finally gets the degree of recognition he was never able to achieve as a cyclist. The film of the interview is moving in its simplicity. A social worker opens the front door of his home and André shuffles into the hall to invite Nelissen into the living room. He is dressed in shirt and vest, blue track suit bottoms and slippers. He has no walking stick or glasses; he doesn't need either. Seated in his antiquated sofa, he tells the Dutch journalist about his adventures in the

long-forgotten Tour of 1926. His lack of teeth (he wears no dentures) sometimes makes him difficult to understand. But much the same is true of Nelissen: like many Hollanders, his French is appalling. *'Et vous... vous cre-, cre-, crevaiser quat' fois... Col de la...?'* (And you... you had pu-, pu-, puncture four times... Col de la...?) And later: *'Aussi, vous êtes le dernier des soldats du guerre de monde numéro un?'* (Also, you are the last of the soldiers of the World War Number One?). Brichard smiles and continues imperturbably with his story. He seems in perfect health, but just three days after the interview his long life finally comes to an end. It almost seems as if he was waiting: waiting for Nelissen, for the newspapers, and for the Tour. A good racer always knows when to choose the right moment. Even in death.

Emile Brichard, the last Belgian soldier of the Great War, here in a painting by Maarten Wydooghe.

HOW THE 'RACE' WAS RIDDEN

25.05.1913 Paul Deman wins the first edition of the Tour of Flanders.

28.05.1913 In Belgium, Minister of War Charles de Broqueville introduces compulsory military service to increase the strength of the army from 180,000 to 340,000, a figure that is never attained.

08.06.1913 The victory in Paris-Brussels goes to the Frenchman Octave Lapize, with Cyrille Van Hauwaert second, Charles Crupelandt third and Paul Deman fourth.

22.06.1913 In Philippeville Joseph Van Daele becomes Belgian national champion on the road.

06.07.1913 Following a first edition for professionals in 1912, this year's Liege-Bastogne-Liège is exclusively for independent riders. The race is won by Maurice Moritz.

22.08.1913 In Paris Oscar Egg (Sw.) sets a new world hour record without pacemaker at 42.360 kilometres.

23.08.1913 The world track racing championships are held in Berlin and Leipzig until 31 August.

11.09.1913 In Koolskamp René Arno wins the sixth edition of the Championship of Flanders.

20.09.1913 Marcel Berthet (Fr.) breaks Oscar Egg's world hour record. The new distance is 42.741 kilometres.

31.10.1913 In Ghent the World Exhibition closes. It began on 6 April and was held in what is now the Citadel Park and the Miljoenen district of the city.

02.11.1913 There is a French one-two-three in the Tour of Lombardy. Henri Pélissier wins, ahead of Maurice Brocco and Marcel Godivier.

15.12.1913 New army reforms in Belgium make the 5th Battalion of the Carabineers Regiment an independent unit. They are renamed the Battalion of Carabineer Cyclists, or the Cyclists for short. The 'steel horse' now has a permanent place in the armed forces alongside the real horses of the cavalry.

08.02.1914 Cyrille Van Hauwaert wins the Six Days of Brussels with the Dutchman John Stol. The French duo Lapize-Miquel is second, with the Australian McNamara and the American Moran in third place.

22.03.1914 Marcel Buysse wins the Tour of Flanders. Henri Vanlerberghe is second and Pier Van de Velde third.

05.04.1914 Ugo Agostoni is best in Milan-Sanremo. The first Belgian is Jules Masselis in 13th position.

12.04.1914 Charles Crupelandt, a native of Roubaix, wins Paris-Roubaix. The Belgians Mottiat, Rossius, Van Hauwaert and Van de Velde finish third, fifth, sixth and seventh.

19.04.1914 Oscar Egg (Sw.) triumphs in Paris-Tours. The best Belgian is Philippe Thys in third place.

10.05.1914 Costante Girardengo (It.) wins Milan-Turin, a race first ridden in 1876, which makes it the oldest cycle competition in the world.

17.05.1914 Paul Deman is victorious in Bordeaux-Paris, ahead of Marcel Buysse and Cyrille Van Hauwaert.

25.05.1914 In Namur Victor Dethier wins the Belgian road championships.

31.05.1914 Paris-Menen is won by Philippe Thys. The Frenchmen Emile Engel and Marcel Godivier fill the other podium places.

03.06.1914 In Antwerp the first edition of *De Volksgazet*, a newspaper started by Camille Huysmans, is published. The paper is not printed during the war.

07.06.1914 Paris-Brussels has a completely Walloon podium. Louis Mottiat wins from Louis Heusghem and Joseph Vandaele.

14.06.1914 The Belgians Oscar Robaye and Charles Chabard finish first and third in Luxembourg-Nancy, with the Frenchman Gustave Lorain separating them in second.

In Paris-Nancy the victory goes to the Frenchman Maurice Brocco, who beats his compatriot Louis Trousselier in the sprint.

18.06.1914 Oscar Egg (Sw.) gets his revenge on Marcel Berthet, regaining the world hour record with a distance of 43.525 kilometres, a record that will remain unbeaten until 1933.

28.06.1914 In Sarajevo the Serbian nationalist Gavrilo Princip assassinates Crown Prince Franz Ferdinand of Austria and his wife, Sophie Chotek.

The 12th edition of the Tour de France starts in Paris. Philippe Thys wins the first stage to Le Havre.

Erich Aberger is the winner of the two-day Vienna-Berlin race. Fritz Bauer is second and Adolf Huschke third.

26.07.1914 Philippe Thys is the overall winner of the Tour de France, ahead of Henri Pélissier and Jean Alavoine.

28.07.1914 Austria-Hungary declares war on Serbia.

In Winterslag, the first layer of coal is cut from the seam in the Limburg basin.

29.07.1914 Stijn Streuvels starts his war diary. At the end of 1915 and the start of 1916 it will be published in six parts under the title *In Oorlogstijd* (In time of war).

The Ghent authoress Virginie Loveling, the aunt of Cyriel Buysse, also starts a war diary, in which she writes her critical appraisal of events. This will not be published in book form until 2006.

01.08.1914 Germany, the ally of Austria-Hungary, declares war on the Russian Empire, the ally of Serbia.

02.08.1914 Germany occupies Luxembourg and demands free passage through Belgium to attack France, Russia's ally. The Belgian government rejects the demand out of hand.

03.08.1914 Germany declares war on France.

04.08.1914 Following the rejection of the German demand by King Albert I, German troops cross the border at Gemmenich at 7.30 in the morning. Twenty-two Belgian soldiers are killed that day.

Marcel Kerff, the best placed Belgian in the first Tour de France in 1903, is arrested in Moelingen. A few days later, he is hanged with other civilians and his body dumped in a mass grave.

The British Empire declares war on Germany.

In Rome Pope Pius X, the leader of the Catholic Church since 1903, dies.

06.08.1914 Liege falls to the Germans, although some of the 12 forts around the city hold out until 17 August.

In Labouxhe Jacques Julémont is executed by firing squad. He is the first Belgian bike racer to die in the war.

08.08.1914 After heavy fighting, German troops capture the fort at Barchon.

09.08.1914 One of the nine Zeppelin airships available to the German Army carries out the first aerial bombardment in history on Liege.

12.08.1914 At Halen the German cavalry are repulsed during the Battle of the Silver Helmets, in which the Carabineer Cyclists play an important role.

15.08.1914 A German shell penetrates the magazine of Fort Loncin near Liege, causing a huge explosion. The fort falls and is turned into a mass grave for the Belgian soldiers inside.

The Belgian king, queen and government move to Antwerp. Albert I assumes command of the Belgian Army.

The opening of the Panama Canal. The American steamer *Ancon* is the first ship to sail directly from the Atlantic to the Pacific Ocean.

18.08.1914 Following a fierce rearguard action at Gete, the Belgian Army fails to stop the German advance. In the fighting at Sint-Margriete-Houtem, Grimde and Oplinter, the 3rd Line Regiment loses almost half its troops.

19.08.1914 The Germans cross the River Meuse and take Aarschot and Leuven.

20.08.1914 The Germans occupy Brussels.

21.08.1914 Tamines is the victim of German atrocities. All the houses are burnt and 384 innocent civilians are killed.

22.08.1914 The Germans attempt to attack the French through Belgian Luxembourg. In a single day, 22,000 soldiers die in the fighting around Rossignol, Virton and Herbeumont. Several villages are plundered and burnt to the ground. This Battle of the Frontiers is one of the bloodiest days of the entire war.

In Binche, the Germans are temporarily held up by the newly arrived British Expeditionary Force (BEF).

23.08.1914 Because the Belgian government still refuses the Germans right of free passage over Belgian territory, the invaders vent their anger on the civilian population of Dinant. Six hundred and seventy-four innocent civilians are executed. Two-thirds of the city is reduced to ashes.

Namur is also plundered and many buildings burnt. Seventy-five civilians lose their lives.

In Aarschot a German officer is hit by a stray (Belgian?) bullet. As a reprisal, the town is razed to the ground and 183 civilians are executed.

The so-called Battle of the Angels in Mons sees the first serious confrontation between British and German troops.

24.08.1914 A rumour that the Germans are rounding up all men between the ages of 18 and 50 causes a mass exodus from East and West Flanders. The day goes down in history as 'Flight Monday' or 'Fleeing Monday'.

25.08.1914 For four days the Germans sow terror and destruction in Leuven. Two hundred and eighteen civilians are killed and 1,128 buildings are destroyed, including the world-famous university library.

27.08.1914 British marines land at Ostend to help the Belgian Army in the defence of Antwerp.

31.08.1914 The Belgian queen, Elisabeth, leaves with her three children — Leopold, Karel and Marie-José — by mail boat from Ostend for the safety of England.

04.09.1914 German troops storm Dendermonde. During the following several days, countless civilians are executed and houses are plundered, before being burnt to the ground. At the end of the destruction, only 100 buildings are still intact.

07.09.1914 The Belgian Army puts up fierce resistance against the Germans on the River Schelde at Kwatrecht and Melle. As an act of revenge, the invaders kill ten civilians and burn down 45 houses.

09.09.1914 Benedict XV, who is regarded by the Allies as being pro-German, becomes the new pope.

During the Battle of the Marne, the German advance on Paris is finally halted. The French dig in. Trench warfare begins.

10.09.1914 The French racer Emile Engel is killed in the Battle of the Marne.

11.09.1914 The mail boat *Rapide* takes part of Belgium's bullion reserves from Ostend to Dover.

23.09.1914 The Bruges newspaper *Burgerwelzijn* publishes an official text stating that anyone who offers shelter to German troops will be regarded as a spy.

24.09.1914 A German Zeppelin bombs Ostend, causing serious damage.

29.09.1914 A large part of the Belgian Army retreats from Antwerp. This happens mainly at night, by train to Ostend.

02.10.1914 A German spy, Karl Lody, is caught in Edinburgh. He is executed by firing squad in the Tower of London on 6 November.

04.10.1914 The Belgian Army is forced to withdraw behind the Rivers Nete and Rupel.

06.10.1914 More than 4,000 shells and 140 bombs from Zeppelins fall on Antwerp.

An exodus begins along the River Schelde. More than one million Belgians flee to the neutral Netherlands. Others head for West Flanders and France, or else try to reach England via the port at Ostend.

08.10.1914 The Second Battle of Melle. Six thousand French marines on their way to help with the defence of Antwerp run into the advancing Germans.

09.10.1914 Antwerp is occupied by the Germans.

11.10.1914 After the French promise support, King Albert decides to make a final stand on the line of the River IJzer.

13.10.1914 Ghent and Oudenaarde fall to the Germans, followed by Bruges the next day. British troops arrive in Ieper.

The mail boat *Pieter De Coninck* takes the Belgian government from Ostend to Le Havre. The king and queen decide to stay in De Panne.

15.10.1914 As the last ship leaves the harbour, the Germans take Ostend.

18.10.1914 The Germans launch a massive attack over a 100-kilometre wide front, from Nieuwpoort to La Bassée — the so-called Battle of the IJzer.

19.10.1914 Based on nothing more than rumours, the Germans carry out savage reprisals in Roeselare on the day that becomes known as 'Black Monday'.

20.10.1914   Tielt becomes the administrative centre of the Germans' exclusion zone, the zone to the west of the River Schelde occupied by their army.

21.10.1914   The fighting at Langemark opens the First Battle of Ieper.

22.10.1914   Near Diksmuide the German soldier Peter Kollwitz is killed in action. His mother, Käthe Kollwitz, later creates the 'Grieving Parents' sculpture to mark his grave in the German cemetery at Vladslo.

The Germans break through at the bend in the River IJzer at Tervate. The Belgians drive them back, but at a huge cost.

25.10.1914   Only Italian riders take part in the Tour of Lombardy. Bordin wins, ahead of Azzini and Piacco.

27.10.1914   Admiral von Schröder takes up residence in the Provincial Court in Bruges, which becomes the headquarters of the German Flanders Marine Corps.

28.10.1914   The Germans stop all postal communication in the occupied zone. It will only be resumed on 5 November 1915, under strict conditions of censorship.

29.10.1914   The 16th Bavarian Infantry Regiment, with a certain Adolf Hitler in its ranks, makes a second attempt at Geluveld to break though to Ieper.

30.10.1914   Hendrik Geeraert and Karel Cogge open the sea locks at Nieuwpoort to flood the IJzer plain. The Battle of the IJzer comes to a standstill. The war of movement degenerates into trench warfare.

01.11.1914   While visiting Duke Albrecht of Württemberg, commander of the German 4th Army, at Tielt, Kaiser Wilhelm only narrowly escapes an attack.

The German Army of Occupation closes the border between Belgium and the neutral Netherlands. From April 1915 onwards, the frontier will be blocked with an electrified fence.

03.11.1914   All telephones must be surrendered to the German authorities, the first of many such requisitioning orders.

08.11.1914   'German time' is introduced in the occupied zone. All clocks are moved forwards by one hour.

10.11.1914   The Germans capture the centre of Diksmuide — or what remains of it.

14.11.1914   The Germans announce their arrangements for the military and civil governance of the occupied zone. Each town will have a military commander with a *Kommandatur*; smaller municipalities will have an *Ortskommandatur*.

22.11.1914   The German High Command decides to break off their offensive at Ieper. They shell the town mercilessly, but the British refuse to withdraw.

24.11.1914   The Belgian queen, Elisabeth, asks the Brussels doctor Antoine Depage to set up a hospital behind the front in a large hotel — L'Océan — on the promenade in De Panne.

The Germans introduce a compulsory *Ausweiss* or identity card for all Belgian citizens older than 15 — a symbol of their control over the civilian population.

02.12.1914   The headquarters of the Belgian 6th Division takes up residence at Beauvoorde Castle in Wulveringem.

03.12.1914   The Frenchman Auguste Succaud is executed in Bruges for spying.

04.12.1914   The British king, George V, visits the Westhoek and inspects the British part of the front.

07.12.1914   The German occupiers introduce the rationing of bread.

10.12.1914   The German authorities announce that the damaging of telegraph and telephone lines will henceforth be punishable by death.

15.12.1914   A typhus epidemic breaks out in the Westhoek. Notwithstanding an inoculation campaign, it proves difficult to stop.

22.12.1914   The Red Cross hospital at the L'Océan hotel receives its first group of wounded patients.

At the initiative of the American Herbert Hoover, the Commission for Relief in Belgium is set up in London. The Commission purchases and transports foodstuffs to Belgium.

23.12.1914   The National Food and Aid Committee is set up in Brussels to help distribute food aid received from England.

In Izegem, German lorries arrive with Christmas trees for their troops — a custom previously unknown in Belgium.

25.12.1914   A series of 'Christmas truces' take place along the front near Ieper. Much to the displeasure of the high commands on both sides, the troops lay down their arms and meet in no-man's-land.

01.01.1915   Belgian soldiers training in France receive five cigars, an apple and half an orange as a present for New Year.

It is no longer possible to race in the covered winter velodrome in Schaarbeek, since it has been taken over by the National Food and Aid Committee.

03.01.1915 German troops are also hit by typhus. Operations and even amputations need to be carried out.

10.01.1915 Father Ildefons Peeters publishes the first number of *De Belgische Standaard*, the only newspaper that will appear in the unoccupied zone of Belgium behind the IJzer Front during the war.

15.01.1915 From this date on, Belgium must pay 40 million francs per month in war tax to Germany.

19.01.1915 Marie Curie sends a mobile X-ray unit to Poperinge, which is used to locate bullets and shell fragments in wounded soldiers.

20.01.1915 The Dutch newspaper *De Telegraaf* reports that the British Cycling Federation cannot organize the cycling world championships '... because of the war.'

22.01.1915 Belgians in the occupied zone are ordered to register their cars, motorbikes and any spare parts.

23.01.1915 Because Veurne is being shelled by German artillery, the General Headquarters of the Belgian Army withdraws to the vicarage in Houtem.

01.02.1915 Germany decides to engage in submarine warfare. Their U-boats are based in Ostend and Zeebrugge.

15.03.1915 George Llewellyn Davis is killed by a sniper. This British officer was J.M. Barrie's inspiration for the figure of Peter Pan. Davis is buried in Voormezele.

17.03.1915 The Belgian Cycling Federation closes down its operations, officially as a gesture of 'national mourning' in response to the German occupation.

26.03.1915 The track at Karreveld in Brussels reopens its door for racing. During the summer there will be competitions almost every weekend.

28.03.1915 Ezio Corlaita wins Milan-Sanremo. There are no Belgians in the field.

31.03.1915 The 400 children who until now have been sheltered in the abbey at Westvleteren are sent to the Belgian school colonies in France.

05.04.1915 The German Fritz Bauer is the best in Berlin-Cottbus-Berlin, ahead of his compatriots Paul Arnhold and Alfred Kebel.

17.04.1915 In the skies above Roeselare, Fernand Jacquet shoots down a German aeroplane, the first victory scored by a Belgian pilot in the war.

18.04.1915 Following a spectacular emergency landing in Hulste, the French pilot Roland Garros is captured by the Germans. His plane is displayed as a 'trophy of war' on the market square in Izegem.

19.04.1915 Lieutenant Hawker bombs the Zeppelin hangars near the East Flanders village of Gontrode.

22.04.1915 Between Steenstrate and Langemark the Germans employ a new and terrible weapon of war: chlorine gas. This marks the opening of the Second Battle of Ieper.

24.04.1915 The Turkish authorities imprison hundreds of Armenians. In the weeks and months that follow, more than one million Armenians are deported to the Syrian desert. Many hundreds of thousands will not survive.

25.04.1915 The Australian and New Zealand Army Corps (ANZAC) lands on the Gallipoli peninsula in Turkey at the beginning of the Dardanelles campaign. It is both nations' first involvement in the war.

At the request of the Belgian government, Edith Wharton (an American novelist living in Paris) sets up a committee to help Flemish children from the front region.

Milan-Turin is won for the second year in a row by Costante Girardengo, with Guiseppe Azzini in second and Carlo Durando in third.

02.05.1915 The German authorities in Belgium order the population to hand in all their bicycles.

The Germans intercept racing pigeons in the act of carrying secret information to England. As a result, they order that all pigeons in the occupied zone must be killed.

At the front, John McCrae writes his famous poem 'In Flanders Fields'.

Fritz Bauer triumphs in the Berlin-Hannover race, followed by Max Hildebrandt and Karl Gröhl.

06.05.1915 As a result of the continuing gas attacks and bombardments, the governor of West Flanders encourages parents in the unoccupied zone to send their children to the Belgian school colonies in France.

07.05.1915 The American passenger liner *Lusitania* is sunk off the Irish coast without warning by a German submarine. Some 1,198 of the 1,962 people on board lose their lives, including 128 American citizens. The attack provokes a strong reaction from the United States, at that time still a neutral country.

09.05.1915 François Faber, a former winner of the Tour de France, is killed at the front near Carency.

12.05.1915 The Belgians start to dig new trenches very close to the German lines in the dyke of the River IJzer at Diksmuide. These trenches later become known as the Trench of Death.

17.05.1915 A first convoy of trains leaves Adinkerke to take 300 children from the Westhoek to Paris. They are each given a bar of chocolate from Queen Elisabeth.

20.05.1915 The Germans prohibit the breeding of mares without their prior permission.

22.05.1915 In the Netherlands, the Groningen Cycling Club celebrates its fifth anniversary with a series of athletics and cycling competitions. There is also a special 'Belgian-Dutch-English' race on the programme.

30.05.1915 Fritz Bauer is fastest in the Hannover Street Grand Prix, ahead of Hermann Facklam and Peter Böhm.

17.06.1915 Near Maldegem, the Germans begin the construction of an electrified fence with the intention of closing off the full length of the border (449 kilometres) between Belgium and the Netherlands.

25.07.1915 Jan Van Ingelghem wins 'Bordeaux-Paris'; not the real race, but a surrogate version held on the Karreveld track in Brussels.

01.08.1915 Stijn Streuvels and two companions begin a six-day bike journey through the occupied territories. Among other places, they visit Halen, Leuven, Aarschot and Antwerp.

10.08.1915 The Germans confiscate all pigeon baskets, pigeon food, pigeon water troughs, nesting materials and racing clocks.

15.08.1915 A team race (with Cyrille Van Hauwaert as one of the competitors) at the Zurenborg velodrome in Antwerp attracts 6,000 spectators.

22.08.1915 An 'ersatz' Tour of Flanders is held on the race track in Evergem over an imaginary course of 150 kilometres. The winner is Leon Buysse.

29.08.1915 This day sees the start of a surrogate Tour of Belgium, ridden on the Karreveld track. The five 'stages' are each given the names of pre-war starting and finishing towns. On 6 September, Pier Van de Velde wins the race ahead of Jean Rossius and Marcel Buysse.

In Germany, Karl Wittig is victorious in the Tour of Berlin. It will be 1919 before the next edition of this race is held.

12.09.1915 The duo Van de Velde-Vanderstuyft triumph in the 'Golden Wheel' race at the Zurenborg circuit. The meeting is attended by more than 9,000 spectators.

19.09.1915 Thousands of spectators are present at the Arsenal track in Gentbrugge for a three-hour benefit race to raise money for the Work Group for Prisoners of War. Pier Van de Velde wins ahead of Marcel Buysse and Aloïs Persijn.

26.09.1916 The Arsenal velodrome hosts a race over 100 kilometres, with the duos Marcel and Lucien Buysse, Van de Velde-De Jaegher, Persijn-Cocquyt and César Debaets-Demiddel among the competitors.

10.10.1915 The Six Days of Brussels is contested at the Karreveld circuit. Van Hauwaert-Van Bever win, with Spiessens-Vandenberghe second and Buysse-Van de Velde third.

11.10.1915 The duo Pol Verstraete and Jules Van Renterghem are the best in the Six Days of Ghent, ahead of the teams Persijn-Cocquyt and Hudsyn-De Leener.

12.10.1915 Having been convicted of espionage, the British nurse Edith Cavell is executed by firing squad at the National Rifle Range in Schaarbeek.

16.10.1915 During a period of home leave from the front, the successful six-day duo of Léon Hourlier and Léon Comès are killed in a plane crash.

24.10.1915 The duo Tuyten-Van Isterdael beat Miel Aerts in a sprint competition at the velodrome in Laken. There is also a pre-programme with races for novices, amateurs and independent riders.

07.11.1915 The Tour of Lombardy is an all-Italian affair, with Gaetono Belloni ending as winner.

11.12.1915 In Poperinge, two British Army chaplains found Talbot House, an 'Everyman's club' that provides rest, recreation and support to more than half a million British soldiers before the war ends.

10.01.1916 All rubber must be surrendered to the German authorities. From now on, racers can only get new tyres for their bikes if they are smuggled in from the Netherlands.

27.01.1916 The United Kingdom is the last of the major powers to introduce compulsory military service.

21.02.1916 In an attempt to break the stalemate on the Western Front, the German High Command launches an offensive at Verdun that intends to 'bleed the French dry'. The fighting lasts until 15 December.

20.03.1916 Potatoes are rationed in the occupied zone.

01.04.1916 The 22-year-old Gabriëlle Petit faces a firing squad at the National Rifle Range in Schaarbeek for her part in passing on secret information to the Allies. The continuing execution of women raises a storm of international protest.

02.04.1916 Franz Bauer wins Berlin-Cottbus-Berlin for the second year in a row, with Walter Braeckow in second and the Austrian Ernst Duschinski in third.

14.04.1916 Ludwig Opel, second in the world sprint championship of 1898 and scion of the famous family of bike and car makers, dies on the Eastern Front at Hoduzischki (Russia) at the age of 36.

23.04.1916 The Germans introduce meat rationing in Belgium, with an allowance of 150 grams per person per week. From 18 December, this will be reduced by half to 75 grams per week.

30.04.1916 The occupying authorities introduce summer time into Belgium. The clocks are turned back by one hour.

10.05.1916 With the support of Queen Elisabeth, the Belgian Army sets up an Artistic Documentation Section to record the activities of the Belgian armed forces in the field.

14.05.1916 The Hannover Street Grand Prix is a triumph for Robert Tartsch, with Ernst Duschinski second and Walter Wendt third.

The Schelde Prize is ridden on the velodrome in Hemiksem.

15.05.1916 The German governor-general, von Bissing, signs the decree that obliges unemployed Belgians to work for the German military authorities. In total, 180,000 men and women will be deported to work in German factories and fields.

30.06.1916 The Dutch printing house Van Kampen publishes *Pallieter* by Felix Timmermans.

01.07.1916 The opening day of the Battle of the Somme. The British lose 60,000 men, killed, wounded or missing.

Bike racing returns to Paris, with meetings being held roughly once every two weeks at the Parc des Princes.

16.07.1916 The velodrome at the Garden City in Wilrijk is 'festively' reopened. The main attraction is a race between Cyrille Van Hauwaert and Arthur Vanderstuyft.

23.07.1916 The Arsenal track in Gentbrugge is the venue for an 'alternative' Tour of Flanders. Pier Van de Velde is the best of the 12 participants.

29.07.1916 Paul von Hindenburg replaces Erich von Falkenhayn as commander-in-chief of the German Army.

13.08.1916 Charles Deruyter wins Paris-Orleans, ahead of the Frenchman Hubert Samyn and the Belgian Edward Bonheurre.

16.08 1916 The German racer Alex Benscheck accidentally shoots himself in the chest while cleaning his rifle and dies soon afterwards.

20.08.1916 The Tour of Belgium is ridden as a one-day race on the Arsenal track in Gentbrugge. After 175 kilometres, Pier Van de Velde is first across the line, followed by Lucien Buysse and César Debaets.

27.08.1916 Rumania joins the war on the side of the Allies.

15.09.1916 The British Army employs tanks in battle for the first time.

18.09.1916 The *Force Publique*, the Belgian Defence Force in the Congo, defeats the Germans at Tabora, in what is now Tanzania. A large part of German East Africa comes under Allied control.

20.09.1916 The Germans order the surrender of all bicycles in both the *Etappengebiet* and the zone administered by the General-Government.

02.10.1916 On the improvised track in the internment camp for Belgian soldiers in Hardewijk, some 2,000 spectators see Urbain Anseeuw and Jan Somers win an American style relay race, ahead of the Dutch duo Biezembos-Deuts.

15.10.1916 A benefit meeting is held at the Arsenal velodrome in Gentbrugge on behalf of the 'Public Aid' and 'Help the Prisoners of War' organizations.

05.11.1916 Victory in the Tour of Lombardy goes to Leopoldo Torricelli.

In Paris, the Velodrome d'Hiver reopens its doors. Regular meetings are held in the following months.

16.11.1916 The world sprint champion (1907, 1910) Emile Friol dies in a traffic accident while serving at the front.

18.11.1916 Oscar Egg and Henri Contenet win a team event on the Vel' d'Hiv in Paris. The Belgian duo of Charles Deruyter and Philippe Thys are runners-up.

The Battle of the Somme finally draws to a close. More than one million soldiers are killed, wounded or missing. The Germans have been pushed back some ten kilometres.

01.12.1916 The German occupiers significantly increase taxation on events and entertainments — including track races. More and more men — including cyclists — are compelled to go and work in Germany.

18.12.1916 The Battle of Verdun finally ends. In ten months of fighting, more than 300,000 French and German troops have been killed.

29.12.1916 Fearing his great influence at the court of Tsar Nicholas II — and in particular his pacifist stance against the war — Grigori Rasputin is murdered by a monarchist group in Petrograd.

02.01.1917 Léon Flameng — in 1896 the first ever Olympic champion in the 100-kilometre track race — dies of his injuries near Paris, when his parachute fails to open after his plane gets into technical difficulties.

14.02.1917 In the occupied zone it becomes compulsory to hang a list of the inhabitants on the door of every house — supposedly to make it easier to trace possible victims in the event of enemy bombing.

08.03.1917 The Russian people revolt against Tsar Nicholas and Tsarina Alexandra. It is the start of the February Revolution (8 March is 22 February in the Russian calendar). Power passes into the hands of a provisional government.

22.03.1917 The German authorities introduce the compulsory registration of all sick people, pregnant women, breast-feeding women and children under the age of six years to whom doctors can prescribe milk.

06.04.1917 The United States joins the Allied cause and declares war on Germany.

09.04.1917 To fill out the sporting calendar, the French organize Tours-Paris in addition to Paris-Tours. Charles Deruyter wins the first of the two wartime editions of this 'reverse' race.

15.04.1917 Gaetano Belloni wins Milan-Sanremo with a lead of more than 12 minutes over Costante Girardengo.

06.05.1917 Philippe Thys is the best in Paris-Tours, ahead of Marcel Godivier and Eugène Christophe.

28.05.1917 For the first and only time, the *L'Auto* newspaper organizes a race from Mont-Saint-Michel to Paris. It is won by Marcel Godivier, with the Belgian Charles Juseret in second and Eugène Christophe in third.

07.06.1917 At Zero Hour (4.10am local time), the British detonate 19 mines under the Messines-Wijtschate ridge, completely destroying the German front line positions.

26.06.1917 The first American troops arrive in Europe. Before the end of the war, the United States will send almost two million men to the Western Front.

10.07.1917 Under the codename *Strandfest* (Beach Party), the Germans launch a successful surprise attack against British positions near the mouth of the River IJzer in Nieuwpoort. It is also the first recorded use of mustard gas.

11.07.1917 In an open letter to King Albert, the Front Movement complains about the discrimination and harassment of Flemish soldiers in the Belgian Army.

14.07.1917 During a routine flight over the Moselle valley, former Tour winner Octave Lapize is shot down and killed.

The Belgian Charles Juseret is first over the line in Paris-Bourges, followed by the Frenchman André Noël and another Belgian, Eugène Platteau.

31.07.1917 The opening of the Third Battle of Ieper, also known as Passchendaele (Passendale). With the help of Belgian, Canadian and ANZAC troops, the British commander, Field Marshall Haig, hopes to finally break through the German defences.

19.08.1917 Henri Pélissier wins Trouville-Paris. His compatriot Marcel Godivier is second and the Belgian Charles Deruyter is third.

21.08.1917 In Poperinge, the British nurse Nellie Spindler is killed by a shell. She is one of the two female victims of the war from the United Kingdom buried in Belgium.

02.09.1917 After a gap of a year, the Milan-Turin race is resumed. The winner is Oscar Egg, followed by the Italians Torricelli and Lucotti.

11.09.1917 The famous French pilot Georges Guynemer, with a record score of 53 'kills', is shot down near the village of Poelkapelle. His body is never found.

15.10.1917 At Vincennes near Paris, the Dutch spy Margaretha Geertruida Zelle — better known as the exotic dancer Mata Hari — is executed by firing squad for passing secret information to the Germans.

24.10.1917 The Bolsheviks, led by Vladimir Lenin, seize power from the provisional government in Russia. It is the start of the communist era.

04.11.1917 Philippe Thys wins the Tour of Lombardy, ahead of the Frenchman Henri Pélissier and the Italian Leopoldo Torricelli.

10.11.1917 The Third Battle of Ieper draws to a close. The village of Passendale finally falls to the Allies. However, an advance of just eight kilometres in 100 days of fighting has cost them 245,000 killed, wounded and missing, with the Germans also suffering 215,000 casualties. The offensive is condemned as a senseless slaughter.

20.11.1917 The British score a surprise victory over the Germans at Cambrai, mainly through the first large-scale use of tanks en masse on the battlefield.

03.12.1917 The Bolsheviks agree a cease-fire with the Germans. This releases almost a million German troops, who can now be transferred from Russia to the Western Front.

Carlo Oriani, the winner of the 1913 Giro but now a soldier in the Italian Bersaglieri, dies of pneumonia contracted as a result of swimming the Isonzo River to escape from the advancing Germans.

20.12.1917 Ex-Tour winner Lucien Petit-Breton dies as a result of a traffic accident at Vouziers near Troyes, while delivering a message in his capacity as an orderly officer.

08.01.1918 The American president Wilson sets out his so-called Fourteen Points, a blueprint for a new world order after the war.

06.03.1918 The 2nd Battalion of the Carabineer Cyclists beats off a German attack on the advanced post at Old-Stuivekenskerke.

08.03.1918 The first case of Spanish flu is confirmed at an army base in Kansas. The disease spreads to Europe, probably through American troops. The resulting epidemic kills 20 million people, more than the war itself.

21.03.1918 The Germans launch their Spring Offensive, the *Kaiserschlacht*. They break through the British lines between the rivers Somme, Oise and Sensée.

26.03.1918 The French general Ferdinand Foch is appointed supreme commander of all the Allied armies.

15.04.1918 The Italian Costante Girardengo triumphs in Milan-Sanremo. In the years ahead, he will win the race a further five times.

21.04.1918 Manfred von Richthofen, known as the Red Baron, is shot down and killed. With 80 victories to his credit, he is the most successful fighter pilot on both sides during the war.

22.04.1918 The British raid the port of Zeebrugge, in the hope of blocking the harbour entrance to prevent its further use by German submarines.

09.05.1918 The Championship of Champions is ridden at the Parc des Princes in Paris over 100 kilometres. The winner is the Frenchman Charles Mantelet.

19.05.1918 Charles Mantelet also wins Paris-Tours, ahead of the Swiss Lucien Cazalis and the Belgian Alexis Michiels.

27.05.1918 The Germans launch their third great offensive of the year, this time against the French on the Chemin des Dames. They quickly reach the River Marne —just 70 kilometres from Paris — for the second time in the war.

09.06.1918 The second and final edition of Tours-Paris is won by Philippe Thys, with the Frenchmen Charles Mantelet and Georges Sérès in second and third.

15.07.1918 The Germans launch their fourth and final offensive — Friedenstorm — near Rheims, but are halted by the French on the Marne. It is the beginning of the end for the German cause.

17.07.1918 Tsar Nicholas and his family are executed by the Bolshevik.

11.08.1918 Dresden-Berlin-Dresden is won by the Austrian Ernst Duschinski, ahead of the Germans Emiel Kleikamp and Fritz Bauer.

15.08.1918 The Trouville-Paris race has an international podium. The Belgian Alexis Michiels wins, with the Swiss Oscar Egg in second and the Frenchman Honoré Barthélémy in third.

08.09.1918 Jules Van Hevel is victorious in a 100-kilometre race at Gravelines in northern France, beating his compatriots Stockelynck and Van Herck.

15.09.1918 Napoléon Paoli is the best in Nice-Annot-Nice, pushing Ernest-Paul Bottero and the Spaniard Juan Arbonna into second and third places.

18.09.1918 Jules Masselis wins Bourges-Paris, ahead of Henri Pélissier and Oscar Egg.

28.09.1918 Under the command of Field Marshall Foch, the Allies begin their great Final Offensive. The breaking of the Hindenburg Line at Saint-Quentin heralds a general German retreat.

29.09.1918 The Schelde Prize is ridden on the Garden City velodrome in Wilrijk over 175 kilometres. The winner is Karel Block.

06.10.1918 The home rider Gaetano Belloni wins Turin-Milan, with Alfredo Sivocci in second place and Angelo Vay in third.

07.10.1918 The German Peter Günther crashes during the Grand Autumn Prize on the track in Dusseldorf and dies soon after from his injuries. Günther was the 1911 world champion in the stayer discipline.

18.10.1918 Czechoslovakia declares independence from Austria-Hungary.

26.10.1918 Ingooigem is liberated by the British. Stijn Streuvels' house — *het Lijsternest* (The Thrush's Nest) — is damaged during the fighting but Streuvels and his family have already fled to Kortrijk.

01.11.1918 The Americans break through the German lines at Stenay on the River Meuse. Belgian, French and American troops liberate Oudenaarde, although the Germans continue to bombard the city with gas shells in the following days.

09.11.1918 Kaiser Wilhelm II of Germany abdicates.

10.11.1918 Gaetano Belloni is victorious in the Tour of Lombardy. Alexis Michiels is the only Belgian participant, finishing in fourth place.

Kaiser Wilhelm seeks asylum in the Netherlands. Emperor Karl I of Austria-Hungary abdicates.

11.11.1918 The Armistice is signed in a train wagon in the Forest of Compiègne. The war is over.

16.11.1918 Even while there are still German troops in the city, the first post-war edition of *Vélo-Sport* is published in Brussels.

All clocks are reset to Belgian time.

17.12.1918 The Belgian government asks all its citizens to submit lists of furniture they hold that does not belong to them, reminding them that the sale of such furniture is illegal.

01.01.1919 The newspaper *Sportwereld* makes its reappearance.

18.01.1919 The post-war peace conference gets under way in the Hall of Mirrors in the Palace of Versailles. The negotiations between Germany and the representatives of 26 Allied governments will lead to the signing of the Treaty of Versailles on 28 June.

25.01.1919 The Versailles conference decides to set up a League of Nations, which must prevent new wars from breaking out.

16.03.1919 The Mechelen Grand Prix is the first post-war cycle race to take place in liberated Belgium, although it is restricted to independent riders. Victory goes to Jules Van Hevel.

23.03.1919 Henri Vanlerberghe wins the Tour of Flanders by the massive margin of 14 minutes, which is still a record.

05.04.1919 The duo of Philippe Thys and Marcel Dupuy wins the Six Days of Brussels. They have a lead of one lap over Aerts-Spiessens, Persijn-Van de Velde and Leon Buysse-Vanlerberghe.

06.04.1919 Victory in Milan-Sanremo goes to the Italian Angelo Gremo. Lucien Buysse is the only Belgian finisher, in tenth position.

19.04.1919 The Frenchman Henri Pélissier wins Paris-Roubaix ahead of Philippe Thys and another Frenchman, Honoré Barthélémy.

28.04.1919 The Tour of the Battlefields — a seven-stage race around the old Western Front over 14 days — starts in Strasbourg.

02.05.1919 The third stage in the Tour of the Battlefields takes the riders to the IJzer, Ieper and the Somme. It is one of the strangest and toughest races ever ridden and is eventually won after more than 18 hours by Charles Deruyter.

11.05.1919 Charles Deruyter wins the seventh and final stage in the Tour of the Battlefields, and is also best in the overall standings, ahead of Urbain Anseeuw and Henri Vanlerberghe.

THE RACE LINE-UP

A

Emiel Aalman 146
Erich Aberger 193
Emile Aerts 64, 128, 131, 166, 197, 201
François Aerts 131
Ugo Agostoni 55, 192
Bartolomeo Aimo 190
Alain-Fournier 83
Henri Alavoine 83
Jean Alavoine 55, 64, 83, 180, 183, 184, 193
King Albert I 46, 66, 68, 73, 78, 82, 88, 90, 114, 139, 144, 148, 193, 194, 199
Cyril Alden 90
Tsarina Alexandra 199
René Anno 168, 192
Jacques Anquetil 149
Urbain Anseeuw 82, 144, 180, 182, 183, 184, 198, 201
Jos Apostel 64
Willy Appelhans 64
Juan Arbonna 200
Willy Arend 24, 40, 64, 136
Neil Armstrong 175
Paul Arnhold 196
John Arnst 165
Richard Arnst 165
Fabio Aru 71
André Auffray 50
Donald Hugh Austin 159
Matthew Herbert Austin 159
Carlo Azzini 195, 196

B

Willy Bader 29
Eddi Bald 20
Georges Banker 20, 157
Romain Bardet 71
Honoré Barthélémy 70, 168, 178, 200, 201
Fritz Bauer 193, 196, 197, 198, 200
Jack Bauer 163
Erich Bäumler 135
Charles Bean 158
John Bedell 158
Aimé Behaeghe 137, 138, 139
Joseph Behaeghe 137, 138, 139
Gaston Beirlaen 18
Henri Beirnaert 190
Boudewijn of Belgium 90
Karel of Belgium 194

Leopold III of Belgium 194
Marie-José of Belgium 194
Gaetano Belloni 52, 148, 168, 197, 199, 200, 201
Pope Benedict XV 194
Adelin Benoit 190
Auguste Benoit 51
Alex Benscheck 135, 198
Marcel Berthet 64, 65, 183, 192, 193
Sam Bewley 163
Eduardo Bianchi 98
André Blaise 55
Cor Blekemolen 144
Louis Blériot 32, 114, 138, 152
Karel Block 200
Peter Böhm 197
Edward Bonheurre 198
Louis Bonino 83, 174
Lauro Bordin 195
Camille Botte 64
Ottavio Bottecchia 185, 186, 190
Ernest-Paul Bottero 200
Oscar Braeckman 45
Walter Braeckow 198
Victor Breyer 177
Emile Brichard 189, 190, 191
Maurice Brocco 49, 178, 180, 183, 192, 193
Georges Bronchard 87
Paul Bruns 99
Cyriel Buysse 52
Jules Buysse 52, 190
Leon Buysse 120, 122, 124, 126, 130, 133, 155, 175, 176, 197, 201
Lucien Buysse 52, 82, 126, 168, 173, 180, 190, 197, 198, 201
Marcel Buysse 40, 18, 51, 52, 55, 82, 106, 111, 122, 126, 128, 129, 131, 133, 172, 173, 192, 197

C

Henri Caesar 49
Fabian Cancellara 191
Girolamo Cardano 12
Clarence Carman 94
George Carptentier 46, 51
Joseph Cassiers 64
Aloïs Catteau 28
Edith Cavell 112, 197

Mark Cavendish 20
Lucien Cazalis 200
Charles Chabard 193
Arthur Chase 20
Sophie Chotek 58, 193
Eugène Christophe 22, 48, 177, 199
Arthur Churchill 102
Jacky Clark 20
Constant Cleiren 174
Avile Cocquyt 126, 128, 130, 133, 155, 197
Karel Cogge 78, 172, 195
Léon Comès 49, 50, 51, 197
Henri Contenet 81, 167, 198
Jacques Coomans 126
François Cordier 83
Henri Cornet 34
René Cottrel 87
Guy Crasset 189
Charles Cruchon 118
Charles Crupelandt 40, 50, 55, 64, 65, 66, 172, 192
August Cuppens 73
Marie Curie 196

D

Louis Darragon 118, 167
George Llewelyn Davis 196
César Debaets 94, 111, 124, 126, 155, 175, 197, 198
Gérard Debaets 94
Michel Debaets 94, 111
Albert De Belder 64
Louise de Bettignies 108, 109
Emile De Beukelaer 20, 28, 47, 113
Jean De Blauwe 156
Charles de Broqueville 114, 192
Jan Debusschère 190
Octaaf Declercq 106, 107
Jozef De Coene 122, 123
Odiel Defraeye 37, 58, 59, 91, 92, 99, 178, 183
Eugène Degrendele 146
Henri De Jaegher 128, 197
Maurice Dejoie 83
Albert De Jonghe 174, 175, 179, 180, 182
Auguste De Maeght 128
Paul Deman 45, 55, 108, 109, 111, 138, 168, 192
Jean Demarteau 72, 73, 84
Frans Demeuyninck 45
Jules Demiddel 197
Bruno Demke 99, 100
Antoine Depage 195
Arthur Depauw 51, 64, 124
Desiré De Poorter 51, 121, 124

Charles Deruyter 62, 81, 178, 180, 182, 183, 184, 185, 198, 199, 201
Florent Desanthoine 64
Georges Descamps 50
Henri Desgrange 58, 59, 60, 87, 162, 190
Maurice Desimpelaere 154
Albert Desmedt 122, 126, 183, 184
Victor Dethier 55, 193
Abel De Vogelaere 156
Frans De Vogelaere 156
Guido De Vogelaere 156
Anna De Vos 104, 171
Jules Dhondt 128, 133
Idalie Dick 133
Raymond Didier 86
Kurt Dierckx 106
August Dierickx 45, 51
Rudolf Diesel 24
Léon Domain 157
Victor Doms 45
Jules Dossche 175
Richard Dottschadis 99
Paul Duboc 62, 87, 180, 182, 184
John Boyd Dunlop 10
Albert Dupont 84
Marcel Dupuy 149, 201
Carlo Durando 196
Ernst Duschinski 198, 200
Eugène Dutrieu 30
Hélène Dutrieu 30, 32, 80
Arthur Duysburgh 128

E

Oscar Egg 50, 55, 64, 65, 81, 93, 144, 178, 180, 187, 192, 193, 198, 199, 200
Albert Eickholl 100
Empress Elisabeth of Austria-Hungary 66
Queen Elisabeth of Belgium 46, 66, 189, 193, 195, 197, 198
Thorvald Ellegaard 24, 136, 142, 187
Emile Engel 55, 58, 64, 65, 71, 193, 194
Raymond Englebert 190
Jean Esser 64
René Etien 83
Charles Evans 151
Pierre Everaerts 126

F

François Faber 55, 58, 59, 117, 118, 119, 168, 170, 178, 197
Hermann Facklam 197
Henry Farman 28
Victor Fastré 84
William Fenn 158

BOUQUETS

— Ronald J. Austin: *Cycling to War. The history of the AIF/NZ Cyclist Corps 1916-1919* – Mc Crea Victoria, Slouch Hat Publications, 2008;
— Frederik Backelandt, Patrick Cornillie and Rik Vanwalleghem: *Koarle. Vader van de Ronde van Vlaanderen* – Balegem, Pinguin Productions, 2006;
— Frank Becuwe: *Omloop van de Slagvelden. De meest heroïsche wedstrijd ooit* – Leuven, Davidsfonds, 2013;
— Jean-Paul Bourgier: *Le Tour de France 1914, de la fleur au guidon à la baïon-nette au canon* – Toulouse, Le Pas d'oiseau, 2010;
— Jean-Paul Bourgier: *1919: Le Tour renaît de l'enfer* – Toulouse, Le Pas d'oiseau, 2014;
— Lucas Catherine: *Loopgraven in Afrika (1914-1918). De vergeten oorlog van de Congolezen tegen de Duitsers* – Berchem, EPO, 2013;
— Hannes Cattebeke: *Gérard Debaets. De gouden jaren van de koers* – Veurne, Kannibaal, 2015;
— Herman Chevrolet: *De Flandriens. Opkomst en ondergang van een wielersoort* – Amsterdam, De Arbeiderspers, 2007;
— Ria Christens and Koen De Clercq: *Frontleven 14/18. Het dagelijks leven van de Belgische soldaat aan de IJzer* – Tielt, Lannoo, 1987;
— Patrick Cornillie: *Den Doodrijder van Lichtervelde. Het verhaal van Ritten de Coureur* – Lichtervelde, Comité Dorp van de Ronde, 2004;
— Patrick Cornillie, Patrieck Geldhof and Dries Vanysacker: *Helden van het veld* – Roeselare, Roularta Books, 2006;
— Patrick Cornillie: *De zeer schone uren van Stijn Streuvels, cyclotoerist* – Elzele, Les Iles, 2018;
— Roger De Maertelaere: *Zesdaagsen* – Ghent, Worldstrips, 1991;
— Gaston Durnez: *Zeg mij waar de bloemen zijn. Vlaanderen 1914-1918* – Leuven, Davidsfonds, 1988;
— Émile Engels: *In de rug van de Duitsers. Het verzet tijdens WO I in België, Luxemburg en Noord-Frankrijk* – Tielt, Lannoo, 2014;
— Patrick Goossens and Lieve Meiresonne: *Vlaanderen Niemandsland 1914. Van gendarmen, vrijwilligers en burgerwachten tijdens de eerste oorlogsmaanden* – Leuven, Davidsfonds, 2009;
— Forster Groom e.a.: *The London Cyclist Battalion. A chronicle of events connected with the 26th Middlesex V.R.C., and the 25th Cyclist Battalion, The London Regiment and military cycling in general* – London, Fulham House, 1932;
— Graham Healy: *The Shattered Peloton. The devastating impact of World War I on the Tour de France* – Halcottsville, Breakaway Books, 2014;
— George J.M. Hogenkamp: *Een halve eeuw wielersport. 1867-1917* – Amsterdam, private publication, 1916;
— Herman Laitem: *Odiel Defraeye. Het pakkende leven van de eerste Belgische Tourwinnaar* – Balegem, Pinguin Productions, 2012;
— Pascal Leroy: *François Faber. Du Tour de France au champ d'honneur* – Paris, l'Harmattan, 2006;
— Virginie Loveling: *Oorlogsdagboeken 1914-1918* – Antwerp, De Bezige Bij, 2010;
— Jan Luitzen and Ad van Liempt: *Sportlegendes* – Amsterdam, Uitg. Balans, 2013;
— Georges Matthys: *De galerij der wielerkampioenen (1ste deel 1860-1900, 2de deel 1901-1914, 3de deel 1915-1920)* – Ghent, Het Volk, 1947;
— Bart Moeyaert: *Van wielerbaan tot... 'Velodroom'. De geschiedenis van het baanwielrennen in België van 1890 tot 2003* – Leuven, KUL fac. Letteren en Wijsbegeerte, 2003;
— Rudy Neve: *Gent-Wevelgem* – Wevelgem, Wibilinga, 2003;
— Marc Pyncket: *Paul Deman won de eerste Ronde van Vlaanderen* – Menen, Heemkring, 2013;
— Luc Schepens: *14/18. Een oorlog in Vlaanderen* – Tielt, Lannoo, 1984;
— Gunter Segers: *Hélène Dutrieu. Biografie van een fenomeen* – Elzele, Les Iles, 2018;
— Adolf Sempf: *De dood op de Kemmel* – Kemmel, VVV Westvlaamse Bergen, 1968;
— Pascal Sergent: *Charles Crupelandt. Le champion des brumes* – Eeklo, De Eecloonaar, 1999;
— Arthur Soetens: *Jules Van Hevel. De levensschets van den kampioen der kampioenen* – Borgerhout, Constant Cleiren, 1925;
— Stijn Streuvels: *Herinneringen uit het verleden* – Amsterdam, L.J. Veen, 1924;
— Stijn Streuvels: *In oorlogstijd. Deel 1: 1914* – Tielt, Lannoo, 2015;
— August Thiry: *Reizigers door de Grote Oorlog* – Leuven, Davidsfonds, 2008;
— Robert Thys: *Les inondations de l'Yser et la Compagnie des sapeurs-pontonniers du Génie belge* – Liege, Henri Desoer, 1922;
— Philippe Vandenbergh: *Wielermonumenten. Het verhaal van de vijf grootste wielerklassiekers* – Leuven, Davidsfonds, 2016;
— Luc Vandeweyer: *Koning Albert en zijn soldaten* – Antwerp, Standaard Uitgeverij, 2005;
— Karel Van Wijnendaele: *Het rijke Vlaamsche Wielerleven* – Ghent, Snoeck-Ducaju, 1942;
— Dries Vanysacker: *Koersend door een eeuw Italiaanse en Belgische geschiedenis* – Leuven, Acco, 2009;
— Dries Vanysacker: *Vlaamse wielerkoppen. 150 jaar drama en heroïek* – Leuven, Davidsfonds, 2011;
— Rik Vanwalleghem: *De Ronde van Vlaanderen* – Ghent, Pinguin Productions, 1991;
— Johan Van Win: *Philippe Thys. De vergeten drievoudige Tourwinnaar* – Elzele, Les Iles, 2014;
— Benedict Wydooghe: *De sluiswachter van de IJzer* – Antwerp, Witsand, 2013.

— Patrick Cornillie: *Wallonië 1815, 1914-'18, 1944-'45*, in Krant van West-Vlaanderen – Roeselare, 13.06.2014;
— Patrick Cornillie: *Roeselare, Duitse garnizoenstad*, in Krant van West-Vlaanderen – Roeselare, 13.06.2014;
— Patrick Cornillie: *Torhout, een Duitse evacuatiestad*, in Krant van West-Vlaanderen – Roeselare, 13.06.2014;
— Patrick Cornillie: *Emile Brichard. De laatste der (Tour)veteranen*, in Etappe #03 – Roeselare, Wieler-museum, 2014;
— Patrick Cornillie: *In het zicht van de vijand*, in Knack and in Krant van West-Vlaanderen – Roeselare, February 2015;
— Patrick Cornillie: *De uitbouw van de Dodengang*, in Knack and in Krant van West-Vlaanderen – Roeselare, February 2015;
— Patrick Cornillie: *De ondergrondse oorlog*, in Knack and in Krant van West-Vlaanderen – Roeselare, February 2015;
— Jean-Paul Delcroix: *Il y a 100 ans*, in Coups de Pédales nº 181 – Seraing, 2017;
— Stefaan De Groote: *De gebroeders De Vogelaere of de Flandriens van Bachte-Maria-Leerne*, in Het Land van Nevele – Nevele, heemkundige kring, 1997;
— Jean-Pierre Deweer: *De militaire gebeurtenissen tijdens de 20ste eeuw te Oudenaarde*, in Handelingen van de Geschied- en Oudheidkundige Kring van Oudenaarde, 2005;
— Dries De Zaeytijd: *Jules Van Hevel. Cyclist voor, tijdens en na de Groote Oorlog*, in Etappe #03 – Roeselare, Wielermuseum, 2014;
— Marc Holderbeke: *In memoriam Belgische renners*, in Handelingen. XVII, Zottegems Genootschap voor Geschiedenis en Oudheidkunde, 2015;
— Stijn Knuts: *Koersen in magere tijden*, in Etappe #03 – Roeselare, Wieler-museum, 2014;
— Stijn Knuts: *Leeuw in zakenpak. Cycles Van Hauwaert, het fietsmerk van een flandrien*, in Etappe #06 – Roeselare, Wielermuseum, 2017;

— Peter Laroy: *Wielrenner Urbain Anseeuw en de Eerste Wereldoorlog*, on geschiedenisvanaalter.blogspot.be, 2015;
— n.n., *How cyclist battalions would meet invaders*, in Cycling – London, 10.06.1915;
— Nico Oudhof: *Kamp Harderwijk. Belgische wielerpiste in Nederlands interneringskamp*, in Etappe #03 – Roeselare, Wielermuseum, 2014;
— Raymond Raife: *Bicycles in real war today*, in Cycling – London, 03.10.1912;
— Pieter Troch and Annick Vanden-bilcke: *Fairplay? Sport en de Eerste Wereldoorlog* – Ieper, In Flanders Fields Museum, 2014;
— Filip Van Devyvere: *Lichterveldenaren bij het Speciaal Contingent 1915*, in Dertigste Jaarboek – Lichtervelde, Heemkundige Kring Karel Van de Poele, 2014;
— Roger Verbeke: *De Zwarte Duivels. De Belgische karabiniers-cyclisten voor en tijdens de Eerste Wereldoorlog*, in Etappe #03 – Roeselare, Wielermuseum, 2014;

————————————

— l'Auto, 04.08.1914 – 29.06.1919
— Gazet van Antwerpen, 10.04.1915
— Gazet van Brussel, 03.10.1915 – 26.10.1915
— Coups de Pédales, 09.2015 – 10.2017
— Cycling, 03.10.1912 – 10.06.1915
— La Dernière Heure, 23.07.1911
— l'Echo de la Presse, 10.02.1915 – 24.08.1915 – 29.08.1915
— Gazette van Iseghem, 25.03 1911
— De Gentenaar, 31.07.1915 – 10.08.1915 – 14.08.1915 – 20.08.1915 – 22.08.1915 – 21.09.1915
— 't Getrouwe Maldegem, 28.08.1910 – 18.09.1910
— The Guardian, 01.07.1914
— InterNos Revue, years 1916-1918
— De Legerbode, 27.09.1917 – 30.10.1917
— Het Morgenblad, 06.05.1914
— La Nation Belge, 17.11.1918
— Het Nieuws van den Dag, 28.11.1918
— De Oude Thorhoutenaar, years 1965-1966
— Le Petit Journal, 19.12.1918
— Le Quotidien, 03.05.1915

— De Revue der Sporten, 03.03.1915 – 08.05.1918 – 20.11.1918
— Sportwereld, 30.04.1913 – 24.09.1913 – 24.02.1919 – 17.03.1919 – 22.03.1920
— De Telegraaf-Sportwereld, 03.08.1914 – 05.08.1914 – 08.08.1914 – 09.08.1914 – 10.08.1914
— Het Vlaamsche Nieuws, 11.02.1915 – 17.03.1915 – 20.05.1915 – 14.06.1915 – 02.08.1915 – 09.09.1915 – 30.10.1915 – 14.07.1916 – 22.07.1916 – 23.07.1916 – 26.07.1916 – 18.10.1916 – 28.09.1918 – 05.10.1918
— Vooruit, 07.10.1915 – 16.10.1915 – 21.05.1916 – 08.07.1916 – 25.07.1916 – 17.08.1916 – 29.06.1917 – 16.11.1918
— Het Volk, 24.03.1914 – 12.08.1915 – 15.08.1915 – 17.08.1915 – 21.08.1915 – 25.08.1915 – 01.10.1915 – 16.02.1916 – 25.07.1916 – 27.07.1916
— De Volksstem, 02.03.1913 – 08.11.1914 – 22.03.1916
— Geïllustreerde Zondagsgazet, 07.05.1916

————————————

— hetarchief.be
— www.be14-18.be
— www.thebikecomesfirst.com
— www.canadaatwar.ca
— www.cycling4fans.de
— www.forumeerstewereldoorlog.nl
— www.historischekranten.be
— history.2014-18brussels.be
— karelvanwijnendaele.be
— kbr.be
— hetiskoers.nl
— www.lepetitbraquet.fr
— www.memoire-du-cyclisme.eu
— nzetc.victoria.ac.nz
— opac.kbr.be/belgicapress
— nl.renners-in-de-grote-oorlog.wikia.com
— stuyfssportverhalen.com
— veertienachttien.be
— viaa.be
— wereldoorlog1418.nl
— www.dewielersite.net
— wo1dudzele.brugseverenigingen.be

With thanks to
Jean-Paul Bourgier, Lieven Byls,
    Freddy Declerck, Pieter
    De Messemaeker, Dries De Zaeytijd,
    Gert Dooreman, Johan Drossart,
    Robert Hubrecht, Geert Joris,
    Jan Kolkman, Griet Langedock,
    Simon Louagie, Stijn Lybeert,
    Lynn Maelfeyt, Nico Oudhof,
    Gunter Segers, Pieter Troch,
    Marnix Van Breusegem,
    Annick Vandenbilcke, Philip
    Vanoutrive, Benedict Wydooghe.

Museum van het Kamp van Beverlo,
    Koninklijke Bibliotheek, Geheugen
    Collectief vzw, In Flanders Fields
    Museum Ieper, PeaceVillage Mesen,
    Stadsarchief Oudenaarde, Streek-
    archivariaat Noordwest-Veluwe,
    Vlaams Instituut voor Archivering,
    Wielermuseum Roeselare.

With special thanks to
Marc Holderbeke, Roger Verbeke
    and Filip Walenta.

Picture credits
(the numbers refer to the pages)

Alamy/Imageselect: 14 (bottom)
Australian War Memorial: 116, 150, 159, 163
Becuwe (2013): 181
Belga: 50, 167
Bibliothèque Documentaire Internationale
    Contemporaine: 19 (top), 61 (bottom), 81,
    101 (top and bottom)
Bibliothèque nationale de France: 10 (bottom),
    15 (top), 17 (top), 23 (top), 25, 29, 37, 44, 48, 49
    (top and bottom), 61 (top), 62 (left and right), 63,
    65, 70, 71, 83, 86, 96, 99, 109, 117, 119, 120, 131, 136,
    157, 174, 185 (top)
Centrum Ronde van Vlaanderen: 42 (right), 43, 45,
    129 (bottom), 176
Collection Gunter Segers: 30, 31, 32, 81, 149
Collection Marc Holderbeke: 68 (right), 72 (top),
    85 (left and right), 88, 100, 110, 111, 112 (top),
    127, 135, 156
Collection Patrick Cornillie: 10 (top), 36, 52, 53, 55,
    80, 84, 90 (top), 91, 92, 93 (bottom), 94, 104,
    114, 124, 126 (bottom), 128 (bottom), 130 (left),
    132 (right), 146, 147, 151, 164, 175, 177 (top),
    179, 183
Collection Tillo Behaeghe: 139
De Zwarte Doos, Stadsarchief Gent: 46
Georges Matthys (1947): 64, 145 (top), 177 (bottom),
    178 (bottom)
GM Media: 13 (top and bottom)
Het Utrechts Archief: 113
Imperial War Museum: 93 (top), 105
Library of Congress: 21 (top and bottom)
Lijsternest/Letterenhuis, Antwerp: 74
Maarten Wydooghe: 191
Mémoire des hommes, France: 34
Musée de la poste, Paris: 14 (top)
Museum Kamp van Beverloo/Philip Vanoutrive:
    8, 26 (bottom and top), 27, 38, 39, 56, 66 (bottom),
    67, 72 (bottom), 73, 76, 77, 103, 140-141, 188
N.S.B. Dudzele/Aimé De Clercq: 106, 107
Pyncket (2013): 168
Royal Antwerp Bicycle Club: 166
Sergent (1999): 40, 66 (top)
Stadsarchief Oudenaarde: 153
Streekarchivariaat Noordwest-Veluwe: 82, 144,
    145 (bottom)
Troch e.a. (2014): 22

www.lannoo.com

Register on our website to receive a regular
    newsletter with information about new books
    and interesting exclusive offers.

Translation: Ian Connerty
Graphic design: Dooreman
Typesetting: Keppie & Keppie
Cover photos: Bibliothèque nationale de France,
    Gunter Segers, Imperial War Museum,
    Patrick Cornillie and Marc Holderbeke

D/2018/45/510
ISBN 978 94 014 5502 2
NUR 686

© Lannoo Publishers nv, Tielt
    and Patrick Cornillie, 2018